DATE DUE

*Earning More and
Getting Less*

Earning More and Getting Less

WHY SUCCESSFUL WIVES CAN'T BUY EQUALITY

VERONICA JARIS TICHENOR

RUTGERS UNIVERSITY PRESS
New Brunswick, New Jersey, and London

LIBRARY OF CONGRESS CATALOGING-IN-PUBLICATION DATA

Tichenor, Veronica Jaris, 1963–
   Earning more and getting less : why successful wives can't buy equality /
Veronica Jaris Tichenor.
      p.   cm.
   Includes bibliographical references and index.
   ISBN–13: 978–0–8135–3678–1 (hardcover : alk. paper)
   ISBN–13: 978–0–8135–3679–8 (pbk. : alk. paper)
   1. Marriage—Psychological aspects.   2. Equality—Psychological aspects.
3. Married people—Psychology.   4. Sex differences (Psychology)   5. Power
(Social sciences)   6. Wages—Women.   I. Title.
   HQ734.T526 2005
   306.81—dc22   2005002580

A British Cataloging-in-Publication record for this book is available
from the British Library.

Manufactured in the United States of America

To my husband, Jim, my partner in the struggle for gender equality, and our daughter, Michael, who reminds us why it is so important

Contents

Preface

THIS PROJECT HAS its beginnings in my graduate-school experience. I was close to finishing my course work in sociology, and wondering how to go about choosing a topic for my dissertation. I knew I was interested in doing work that examined the influence of gender on family relationships. One of my advisors suggested that I read Arlie Hochschild's "new" book, *The Second Shift*. Of course, Hochschild's findings are now widely known, as her work was well received both inside and outside the academy. She documented the staggering load that women in dual-earner families face as they continue to be responsible for housework and child care. She gave us a concrete way to think about this double burden by talking about the "extra month of twenty-four-hour days" that wives put into domestic labor, in comparison to their husbands. The vignettes she presented brought to life the difficulties these women faced in trying to balance work and family obligations; this load taxed women both physically and emotionally and often put a tremendous strain on their marriages.

As a young woman and scholar, I was stunned and depressed by her report because it was too easy to see my future in Hochschild's couples. At the time I read *The Second Shift*, I was twenty-five, had just celebrated my fourth wedding anniversary, and had a six-month-old daughter. My husband was in medical school, and though it was a struggle to be in training at the same time (and to be new parents), we were preparing for professions that we both wanted to pursue, and we knew all the sacrifices and hard work would eventually be worth it. In short, we were paying our dues, on our way to "having it all"—the perfect balance between work and family—and here was Hochschild, telling me that it was all a lie.

Fortunately, my personal pessimism was temporary—eroded by my husband's continued commitment to being an involved father and doing his share at home. However, I remained disturbed that women's incomes did not seem to "buy" them very much in their private lives. After all, the women's movement promoted higher education and employment as the keys to personal empowerment for women, as well as increased status and power within marriage. But as I began to review the literature on marital power, it became clear that working *outside* the home had not done much to increase women's power *within* the home. Women did not seem to have much more influence in decision making or financial matters in their marriages, and they were not getting much relief from housework and child care. Employed wives were getting a raw deal.

I started asking, Under what circumstances would it be possible, or likely, for women to get a better deal in their relationships? It seemed clear that simply earning an income was not enough to ensure equitable treatment. Perhaps this was because women typically earned a rather small fraction of the family's total income. If this was the reason, then what would happen if women earned the bulk of the family's income? If men have enjoyed more control in their marriages and relief from domestic labor based on their income advantage, could women with the same kind of advantage enjoy the same privileges?

As the rest of the book makes clear, the short answer to this question is no. The higher-earning wives profiled are unable or unwilling to use their substantial incomes to dramatically alter the balance of power in their marriages, and I admit that I am disappointed to report these findings. I did not set out to tell the story of the intransigence of gender inequality in marriage. On the contrary, I thought I would be profiling gender revolutionaries who could show the rest of us how men's dominance could be dismantled or undermined. I did not expect to find marriages dominated by women, but it seemed likely that wives could use their substantial resources to bargain for more help on the home front and more equal control over household decisions. Surely their incomes would be important enough to their families that these women would be in a better position to negotiate more equitable treatment. However, much like Hochschild, I found that my optimistic assumptions about the progress toward gender equality were largely unwarranted. Rather than toppling the gender structure, these couples with higher-earning wives are largely reproducing it. On the face of it, my results are as depressing as those of Hochschild.

Despite these conservative findings, I argue that these couples have much to teach us about gender equality. As their experiences highlight the resilience of the current gender structure, they also give us a window on the subtle, even hidden, ways in which men's power is reproduced within marriage. This means that, ironically, these results have the potential to move us closer to gender equality. A more complete understanding of how men's dominance is perpetuated means that we can develop more effective ways to undermine it. It is my hope that these findings will be used to that end.

Acknowledgments

Over the years it has taken to complete this project, I have written these acknowledgements in my head dozens of times. All along the way I have been acutely aware of the debts I owe to so many people, and eagerly looked forward to being able to thank them all in a public and meaningful way. Now that the work is complete, it is an enormous pleasure to recognize those who have helped move me along on this intellectual journey.

First, I'd like to acknowledge the members of my dissertation committee at the University of Michigan: Linda Blum, Renee Anspach, and Abby Stewart. These individuals guided my work and offered tremendous support despite increasingly complicated logistics. (For example, I was living in Iceland as I began writing the dissertation.) A special thank you goes to my committee chair, Marty Whyte, who even now is one of my most enthusiastic supporters, and who never fails to meet a request for help with a speedy and cheerful reply. Tom Gerschick, a fellow Wolverine, also deserves special recognition. He, too, has been incredibly supportive, and his comments and insights from an earlier draft of this book helped sharpen my thinking and move the analysis forward. He also offered the one piece of advice that kept me going, through both the dissertation and the writing of this manuscript: "Just do what you can do each day, then put your work away and start again tomorrow." That, Tom assured me, is how dissertations get done. Come to think of it, that's how just about everything gets done.

Several people have read drafts of this manuscript (in whole or part) along the way: Julia McQuillan, Pepper Schwartz, Mitchell Stevens, and Alphonse Sallett. The final product has benefited from your combined encouragement and feedback, and I thank you all. I owe a special debt of gratitude to Barbara Risman. I approached her at a meeting of the Sociologists for Women in Society, hoping to be able to introduce myself, briefly explain my project to her, and get some quick advice on which publishers she thought would be most interested in it. Within five minutes, she was offering to read a chapter, as well as my prospectus, in addition to offering publishing advice. Barbara is one of the busiest women I have ever met, and yet she offered her help without a second thought; her energy and generosity continue to astound me. It was Barbara's suggestion to use my data to highlight a gender-structure argument, and it is for that advice that I am most grateful. I also owe a special thank you to Kris Paap. As my friend, colleague, and intellectual partner, Kris has been my most reliable sounding board. We met as I began to transform the dissertation into the book, and I don't know what I would have done without her. She has an uncanny eye for editing; to her, a manuscript is a puzzle, and she can see where the pieces should fit. She also has the ability to discover what I am trying to say, even when I don't know myself. She has read more versions of my work than anyone and provided the most consistent support and feedback, and I am truly grateful. Kris and I also started a writing group, whose members have provided much needed encouragement along the way: Judy Owens-Manley, Judy Wolf, Gillian Gane, and Henry Rubin. Just knowing I would have to have something to report at our next meeting was often enough to keep me plugging along. Finally, I thank my editor at Rutgers, Kristi Long. Her excitement about this project made Rutgers my first choice for publisher, and her encouragement and helpful feedback have made the final stages of preparing this manuscript more painless than I thought possible.

In any project like this, it is easy to see the intellectual debts one owes, but there are emotional debts as well. As I think about myself as a scholar, I realize that I owe my first thanks to Bob Stauffer, my undergraduate advisor at Kalamazoo College. He once asked me if I had ever thought about becoming a professional sociologist. I so highly respected his opinion that I began to seriously consider it, and here I am. I'm also grateful to my sister, Jennie, who is my best friend. She periodically pumps me up with the most inflated predictions of success for this book.

On a daily basis, my strength and support come from my husband, Jim, and my daughter, Michael. Michael has tremendous energy and enthusiasm. She has buoyed me with her pride in my efforts, largely by bragging to everyone she knows that her mom is writing a book and forcing all of her friends to promise to buy a copy. Jim has provided the kind of support that only a partner can—listening to ideas, theories, anxieties, and hopes. He talked me out of setting the whole project on fire more than once, reminding me to think about how far I've come, rather than how far I have to go. He also provides an important touchstone in my work on gender inequality in marriage by reminding me that true egalitarian partnerships are more than possible. His love, support, and commitment to fairness mean more than mere words can convey.

Finally, my most profound thanks go to the couples who shared their lives and stories with me. As the coming pages reveal, they were often painfully honest about their experiences, in the hopes that others might learn from them. They were keenly interested in discovering that there were other families like them and looked forward to reading what I found. I hope I don't disappoint them.

*Earning More and
Getting Less*

CHAPTER 1

Higher-Earning Wives

SWIMMING AGAINST THE TIDE

WOMEN WHO MAKE more money than their husbands are a hot topic. They have commanded quite a bit of interest in the national media in the last several years. Articles have appeared in the *New York Times,* the *Boston Globe, Jet, More,* and *Newsweek,* with such eye-catching headlines as "When the Big Paycheck Is Hers" (Spragins 2002b) and "Why a Wife's Earnings Can Strain a Marriage" (1999). These articles tap into their audience's natural curiosity about these unusual couples, playing on both the novelty of the situation and a sense of unease about women who are more successful than their husbands.

Stories about higher-earning wives grab the reader's attention because they fly in the face of cultural assumptions that men should be the major breadwinners in their families. Though married women have long been part of the labor force (especially working-class and poor women) and have contributed important assets to their families, they have been largely seen as secondary earners. Providing economically for the family is a masculine imperative—the central responsibility of manhood. These articles imply that, while women's "helping out" is now normal, taking over the job of providing is not.

The assumption that men will be the (major) providers in their families runs so deep that families with higher-earning wives seem not only abnormal but also almost dysfunctional. This is what makes their stories so compelling. Readers want to know: How can he stand the blow to his ego? How can a wife still respect a man who earns less? And what do they tell their family and friends? Her earnings could easily become a dirty little secret, or a burden that they both must try to bear (Hochschild 1989; Pyke 1994). The situation is assumed to be stressful, and the implication is clear: When a wife earns more, the relationship is likely to suffer.

However, the reality of these marriages is more complex. Some of the couples profiled in these articles seem to escape the presumed peril of having or being a higher-earning wife. Younger couples, as well as those who hold less traditional expectations regarding the proper roles of men and women, seem quite comfortable with this arrangement. These are often dual-professional couples, with both spouses working in their chosen fields and possibly quite successful; the wife just happens to earn more. In a smaller number of cases, couples consciously agree that the wife should concentrate her efforts at work while the husband gives up paid employment altogether to stay home with the children. Often they make this decision because her earning potential is higher and it is important to them that one partner be available for the children (rather than relying on day care). In other cases, the wife wants to give her partner the opportunity to try an unconventional line of work that is less financially secure or stable. Under these circumstances, couples with higher-earning wives are basically content (Tyre and McGinn 2003).

However, the stories of most of the couples in these articles paint a far less harmonious and satisfying picture, and their experiences underscore the fears conveyed in the headlines. This is because most couples are thrown unexpectedly into a situation in which the wife earns more. In many of these cases, the husbands have been victims of the economic downturn of the last decade and have experienced a sudden job loss. Consequently, their wives have been thrust into the role of major earner. While occupational instability has been common for men among poor and working-class families, it is a new experience for middle- to upper-middle-class families who have seen husbands "downsized" out of significant paychecks, and these couples struggle to cope with this major shift in their relationships.

Wives in these circumstances are described as disappointed, resentful, anxious, and even angry. They feel intense pressure to continue to provide and are frustrated that their husbands are not "pulling their weight" financially. Wives are also embarrassed to be the major earners. One such wife is quoted as saying, "I make more money and he has no trouble with that, but would you please not mention it?" (Grant 2002). Others ask to have their names changed for or withheld from the articles, to avoid having others know that they outearn their spouses.

Husbands in these marriages are also uncomfortable. They feel like "outcasts" and "freeloaders." Like their wives, they feel they are not pulling their weight financially; some even describe themselves as "failing" because they are not the major providers in their families. In short, the experiences of these couples, as described in the articles, confirm the common assumption that these relationships are likely to be problematic; they leave the reader with the lingering question, "Is he less because she earns more?" (Grant 2002).

The issues raised by these articles seem even more salient because couples with higher-earning wives are growing in number. Though they make up a mere 7 percent of all married couples, as a proportion of the married population their numbers have more than tripled in the last thirty years (Raley et al. 2003). News reports on these couples often emphasize this rapid growth and make them sound like the wave of the future, implying that the twenty-first century will lead us into a brave new world where none of the old rules of marriage apply.

Though probably not the wave of the foreseeable future, couples with higher-earning wives should nonetheless command serious attention. Not because they represent a dominant pattern in married life, but because of the questions they raise about the nature of the relationship between husband and wife. Clearly, they disrupt the expectation that men are the (major) breadwinners in their families. However, the discomfort surrounding having or being a wife who earns more is not simply about challenging conventional gender expectations. These wives also threaten to disrupt the conventional power relationship within marriage. After all, money equals power in U.S. culture, so the question then becomes, Does earning more money give these wives power over their husbands? That seems to be the fear implicit in the reports on these couples. Something dangerous can happen when women earn more than their husbands. Men are diminished, marriages are threatened, and the whole prospect makes readers uncomfortable. But is there really that much power in a woman's paycheck?

A serious examination of couples with higher-earning wives would offer us the opportunity to ask some critical questions about the balance of power within marriage. These couples are both intellectually interesting and theoretically important because they sit at a crossroad of competing cultural imperatives; for them, the lingering expectation that masculinity equals power exists in tension with the expectation that money equals power. Examining how these couples resolve this tension could tell us a great deal about how spouses exercise power within marriage. If wives who earn more than their husbands are able to use their incomes to increase their power within their relationships, then we can think of money as an equal-opportunity source of power. However, if these wives still find themselves at a power disadvantage vis-à-vis their husbands, that tells us something equally important—that gendered expectations exert a force strong enough to undermine the logic of other social practices (i.e., the general rule that money equals power). Because of their unique circumstances, these couples can tell us whether money or gender has a greater influence on the balance of power in marriage.

Of course, it is possible that these couples will use their unconventional position to rethink power issues altogether. Having or being a wife who earns more may indicate a certain willingness to challenge other assumptions that are built into marriage, such as men's dominance. These couples may decide to reject the cultural link between money and power in favor of constructing more egalitarian relationships, where power is not rooted in gender or income earned. If so, they could give us alternative ways to think about gender and provide a model that would move us closer to equality in marriage.

Couples with higher-earning wives face a number of possibilities as they attempt to negotiate issues of power and make sense of their unconventional relationships. The tensions they live with are profound, and their experiences throw into sharp relief our assumptions about marriage. Exploring these tensions and assumptions gives us new ways to think about how power operates within marriage. And, as I will argue, understanding the dynamics among these couples is fundamental to understanding the nature of the relationship between gender and power.

THE LINK BETWEEN MONEY AND POWER IN MARRIAGE

Historically, for men, money equals power. As breadwinners, men have enjoyed a great deal of authority and control within marriage (Hertz 1986). First, since a man's earnings have been central to the family's economic survival, family life has often been organized around the needs of his work. Most fundamentally, the family moves to wherever the husband can find employment and may have to move often as jobs disappear or new opportunities arise. Even the rhythms of family life, such as bedtime, rising, and mealtimes, are often dictated by the husband's work demands and schedule.

Second, by earning the money, men have also earned the right to control it, often managing the family purse and controlling other family members' access to it. This control means that men have typically had access to money "off the top"; no matter how strained the family's financial circumstances, men still retain some money for their personal use (Blumberg and Coleman 1989; Ferree 1990). In addition to controlling and managing the economic resources of the family, men have also had the freedom and authority to control household decisions, both large and small. Husbands may delegate the daily running of the household to their wives, but they reserve the right to make final decisions on matters that they deem important.

Finally, bringing home the bacon has assured men more subtle privileges within marriage. To ensure that men could continue to provide well, they enjoyed the best food the family table had to offer, as well as ample leisure time to recover from the mental and physical strains of hard labor (Bernard 1981). Male breadwinners were also free from participating in domestic labor, leaving responsibility for household chores and child care to their wives. In these ways, a man's income has been the ticket to greater power and privilege within marriage.

This equation of money with power has led millions of women to pursue education and employment as the keys to both personal empowerment and relationships with men that were more egalitarian. If men's power is rooted in their incomes, then women need access to independent wages to increase their power vis-à-vis their husbands. Indeed, this logic drove the second wave of the feminist movement in the 1960s and 1970s. Popular writers and scholars urged women to pursue higher education and prepare to enter the world of paid work on the same footing as men, so that women could both improve their sense of personal competence and increase their autonomy and power within their most intimate relationships. Women responded to these new opportunities outside the home, fueling one of the most dramatic social shifts of the twentieth century (Mintz and Kellogg 1988). Of course, many women also pursued paid employment during this time to meet the very real material needs of their families, and these needs continue to push women into the workforce. But whatever women's motivations, the expectation remains that they can use their incomes to increase their power in their marriages.

Along with this movement toward labor-force participation has come a change in people's attitudes about the proper roles for men and women. Fewer people believe that a woman's working necessarily harms her child, or that it is better if women stay at home and leave the work of running the country to men. This is taken to mean that gender attitudes have become increasingly egalitarian over the last several decades (Brewster and Padavic 2000). Women are more accepted in the labor force, even in traditionally male-dominated occupations; husbands have been urged to become more "involved fathers" rather than leave all parenting activities and responsibilities to their wives. Opportunities and gender definitions have begun to expand for both men and women.

In spite of these important changes in behavior and expectations, working for wages has not paid off for women in the way feminism expected. Even as wives have moved into the labor force in great numbers over the last several decades, men's power and privileges within the home have been largely preserved. Their privilege at home is manifested in three fundamental ways: control over the family purse, authority in decision making, and the ability to avoid household chores and child-care responsibilities. Measured in these terms, wives still seem to be at a substantial disadvantage. On the whole, women's employment has given them only a small increase in control over family finances and decision making, and women still bear the disproportionate burden of domestic labor and child care (Blumberg 1991; Coltrane 2000; Fox and Murry 2000; Williams 2000). In other words, working outside the home has not done much to increase women's power within the home.

Still, the logic that links power to income is compelling (Blumberg and Coleman 1989). By all rights, earning a wage should increase women's power within marriage. Perhaps women are still at a disadvantage because they typically earn a smaller fraction of the family's total income (Raley et al. 2003). Most men still outearn their wives and seem to retain substantial power based on their larger incomes and their status as the major breadwinners. If this is the reason for men's continued power advantage, the question then becomes, what happens when women earn the bulk of the family income? It is tempting to think that enjoying income and status advantages over their husbands would allow women to negotiate more egalitarian power relations within their marriages, where merely working and earning a (lesser) wage have not.

However, the available evidence suggests that earning more than one's husband does not translate into other advantages within the marital relationship. For example, several studies have found that as a woman's income surpasses that of her husband, she performs more housework rather than less (Bittman et al. 2003; Brines 1994; Greenstein 2000). In fact, wives who earn all the family's income perform about as much housework as wives who earn no income at all. This clearly undermines the money-equals-power equation, at least for women.

These findings are difficult to explain. It appears that these couples are trying to find some way to normalize an unconventional (and uncomfortable) situation. Either husbands refuse to engage in housework, or higher-earning wives willingly take on more to restore the relationship to some balance that feels right. The exact dynamic that produces these results is unclear.

Certainly these quantitative studies demonstrate that gender problematizes the link between money and power, but they are unable to describe either the dynamics between these spouses or the ways couples come to construct relationships where wives contribute so much and husbands contribute so little. This book reports on a qualitative study of couples with higher-earning wives that addresses this crucial gap in our understanding of the interaction between income and gender and its effect on marital power dynamics. By drawing on in-depth interview data, I illuminate how these spouses work together to reproduce men's dominance within their relationships. That is, rather than using their unconventional circumstances to negotiate more egalitarian power relations, couples attempt to hide or ignore wives' income advantage to preserve men's power and privileges within marriage.

CENTRAL CLAIMS OF *EARNING MORE AND GETTING LESS*

Though linking money and power makes intuitive sense and may seem only fair, the data presented here suggest that this equation works only for men. Higher-earning wives are unable to use their incomes to negotiate more egalitarian power relationships with their husbands. Rather, the potential power in women's greater incomes is largely hidden or ignored, and men's dominance is preserved in these marriages. Wives work with their husbands to preserve men's privileges within marriage by continuing to perform the bulk of the domestic labor and by deferring to their husbands' authority in financial and other matters.

But it is not simply that women's greater incomes do not significantly enhance their power within their relationships. More importantly, their incomes actually become liabilities for them. Wives seem to feel that they have to make up for their income advantage by taking on the greater share of the domestic labor burden or by deferring to their husbands in decision making. This puts an additional burden on wives—that of maintaining harmony within their relationships by working to (re)create a balance of power that feels culturally "right." The income advantage that has historically given men a great deal of power within marriage does not offer the same benefits to these wives.

I draw on these results to make several larger claims about the nature of gender and power. The first is that the experiences of these couples demonstrate that gender, and not economics, is at the heart of men's privilege within marriage. Gender ideology—specifically, conventional beliefs defining what husbands and wives are or should do—overrides the cultural link between money and power for women in these marriages. Conventional gendered beliefs and practices, such as men's dominance within marriage, persist even without the support of other social structures, such as men's economic dominance.

This means that we can talk about gender as a separate structure that exerts on these marriages an influence both distinct from other social forces and extremely compelling (Lorber 1994). I build on the work of Barbara Risman (1998), who argues that gender exists as a structure that operates on three levels of social life: the institutional, interactional, and individual. My data demonstrate that to understand marital power dynamics, it is important to examine the gendered cultural expectations at the institutional level (including notions of what a good wife or husband should be), the face-to-face communications of couples at the interactional level, and the efforts of each spouse to construct appropriate gender identities at the individual level. The influence and contradictions of gender make themselves felt at each of these levels as spouses work together to negotiate and construct meaningful and comfortable relationships, and the contradictions are typically resolved in ways that support conventional gendered constructions and reproduce men's power advantage.

My second claim about the nature of gender and power is that the most important power dynamics in these relationships are hidden. This means that conventional tools for assessing marital power fail to reveal either the scope of men's power within marriage or exactly how men's power is reproduced. Only by listening carefully to how couples make decisions and how spouses feel about themselves, their partners, and their relationships can we fully understand the complex dynamics that we call power.

Third, while this study attempts to separate gender from power analytically, the results presented here demonstrate that they are clearly linked in practice. That is, the power dynamics in these relationships are shaped by the gendered expectations that men are to be breadwinners and wives are to be mothers and homemakers. Issues of what it means to be a "real" man or woman are tangled up with questions of power in these relationships. As couples attempt to preserve these conventional gender identities, they also preserve the differential power invested in them. Because of this, rather than using their unusual circumstances to challenge conventional gendered practices, these couples are largely reproducing the status quo.

And finally, these results suggest that movement toward greater gender equality has to be addressed at all three levels of the gender structure. Equality must involve more than changing attitudes at the cultural level or behavior at the interactional level. It is not enough to argue that women deserve the access to education, jobs, and income that men have. It is not enough to attempt to negotiate equal power in decision making with one's partner or a more equitable sharing of domestic labor. Real movement toward gender equality must also address issues of identity. To strike at the heart of the gender structure, we must aggressively disrupt and reconstruct assumptions that lie at the very core of who we think we are.

ORGANIZATION OF *EARNING MORE AND* *GETTING LESS*

The book is organized with several goals in mind: to assess what higher-earning wives are able to "buy" with their incomes within the context of their relationships; to explore the assumptions about gender and power that are built into the institution of marriage; and to illuminate the subtle dynamics of these relationships that undermine wives' power and reproduce men's privileges. Chapter 2 explores our cultural assumptions about gender and power within the context of heterosexual love relationships. I examine the cultural contract that has existed between husbands and wives since the Industrial Revolution. This contract rests on the ideology of separate spheres, which links men with the public realm and the world of paid work, and women with the domestic realm and the world of hearth and home. As breadwinners and mothers/homemakers, men and women have different responsibilities and enjoy different rights within marriage. I explore the power implications of these gendered responsibilities and discuss how this contract has largely endured, even as wives have crossed over from the domestic sphere to the public sphere in pursuit of paid employment.

In Chapter 2 I also present the design of my investigation. I begin by discussing how to conceptualize and measure power in love relationships. Because of the cultural reluctance to admit that power operates within the context of our most intimate relationships, I explore the challenge of trying to link love and power, review past conceptualizations of power, and offer an alternative way to think about power that reveals the subtle gendered dynamics that help reproduce men's dominance within marriage.

The central findings of my exploration demonstrate that higher-earning wives are unable to use their substantial resources to negotiate more egalitarian power relationships with their husbands. Their incomes do not ensure them access to the same kinds of privileges that men have historically enjoyed. Chapters 3, 4, and 5 demonstrate that, based on their income advantage, these wives receive relatively little relief from domestic labor, do not typically enjoy greater (or even equal) control over the family's financial resources, and are unable to gain equal footing in family decision making. In short, the substantial incomes of higher-earning wives buy them very little in their relationships.

Instead, wives work with their husbands to reproduce men's dominance within their relationships as part of an effort to make their marriages look and feel like more conventional ones. Chapter 6 shows how spouses struggle to construct appropriate gender identities in these marriages. That is, rather than using their experiences to rewrite the marital contract, spouses seem committed to the identities of mother/homemaker and breadwinner that make it appear they are conforming to this contract. This strategy allows couples to feel better about their relationships but seems to undercut any potential for transforming conventional gender constructions that may exist in these marriages. These results make clear why women's resources do not automatically afford them greater power inside their marriages, and how both men and women actively work to reproduce men's dominance within the marital relationship.

In Chapter 7, I explore how couples manage the tensions created by having or being a wife who earns more. I present both the satisfactions and disappointments spouses express about their relationships, and I discuss the strategies they use to make their relationships feel more comfortable. For example, many spouses find ways to hide or ignore the income and status differences between them. Their systems of money management may make the woman's income much less visible, or spouses may choose to live in separate social worlds to manage the status differences between them. These strategies make their marriages look and feel like more conventional ones, and spouses seem more comfortable with each other.

In the final chapter, I explore the implications of these findings for our understanding of the gendered power dynamics within marriage. That men retain their privileges in these marriages demonstrates the resilience of the gender structure and of conventional gendered understandings, even in the face of dramatic social change. On the surface, then, these couples do not offer much hope for the prospects of long-term gender change. However, while these findings may seem conservative—even regressive—I argue that these couples offer the potential for new gender constructions that could help move marriages toward more egalitarian sharing of power. That is, by showing us how spouses can rework gendered understandings in ways that support the status quo, these couples open up the possibility that gendered expectations can also be reworked to dismantle conventional privilege and support new, more egalitarian relationships.

CHAPTER 2

Thinking about Gender and Power in Marriage

THINKING ABOUT POWER within marriage requires exam-
ining the gendered assumptions upon which marriage as an institution is
built, as well as the difficulties researchers face in trying to conceptualize
and measure power within marriage. In this chapter, I examine how
power has been routinely conceptualized and measured within marriage,
adapt these accepted measures to my work, and offer an alternative conceptualization of power that can illuminate more subtle dynamics in
these marriages.

THE CONVENTIONAL MARITAL CONTRACT

The balance of power in most marriages reflects the ideology of separate spheres in the conventional marital contract. Of course, this contract is
not a written document; it consists of cultural understandings of the recip-
rocal rights and obligations that each spouse has within the institution of
marriage. According to this unwritten contract, these rights and obligations
are divided along gender lines, which construct men as breadwinners and
women as mothers and homemakers. The man's main responsibilities are to
provide for the family economically and to represent the family to the
community or the world at large. The woman's main responsibility is to
care for the home, husband, and children. If spouses hold up their end of
the bargain, this exchange is considered both reasonable and fair.

While this model may seem overstated and outdated, Joan Williams
(2000) argues that the basic assumptions of this contract persist. This
complementary organization of market work and family life exists as a
system that Williams calls "domesticity." Under this system, men are entitled and encouraged to perform as "ideal workers" in the marketplace,
unencumbered by the demands of family life. Women, whether engaged

in paid labor or not, are marginalized in the workplace by their domestic responsibilities. They continue to be seen and treated by employers as mothers or potential mothers, which limits their options and opportunities at work. That women maintain responsibility for domestic labor and child care hampers their ability to engage in paid labor as ideal workers (i.e., men). So while the assumption that women will be engaged only in domestic labor has changed in recent years, the underlying contract that delegates breadwinning responsibility to men and domestic responsibility to women remains largely unchallenged.

The conventional marital contract does not simply divide responsibilities between spouses; it also reinforces men's power within marriage. This is because the responsibilities and tasks of husbands and wives are valued differently. Within most U.S. families, the income that the husband earns is the most highly valued asset. It confers a higher status on the husband, both within and outside the relationship, and has been used to justify men's greater power in marriage, especially in terms of decision-making practices and control over the family's financial resources. Historically, men have wielded power based on their greater incomes, and wives were expected to defer to their husbands' authority. By contrast, women's caring work at home has not been accorded the same status as breadwinning. That it is unpaid work signifies its lesser value, and the ability to refuse to do such work is one of the privileges men typically enjoy in marriage (Hochschild 1989). The conventional marital contract, then, underscores the greater value of the man's contributions (income), while devaluing those of the woman (domestic services). In short, the bargain implied by the conventional marital contract is the key to continued gender inequality in marriage (Williams 2000).

Admittedly, life has changed dramatically for married couples, especially in the last several decades. This model of husband as sole breadwinner and wife as homemaker describes the reality of only 25 percent of married couples in the United States today (Raley et al. 2003). Transformations in the economy have made it impossible for all but a comparative handful of families to enjoy a moderate standard of living on only one income. This makes it tempting to think of the man-as-breadwinner/ woman-as-homemaker model of married life as outdated and irrelevant.

However, marriages are still constructed against the backdrop of the conventional marital contract. Culturally, we still hold men accountable for breadwinning and women for mothering, regardless of whatever additional responsibilities they may take on. In most circles, men are still revered and respected based on the kind of work they perform and the standard of living their families are able to enjoy because of it. Remember that most of the men with higher-earning wives profiled in recent news articles felt like outcasts or failures for not being the major earners. Women are still expected to keep neat homes and present clean, well-adjusted, and well-mannered children to the outside world. Poorly behaved children might still be asked, "Didn't your mother teach you any better than that?"

This means that men and women get more "credit," both inside and outside the marital relationship, for engaging in activities that are consistent with conventional gender identities. While a wife's income may be important to the family, her employment lacks the social legitimacy accorded her husband's work. Women's paid work is typically seen as an option, rather than a duty. Since social convention does not obligate a woman to provide for her family, she is not protected from housework or other domestic intrusions on her breadwinning activities as a man would be. Women typically retain responsibility for the household and simply add the role of worker onto those of mother and homemaker (Hochschild 1989; Rubin 1994). Women also receive less social approval than do men for engaging in paid work and may even face condemnation for "neglecting" domestic duties (Popenoe 1989). Similarly, while men may help out with the workload at home, and in middle- to upper-middle-class circles might receive a great deal of social approval for doing so, their domestic labor is not a substitute for breadwinning; even the most involved father rarely opts out of providing altogether (Coltrane 1996; Deutsch 1999). In short, the meanings attached to paid work and domestic labor are fundamentally different for men and women, and tend to reinforce the identities of breadwinner and mother/homemaker embedded in the conventional marital contract.

The continued distinction between mothering and breadwinning as gendered activities means that we can think of these identities as enduring "gender boundaries"—ways to mark the difference between women and men (Connell 1987; Potuchek 1997). While women may work outside the home, men still have the responsibility to provide that makes them breadwinners. Though men may help with housework or child care, it is still a woman's duty to provide the level of attention and care associated with mothering. The lines dividing these gendered responsibilities are still clearly drawn (Williams 2000).

If it is true that breadwinning is the central identity for men, and mothering is the central identity for women, this could be problematic for dual-earner couples. If wives are also providing an income, what distinguishes them from their husbands? In most dual-earner couples, men still outearn their wives, often by a large margin (Raley et al. 2003). Couples typically respond to this shift in behavior by thinking of husbands as the primary breadwinners, with wives as secondary earners simply "helping out" (Potuchek 1997; Willinger 1993). Similarly, couples see women's mothering and domestic responsibilities as primary, and their work commitments are often organized around the needs of the family (Hochschild 1989; Williams 2000). In this way, men can see themselves as still meeting the masculine imperative of providing for their families, and wives can see themselves as good mothers, despite being employed outside the home (Coltrane 1996).

Of course, having both spouses in the workforce could represent an opportunity to change the gendered expectations and meanings surrounding breadwinning by rejecting the idea of separate spheres embedded in the conventional marital contract. Husbands and wives could think of themselves as co-providers with a joint responsibility to meet the financial obligations of the family. They could then share the responsibilities for maintaining a clean, orderly home and raising healthy children. Sharing all family work (both paid and unpaid) more equally could break down these rigid gender boundaries.

We know that some couples have worked successfully to erode these boundaries (Coltrane 1996; Deutsch 1999; Risman and Johnson-Sumerford 1998; Schwartz 1994). These couples consciously share the work of providing and caring for a family in ways that begin to undermine the breadwinner/mother identities, as well as the power imbalance associated with them. However, even some of these partnerships contain rumblings of gender unease. For example, men and women in these relationships often collaborate to maintain some gender specialization; women want to guard part of the domestic domain as their own (Hertz 1989) or want to feel like "I'm still the mom" (Coltrane 1996; Deutsch 1999), and men still think of providing as their own responsibility

(Wilkie 1993). Such expectations are so strong that even couples with higher-earning wives continue to cling to them (Brennan, Barnett, and Gareis 2001). These results suggest that spouses are often more comfortable with a certain level of conventional gender asymmetry in their relationships.

Williams (2000) describes this pull toward the conventional as being caught in a "gender force field." While conventional gender expectations do not determine behavior, they can exert a strong pull that can be difficult to resist and can wear people down over time. For example, after couples have their first child, the call of traditional roles and expectations can be particularly loud. With a new life depending on them, men often feel a greater need to be a good provider, and even women who had planned to continue working after their child's birth can feel unexpectedly drawn toward staying at home (Cowan and Cowan 1992; Rexroat and Shehan 1987).

In other words, even though spouses' behavior is changing, as women continue to be a strong presence in the workforce and some men become more engaged in domestic labor, it may be too threatening to give up all their conventional gender expectations—it does not feel right. This means that as men and women are engaged in similar activities, such as providing for the family, the breadwinning and mothering boundaries can take on great importance; that is, these boundaries become a crucial way for husbands and wives to create and maintain a sense of gender difference (Potuchek 1997).

So even though the conventional marital contract no longer describes the reality of most U.S. couples, by maintaining the gender boundaries of mothering and breadwinning, dual-earner couples reinforce the bargain implied by the old contract (Brennan et al. 2001; Coltrane 1996; Potuchek 1997; Wilkie 1993). This finding is significant because of the power dynamics embedded in the contract. As we have seen, the activities associated with mothering and breadwinning are differentially valued, with breadwinning generally conferring more privileges than does mothering. If employed women are not defined as breadwinners, they may lose access to these privileges. In other words, by maintaining the gender boundaries written into the conventional marital contract, spouses may undercut women's power within marriage.

However, all of this assumes that men's power within marriage is truly rooted in their greater economic resources. While this assumption has driven much of the research on marital power, the accumulating evidence suggests that it is flawed. If money is the key to the power dynamics within marriage, we would expect the balance of power to shift as women have begun to share breadwinning with their husbands. In fact, earning an income has done little to increase women's power, which undermines the fair exchange of income earned by male breadwinners for the domestic services of their wives implied by the conventional marital contract. This means that we need to rethink the money/power link within marriage.

MARITAL POWER AS THE EXCHANGE OF RESOURCES

Early attempts to talk about the balance of power within marriages rested on the assumptions embedded in the conventional marital contract. This research (beginning with Blood and Wolfe 1960) was driven by resource and exchange theories that link the balance of power in marriages to the relative contributions, or resources, of spouses. Resources are anything of value, tangible or intangible, that partners bring to a relationship. They include money, occupational or social status, education, love and affection, physical attractiveness, special knowledge or expertise, services (such as performing domestic labor or giving back rubs), and so on. Under the conventional marital contract, men contribute their incomes, as well as the status attached to their occupations, in exchange for domestic labor and child-care services from their wives.

The resource/exchange model views power as the ability to prevail in a variety of household decisions, ranging from how much to spend each week on groceries to when and if the family should move. Since men and women both reported that husbands had more control over most decisions, Blood and Wolfe concluded that husbands had more power in their marriages. They also concluded that this power came, not from the influence of patriarchal ideology, but from husbands' contributing the more socially valued resources (income and status) to the marriage. Thus, resources such as income and status represent the potential for exercising power. And while both spouses have access to some resources, men have more power in marriages because they contribute the more important resources to the relationship.

This logic is compelling and has held sway both inside and outside the academy: The more you give, the more you should receive in return. However, if this conceptualization of power within marriage were accurate, we would expect to see a shift in the balance of power between spouses over the last several decades as women have moved into the paid labor force in great numbers. According to resource and exchange theory assumptions, women who contribute economically to the relationship should be able to exercise greater control over finances and decision making, and buy a certain amount of relief from domestic labor and childrearing responsibilities. However, the marital power literature over the past few decades demonstrates that this is not happening (see, for example, Bianchi et al. 2000; Blumberg 1984; Blumstein and Schwartz 1983, 1991; Hochschild 1989; Perry-Jenkins and Folk 1994; Pleck 1985; Wright et al. 1992). Women may gain a greater measure of control over finances or household decisions, but few couples report patterns that could be characterized as egalitarian. Husbands continue to exercise greater control in financial matters and decision making.

Similarly, women's employment has done little to alter the division of domestic labor. Husbands may help a little more with household chores and child care, but much of the research argues that these changes reflect shifts in the proportion of work being done by each spouse. In other words, it looks like men are doing more because women, who are now further crunched for time, are doing less (see Chapter 3). It is clear that merely earning a wage does not significantly enhance a woman's power in most marriages.

As we have said, one reason for this continued imbalance of power may be that men typically outearn their wives, often by a large margin. This income advantage continues to lend legitimacy to the husband's authority within the marriage. He may not be earning all the money, but he is still earning most of it. This circumstance may allow spouses to continue to think of their economic assets as largely his and to justify his continued control over them. However, this is only a partial explanation for the enduring imbalance of power within marriage. If women's income buys them so little, then power is not about money—or at least, not entirely about money. Gender is also a factor.

Two examples from studies of marital power suggest that this is the case. The first example comes from Blood and Wolfe's (1960) work. One of their most interesting findings, given their reliance on resource and exchange theory, is that the wives in their sample who worked outside the home full time got the least amount of help with domestic labor from their husbands. It is not just that these wives could not exchange their income for more help with domestic labor from their husbands, but that they got the worst deal overall of any group of wives when they were contributing the most (in terms of paid and domestic labor) to their relationships. The second example comes from Arlie Hochschild's *The Second Shift* (1989). Hochschild reported that, while substantial sharing of domestic duties was not common in her sample of dual-earner couples, among couples where women earned more than their husbands, none of the men shared the housework and child-care duties. These results directly challenge the exchange of resources implied by the conventional marital contract, since these wives got no credit for the substantial incomes they contributed.

More recent quantitative research has produced results similar to Hochschild's and demonstrates that there is a curvilinear relationship between income contributed and the amount of housework each spouse performs (Brines 1994; Greenstein 2000; Bittman et al. 2003). Husbands who are sole (or major) breadwinners successfully trade their income for domestic labor, but wives who are the major breadwinners in their families are unable to negotiate a similar deal. That is, wives who earn all a family's income perform about the same amount of housework as wives who earn no income at all. Their husbands seem to receive domestic services, rather than to compensate for their wives' unusually high earnings by taking on more household labor. Their wives' earnings disrupt a balance of power that feels culturally right, and either these men attempt to restore that balance by asserting their right as men to their wives' domestic labor, or wives take on more household work voluntarily to avoid further assaulting their husbands' masculinity. Couples engage in "gender display" (Brines) or "deviance neutralization" (Greenstein) to restore a sense that spouses are meeting their conventional obligations. However, the exact dynamic by which gender overrides the money-equals-power equation among these couples is unclear.

That higher-earning wives cannot trade their income for a reduction in their domestic labor burden undermines the theoretical assumptions of the bulk of research on power in marriages. These results demonstrate that men's power in marriage does not come from their income or their role as (primary) breadwinner—or at least, it does not come from these resources alone. Husbands in dual-earner families retain and enjoy some rights or privileges as men. Thus, it makes sense to talk about gender as exerting an influence on marital power dynamics that is independent of income earned by spouses. We can then think of gender as a separate structure that shapes the balance of power within marriage.

GENDER AS STRUCTURE

Because gender so thoroughly pervades social life, it is often conceptualized as a cultural dynamic that is "woven into" other institutions, meaning that beliefs about gender and gender differences are used to maintain and justify other social practices. However, gender also exists as a separate entity (Lorber 1994). That is, while gender is indeed embedded in and shapes the practices of other social institutions, it also exerts an influence that is separable from all other institutions. In the case of marital power, men's ability to retain their control and privileges, even in the absence of the economic dominance that has legitimated this power advantage, suggests that gender exerts an influence on marital power dynamics that is distinct from men's successful enactment of breadwinner responsibilities. In short, that men retain their power advantages in these circumstances points to gender as both a separate and a stable entity.

This means that we can talk about gender as structure (Risman 1998). This structure exists and operates on multiple levels within social life: institutional, interactional, and individual. At the institutional level, gender exists as beliefs about what men and women are or should be and as organizational practices that serve to reinforce these beliefs. The typing of women and men into particular occupations, the gap in wages between men and women, and the glass ceiling in organizations are all examples of gendered organizational practices. But gender at the institutional level also exists as ideology. Beliefs that men should be stronger and rational and women weaker and emotional are part of conventional gender ideology. The conventional marital contract, with the expectation that men are breadwinners and women are mothers and homemakers, is also part of gendered ideology. These institutional-level beliefs and practices organize the behavior of men and women at the interactional and individual levels.

At the interactional level, gender shapes face-to-face communication. That is, we interact with others as men and women, drawing on the cultural expectations for behavior that exist at the institutional level. Perhaps our best conceptualization of how the gender structure operates at the interactional level comes from West and Zimmerman (1987). They argue that men and women "do gender" as they interact with others in ordinary settings. Within a given context, individuals must clearly demonstrate to others that they are appropriately masculine or feminine. Men and women are aware of the gendered expectations for dress, speech, and behavior that exist at the institutional level, and they manage their conduct in light of the possibility that they may be held accountable to these standards by others.

For example, aside from cassocks or ceremonial kilts, men in Western societies do not wear skirts, but not because of any inherent property of the garment. Skirts are actually quite practical in terms of allowing freedom of movement and can be more comfortable than pants, particularly in warm weather when they generate their own breeze. However, since skirts have been successfully typed as women's clothing, no self-respecting (conventional) male would be caught dead in one. Those rare males who choose to adopt this style of dress risk social sanctions ranging from disapproval to ridicule to physical violence. They also risk being labeled inappropriately feminine and, therefore, not men. This example demonstrates that although conventional gender expectations may not completely determine behavior, even the smallest rules can be quite compelling. So while men and women do not always conform to the expectations for their sex categories, all know that deviations may come at a cost.

While "doing gender" encompasses a wide range of behaviors, the primary activities for men and women are the doing of dominance and submission (Berk 1985; West and Zimmerman 1987). This means that gender differences are not neutral but tied to larger power structures. At the institutional level, men enjoy greater economic and political power. At the interactional level, men assert their authority and women defer to this authority. This gender imperative is particularly salient in the context of heterosexual love relationships and marriage. Cultural notions of a man as "head of the household" or "king of his castle" continue to resonate, even if more subtly than in the past. Correspondingly, being a wife has typically entailed a certain level of service to one's husband. All spouses have to negotiate their relationships against the backdrop of these expectations, whether in congruence with or in opposition to them. That is, while spouses may choose to challenge conventional expectations or practices, others may still hold spouses accountable to conventional standards. These conventional assumptions regarding gender continue to shape the interactions of spouses and remain a central part of how men and women think about themselves as husbands and wives.

Gender is also a fundamental component of identity construction; it is impossible to think of ourselves separately from our identity as a man or woman. At the individual level, the gender structure constrains men and women as they attempt to construct meaningful identities. That is, doing gender is an internal process as well (Acker 1992). Individuals often hold themselves accountable to conventional conceptions of gender-appropriate behavior, regardless of the standards imposed by those around them. That is, it is important to feel that one is behaving in a way consistent with one's identity as a man or woman.

The research reviewed thus far suggests that, within marriage, the gendered identities of breadwinner and mother may still resonate for spouses and represent an important touchstone for constructing individual identities. Still, for husbands and wives, this identity construction occurs in the context of the couple; doing gender is a team performance. One spouse's failure to engage his or her part appropriately may reflect negatively on the partner. For example, having a wife who makes substantially more money may represent a significant threat to a man's gender identity, given that breadwinning is such a fundamental component of masculinity in U.S. culture, and the couple must find a way to manage this tension. Spouses must construct gender identities in tandem to find a balance that feels right to them, both as a couple and as individuals.

Although we can conceptualize these three levels of the gender structure as distinct from one another, they operate simultaneously and reinforce each other. While institutional practices and ideologies shape microlevel behavior, behavior on the interactional and individual levels has an impact on gender at the institutional level, for it is through microlevel dynamics that the larger gender structure is either challenged or reproduced. For example, at the microlevel, couples with higher-earning wives could represent a potential site of gender change. They could challenge the conventional link between breadwinning and power by sharing domestic labor, decision-making power, and the responsibility to provide equally. They could rewrite the gender scripts of the conventional marital contract and expand the possibilities for both men and women in marriage.

In spite of this opportunity, it seems that women's incomes have bought them little in their marriages because the gender structure assures men certain privileges within the marital relationship. As we have seen, the gender structure seems to have accommodated women's paid labor by constructing men as primary breadwinners, and therefore still due the privileges attached to this activity. However, couples with higher-earning wives present a more serious challenge to the gender structure. These couples disrupt the cultural link between gender, money, and power more profoundly and create new tensions for spouses to manage. These couples' efforts to preserve men's authority and interpersonal dominance despite women's economic advantage highlight the difficulty of rewriting conventional gender scripts and demonstrate the resilience of the gender structure in the face of potential challenges to it.

CONCEPTUAL ISSUES IN ANALYZING POWER
Love: What's Power Got to Do with It?

Conducting research on marital power raises some sticky questions, because we are not used to thinking that power operates in our most intimate relationships. In U.S. culture, marriage is supposed to be based on romantic love. This notion requires that our relationships be ruled by our hearts and emotions, as in "I'm so crazy about her" or "He just swept me off my feet." This overpowering emotion often puts us beyond the reach of reason. We do not rationally calculate whether we should be in love with someone; we act largely on the basis of feelings. In fact, thinking rationally about a relationship, or weighing its pros and cons, opens us up to the charge that we are not really in love.

Being involved in a romantic relationship also means being focused on the other. That is, loves requires a certain degree of altruism. One's personal desires cannot always be primary. Romantic love often requires putting the needs of one's partner first to make her or him happy or even to preserve the relationship. This selfless giving is often the standard used to assess the nature of our feelings. Only when we can place the interests of the other before our own is our caring and commitment seen as genuine.

This emphasis on affection and altruism leaves little room for power considerations in a love relationship. In fact, Western culture sets up love and power as opposites. If love means a denial of self for the sake of the other, power implies a calculation of one's rational self-interest above the interests of the other. Power means forcing another to do something she or he would prefer not to do, or even taking advantage of another for personal gain. Power considerations, then, seem anathema to the kind of blissful relationship idealized by our cultural emphasis on romantic love.

It is the equation of power with this kind of domination that makes us reluctant to admit that power plays a role in our love relationships. Few people want to think of having power over (or being subordinate to) their beloved. However, power is not simply domination; power also refers to autonomy—the ability to act according to one's wishes and desires. Using this conceptualization of power, the need for love and the need for power are no longer mutually exclusive dynamics in a love relationship but are intimately connected. Great acts of love depend on a free and autonomous self capable of both feeling and action. In this way, love and power are both fundamental dynamics in any healthy relationship (Nyberg 1981).

Even if we think of power as autonomy rather than domination, we can see how power and love exist in tension with one another in any relationship. Fulfilling one's own desires can sometimes mean thwarting those of one's partner, raising important questions, such as, How much should I give up to make my partner happy? and What do I have a right to expect from my partner in return? Conflicting desires or needs between spouses mean that at some point one person's autonomy will be sacrificed to meet the desires of the other. Often these issues exist on an unconscious level and surface in a relationship only in the context of "fairness," as in, Why do *I* have to do all the cleaning? or Why do you always get your way? Despite the clear power implications of these issues, they are rarely framed as evidence of differential power between spouses.

Conceptualizing and Measuring Power within Marriage

The widespread cultural denial of the presence of power in love relationships makes it difficult to conceptualize and measure power within marriage. Most obviously, one spouse's exerting his or her will over the other (overt power) gives us a concrete way to examine the balance of power in a relationship, and much of the work on marital power has taken this factor as its starting point. Spouses have been asked to report on how much "say" each spouse has in a wide range of decisions commonly made by married couples. One's ability to influence or control decision making is a fundamental indicator of one's power within the relationship.

However, power dynamics, particularly within marriage, can be much more nuanced and subtle, and decision-making outcomes tell only part of the story. The process of making decisions, including the various ways in which partners can influence negotiations, also reveals much about who exerts more control within the relationship. For example, while one spouse may be making what appear to be important decisions, it is possible that these are merely tasks delegated by the other partner. Paying the bills could put one spouse in a position of power by allowing her or him to closely monitor the family's finances and make at least some monetary decisions unilaterally. However, in other circumstances, paying the bills may be a task dumped on a spouse by a partner who considers this job menial and stressful. Therefore, knowing how couples come to decisions can be a more important indicator of the balance of power between spouses than the actual outcome of the decision-making process.

The ability to suppress issues, or "non–decision making," is also an important indicator of power. This kind of power would show up in the successful resolution of conflict or resistance in the past in ways that keep similar conflicts from reemerging (latent power). In this case, the partner who "lost" the first round on a particular issue might fear open confrontation if she or he attempts to renegotiate the outcome, and therefore lives with the past decision rather than actively pursuing her or his desires. Power then lies with the partner who is able to avoid discussion or conflict over an issue once it has been settled to her or his satisfaction.

Considering overt and latent power, as well as power processes, gives us a number of ways to assess the balance of power in a relationship. But even these approaches do not examine all the possible avenues for exercising power. Steven Lukes (1974, 1986) has conceptualized power in a way that allows us to explore power dynamics that are embedded in larger cultural assumptions or ideologies. He advocates what he calls a three-dimensional view of power, which examines overt and latent power but also attempts to uncover power that is "hidden." Lukes argues that the ability to keep particular issues from entering the arena of conflict is a more thoroughgoing exercise of power than any overt struggle for dominance. The most effective exercise of power draws on prevailing ideological constructions, so that an individual's or group's domination seems beneficial, reasonable, or natural. In this way, the most adept uses of power are largely hidden.

Hidden power can be exercised in a variety of ways: through individual decisions, institutional procedures, or by dominant values that shape interaction (e.g., conventional gender expectations). Consensus may seem to exist, as ideology masks the contradictions in lived experience; but uncovering these contradictions reveals the exercise of power. We can easily see the distinction between the various conceptualizations of power by looking at the issue of domestic labor. If a husband and wife struggle over domestic labor, and the husband successfully resists his wife's request for him to do more around the house, he has exercised overt power. If his wife then accepts the situation and avoids raising the issue again out of fear of renewed conflict, he has exercised latent power. But even if this issue is never raised between the two spouses because the wife accepts it as her duty to bear the domestic labor burden—even when she is employed outside the home—her husband has benefited from the hidden power in prevailing gendered practices and ideology.

Aafke Komter (1989) adapted Lukes's framework to her examination of the hidden power in Dutch marriages. She found that husbands benefit from the implicit hierarchy of cultural worth that values men over women, and that couples rely on conventional gender expectations to explain inequities in their relationships. For example, men explained that their wives perform more housework because they were "better at it" or "enjoyed it more." These explanations reinforce conventional gender expectations and obscure men's power advantage in these relationships.

This conceptualization of hidden power is particularly useful given our emphasis on analyzing the effects of gender on multiple levels in the marital relationship. It allows us to assess how cultural expectations regarding gender at the institutional level affect both the interactions between spouses and their attempts to construct meaningful identities. Attention to hidden power can sensitize us to the subtle ways in which gender expectations shape the power dynamics within marriage.

While this conceptualization of power moves us forward theoretically, it represents only half the battle. Measuring power can be equally challenging because power cannot generally be measured in any direct way. Rather, theoretically driven indications of power are measured. Within the context of a marriage, the ability to prevail in the face of conflict is an obvious reflection of one's power. The relative level of control spouses exercise over financial and other family decisions has also been seen as indicative of the relative power of each spouse. More recently, especially as women have moved into the workforce, the division of domestic labor has been used to reflect the balance of power between spouses. The assumption here is that performing such labor is onerous and undesirable, and that a spouse will avoid this labor if she or he has the power to do so. And men's strong resistance to performing household chores, despite women's labor-force participation (as well as their continued efforts to get men to help), has been viewed as a successful expression of men's power or privilege (Hochschild 1989).

To ensure comparability with previous work on power in marriage, I examined these standard indicators: the division of domestic labor and child care, patterns of financial management, decision-making practices, and conflict-resolution strategies. Therefore, I was concerned with such issues as who performed which household or child-care tasks and with what frequency, who managed the money, and who prevailed in both day-to-day conflicts and major decisions. These kinds of outcomes are the most basic indicators of each spouse's relative power within the relationship.

To move beyond these measures of overt power, I looked for subtle expressions of power or privilege. I explored such issues as whether one partner's work defined the family (set the daily schedule, received preference in consideration for family moves, and so on), or whether one job was considered more important than the other, for whatever reason. I wanted to know whether decisions about work were made according to each spouse's occupational potential (assuming in these families that the wife's exceeds her husband's), or whether men received automatic first consideration in job-related decisions. I asked spouses about changes they would like to make—in their jobs, in the division of domestic labor, in their relationships—to see if their lives seemed organized around their preferences or their partners'. I asked whether they felt they could pursue these changes and, if not, why. This gave me a sense of how empowered spouses felt individually, and the extent to which they felt constrained by their partners. And finally, I asked if there had been any disappointments in their relationships and whether they had ever considered leaving. These questions tap into potentially serious frustrations with the relationship. People who consider leaving their spouses are on the verge of deciding that the marriage is not worth it anymore—they are not getting enough of what they want or need, so it is time to move on. All these questions allow me to expand previous ideas and evidence of power within marriages, and to offer a more complete picture of their overt and hidden power dynamics.

RESEARCH DESIGN
The Sample

The sample consists of thirty married couples. I recruited twenty-two couples in which wives' income, occupational status, or both are substantially higher than their husbands'. Deciding what constitutes a substantial disparity in these variables is a rather arbitrary decision. Previous work assessing marital power in couples where wives earn more than their husbands has used income differences as small as a few thousand dollars per year (McRae 1986). To put the maximum stress on the gender structure, I examined larger income and status differences that would be more difficult for couples to ignore. Wives had to earn at least 50 percent more per year than their husbands earned (for example, a woman making $45,000 per year, married to a man making $30,000). Status differences were defined by a combination of factors: established occupational rankings, such as Duncan's Socioeconomic Index; education required for the job; and position within the bureaucratic hierarchy. In practice, I relied largely on the last two factors. For example, I judged a wife who was a midlevel bank manager higher in status than her husband who worked as a car salesperson.

In fifteen of these twenty-two couples, wives surpassed their husbands on both income and occupational status. In four couples, wives earned 50 percent more, but there was no clear status difference between them (for example, an attorney married to a physician). In three couples, wives made $4,000 to $7,000 more per year than their husbands did (which did not meet the 50 percent standard) but held jobs with substantially higher status (for example, a research project manager married to a telephone repairer). I included these couples to get a sense of whether income or occupational status seemed more important in driving the power dynamics of the marriages. However, in the final analysis I collapsed these categories into one because the power dynamics among these three types of couples proved substantially similar; that is, the results demonstrate that surpassing one's husband on either income or occupational status affects the power dynamics in similar ways to surpassing him on both.

I also recruited eight comparison couples (for a total of thirty couples) in which husbands' income and occupational status are higher than their wives', or in which spouses are relatively equal on both variables. The comparison couples provide an important contrast to separate out the effects of wives' employment from the effects of their earning substantially more than their husbands. This contrast can tell us whether the dynamics among couples with higher-earning wives are similar to, or differ substantially from, the dynamics of more conventional two-income couples.

Characteristics of the Couples

In general, the two types of couples are similar on key demographic variables. On average, husbands are only slightly older than their wives (thirty-seven years vs. thirty-six years for couples with higher-earning wives, thirty-five vs. thirty-four years for comparison couples). Couples with higher-earning wives had been married for about eight years, with an average of 1.8 children; comparison couples, for ten years, with 2.0 children. There are also no large discrepancies between the two groups in terms of class background, ethnicity, or religiosity of spouses. All couples in both groups are two-income couples with at least one child at home, and all wives are employed full-time. However, five husbands with higher-earning wives spend most of their time in the home (earning, at most, $3,000 per year) and are classified by their part-time occupations. Note that, although the sample includes men whose primary job is that of stay-at-home father, there are no stay-at-home mothers in the comparison group. I was most interested in contrasting the effects of wives' employment alone with the effects of wives having a higher income and occupational status. Contrasting the experiences of these two groups of women provides a way to separate out the relative effects of gender and income on the balance of marital power.

While the two groups are similar on many key demographic variables, as expected they vary more widely on income. Higher-earning wives made an average of $47,000 to their husbands' $22,000 in the year that preceded the interviews. Comparison wives made an average of $33,000 to their husbands' $45,000. (The five husbands who were primarily at home bring this average down considerably. Without them, the average salary for husbands with higher-earning wives is $30,000, making the income discrepancies between spouses in both groups comparable.) The range in family incomes is also slightly greater for couples with higher-earning wives. Total family income ranged from $27,000 to $175,000, with most couples (sixteen of twenty-two) falling in the $50,000–$80,000 range. The corresponding range of total family income for comparison couples is $35,000 to $150,000. Here the distribution is more bimodal, with half the families below $50,000, and the other half above $70,000. This means that, while most families in both groups would be considered middle to upper-middle class, both groups also included families that would be considered solid working class.

There is also some variation between the groups on educational attainment. Over one-third of higher-earning wives have more education than their husbands have. This gap generally reflects a wife with a master's degree and a husband with a bachelor's degree. Among the comparison couples, the husband's education is equal to or exceeds his wife's in all but one case. In short, couples with higher-earning wives are very similar to comparison couples, with the exception that higher-earning wives are more likely to possess more-advanced degrees than do their husbands, and to outearn them by a considerable margin.

This sample is limited in two ways. First, there is little racial diversity among these couples. The sample includes only two Asian Americans, two African Americans, one Latino, and one émigré from the Middle East; all remaining respondents are European American. Second, the sample is highly educated. Over two-thirds of spouses have bachelor's degrees, and most have at least some graduate training. Therefore, while the sample contains some variation by social class, most spouses in both groups are highly educated and white.

Recruiting Couples and Gathering Data

All couples were living in a major metropolitan area in the eastern United States. Couples were recruited primarily through ads placed in a local newspaper that was delivered free to all households in the surrounding communities once a week. The ad asked for volunteers for a study on work, marriage, and family life, and stated that "especially needed are couples in which the wife's income and/or occupational status is higher than the husband's." I also received several referrals through acquaintances. Recruitment efforts ceased after thirty couples had completed the entire data-collection process.

Potential participants were screened during the initial phone contact to determine their eligibility. Of the couples who agreed to participate, spouses were first mailed separate but identical questionnaires. The questionnaires included fixed-choice items about household decision making and the division of domestic labor and child care. These items were taken directly from Blood and Wolfe's (1960) research. (See Appendix A for a copy of the questionnaire.) The questionnaire also asked for information about the respondent's income, education, occupation, current marriage, and family background. The small size and nonrandom nature of the sample meant that I could not analyze these data using standard statistical techniques. However, the questionnaires did yield background information on the respondents and illuminated areas of disagreement between spouses. This information was helpful in the subsequent interviews.

Once the questionnaires were returned, I contacted respondents to schedule face-to-face interviews. I interviewed spouses individually in their homes, usually consecutively, with interviews lasting from one to four hours. The interviews were structured around an interview guide, but questions were designed to be open-ended to allow respondents to explore issues I had not anticipated. (See Appendix B for a copy of the Interview Guide.) The interview topics included personal background (including information about family of origin), current work and work history, the history of the couple's relationship, the division of household chores and child care, financial organization and practices, decision-making practices, and conflict-resolution strategies. Near the end of the interviews,

I also asked spouses direct questions about the balance of power in their relationships to see who they thought exerted more control and under what circumstances. In short, the interview questions were designed to encourage spouses to reflect on multiple dimensions of their lives and relationships, and to assess how satisfied they are with the amount of control they exercise in each of these areas.

This research design allows us to answer important questions about the complex relationship between money, gender, and power. While I build on previous conceptualizations of power, the emphasis on hidden power dynamics opens a window on the subtle ways in which the link between money and power within these marriages is undermined for women while men's dominance is maintained. This conceptualization of power is especially useful because it gives us a way to assess the impact of the gender structure on the balance of power in these marriages—particularly how the expectations embedded in the marital contract and the conventional gender identities of breadwinner and mother/home-maker continue to shape marital power relations.

The in-depth interview data presented here provide a crucial counterpoint to what little we know about couples with higher-earning wives. As we listen to how spouses feel about themselves and their partners, and how they describe their relationships, we can see how they struggle with and manage the tensions associated with having or being a wife who earns more. These results highlight the stability of the gender structure and demonstrate how men's dominance is reproduced at the interactional and individual levels as spouses work together to construct appropriate gender identities and maintain viable marriages.

CHAPTER 3

Gendered Bargain

WHY WIVES CANNOT TRADE THEIR MONEY FOR HOUSEWORK

THIS CHAPTER EXAMINES the straightforward bargain implied by the conventional marital contract—that income is exchanged for domestic labor. While we know that employed wives have had little success trading their incomes for a reduction in their domestic labor burden, it is tempting to think that wives with substantially greater incomes could use their resources to negotiate a better deal. As the primary breadwinners, they may be able to buy out of a greater proportion of housework than can wives who are secondary earners.

The data presented here are based on reports by husbands and wives from the questionnaires and the interviews. Spouses do not always agree in their reports of who does what and how often. Typically, they give themselves more credit than they give their spouses, which is common for research on domestic labor (Coltrane 2000; Cowan and Cowan 1992; Deutsch, Lozy, and Saxon 1993; Vannoy-Hiller and Philliber 1989). In a few instances, what respondents report on their questionnaires differs from the picture they paint in the interviews. All this makes it difficult to arrive at a precise number of hours spent by each spouse on domestic labor and child rearing. Therefore, I report differences in rough proportions to assess the equity of the arrangements. In cases in which spouses disagree over their relative contributions, I give more weight to the wives' responses, since husbands have been found to overreport their participation in domestic labor at a greater rate than do their wives (Press and Townsley 1998; Wright et al. 1992). Also, since husbands perform so little domestic labor on average, they are likely to underestimate the amount of labor required to run a household, as well as the amount of work their wives perform on a regular basis.

EMPLOYED WIVES AND THE CONVENTIONAL
MARITAL CONTRACT

We saw in the second chapter how the gender structure sets up the bargain between spouses in the conventional marital contract. Husbands trade their income for the domestic labor and child care that wives provide. The bargain is simple and straightforward when husbands are the sole providers but has become more complex as women have moved into the workforce. Under the rules of the contract, as wives begin to share the activity of providing with their husbands, fairness dictates that husbands should respond by performing more domestic labor. This would be a simple and reasonable adaptation of the bargain; however, it does not seem to be happening.

Some of the research on domestic labor argues that men have taken on a greater share of the household burden as their wives moved into paid employment. However, this increased labor amounts to only a few hours per week. More importantly, this increase in men's contributions does not necessarily mean that men are providing their wives with substantial help or relief. Rather, these shifts in numbers suggest that employed women are no longer able to do as much around the house as they have in the past; in short, it looks like men are doing more because women, unable to do it all, are doing less. Therefore, these changes for men seem to reflect only a proportional increase in men's share of domestic labor rather than a substantial increase in real hours (Benokraitis 1985; Berk 1985; Bianchi et al. 2000; Coltrane 2000; Hochschild 1989; Nickols and Metzen 1982; Pleck 1985; Whyte 1990).

These small increases in the contribution of men notwithstanding, the bulk of the literature on the division of domestic labor has made clear that wives have simply added paid employment to their duties as wives and mothers (see, for example, Berk 1985; Coltrane 2000; Hartmann 1981; Peterson and Gerson 1992; Sexton and Perlman 1989; South and Spitze 1994. These results hold cross-culturally as well: see Lewis, Izraeli, and Hootsman 1992). That is, the big story is that even when women are employed outside the home, they still bear the prime responsibility for their homes and children. This combined load of paid and domestic labor means that women work longer days and weeks than do their husbands—or, as

Hochschild (1989) put it, women work an extra month of twenty-four-hour days each year. Women with children feel this burden even more acutely. Having a child increases not only the amount of household labor required, but also the inequity in the division of that labor. Men's participation in housework decreases with the birth of the first child, even among couples who shared household labor equitably before the arrival of children (Cowan and Cowan 1992; Rexroat and Shehan 1987).

Occupational disparities between spouses are often used to explain the continued inequities in domestic labor in dual-income households. Work-related variables such as relative earnings, occupational status, and time demands of spouses are thought to explain their relative contributions to household labor (Barnett and Baruch 1988; Mederer 1993; Perry-Jenkins and Folk 1994; Presser 1994; Shelton 1992; Wright et al. 1992). These results reinforce the logic of the conventional marital contract—if one spouse contributes more at work, she or he should contribute less at home. Since men typically earn more than do their wives and often work longer hours in pursuit of these higher incomes, their lesser contributions to housework and child care are seen as legitimate.

However, other research indicates that the division of domestic labor is not driven by the relative earnings or time demands of spouses (Brayfield 1992; Brines 1994; Greenstein 2000; Gupta 1999; Hochschild 1989). In fact, when wives earn more than their husbands do, men perform little or no domestic labor (Bittman et al. 2003; Brines 1994; Greenstein 2000; Hochschild 1989). In other words, the bargain seems to break down when women bring money to the table, because wives are unable to trade their income for domestic services from their husbands. This suggests that the bargain implied by the conventional marital contract is gendered—certain rights, obligations, or privileges are assigned by gender, rather than on the basis of role performance. Women seem obliged to perform nearly all the domestic labor even though their husbands are no longer providing the family's sole (or even major) financial support.

The "His" and "Hers" of Domestic Labor

The imperatives of the gender structure largely determine the division of domestic labor in households. Certain household chores are considered women's jobs, while others belong to men. Though there is some crossover in tasks, most couples still divide them largely on the basis of conventional gender expectations. Men are more likely to handle the outdoors tasks and household repairs, while women are more likely to tend to the nurturing and physical care of the children, as well as the indoor activities required for daily living (food, laundry, cleaning, etc.). Women perform a greater variety of chores, and most of the domestic labor falls on their side of the marital ledger (see Coltrane 2000 for a review of this literature).

There are also distinct differences in the nature of the tasks that men and women perform. Men have more discretion in taking on household tasks, often choosing those they consider pleasant. For example, playing with the children is generally seen as a more enjoyable activity than scrubbing toilets, and when pushed to provide more help, men often choose the more agreeable tasks. Men also tend to perform chores that are more peripheral to the functioning of the household, rather than tasks that are crucial for daily living. This means that men are more often in a position to choose when they will perform these tasks, which gives them the freedom to postpone them. For example, changing the oil in the car or making a household repair can be put off—in some cases, indefinitely. The family is not likely to suffer if men do not perform these tasks immediately. On the other hand, it is difficult to tell a small child that you do not feel like making dinner or changing a soiled diaper right now. These tasks cannot be put off for a week—or even an hour. In short, men tend to do work that has clearly defined boundaries (mowing the lawn), has an element of discretion in timing (household repairs), and has a great leisure component (playing with the children) (Benokraitis 1985; Berk and Berk 1979; Berk 1985; Coleman 1991).

There are also differences in the way men and women view chores. Men seem to underestimate the work involved in ongoing household responsibilities. For example, one study found that 36 percent of the men interviewed regarded cooking as a "leisure activity," whereas only 14 percent of the wives described cooking in this way (Horna and Leipri 1987). Anyone who has tried to put a hot, nutritious meal on the table in between the after-school and evening activities of three or four people would not describe cooking as a "leisure activity." But viewing domestic labor as leisure, at least in part, may permit husbands to see some chores as discretionary, thus allowing them a sense of freedom from housework and child care that their wives do not share.

More fundamentally, much of the labor women perform at home is not viewed as work—it is "invisible" (Wright et al 1992; Daniels 1987). This invisible work refers to the myriad details that women typically handle in the course of an average day or week and ranges from coordinating the schedules of family members to making sure someone is home to meet the cable repairer. It is the kind of work that family members do not notice unless the woman fails to do it. The very invisibility of this work further burdens wives, because men do not recognize the full measure of domestic labor their wives perform. This makes it easier for men to see themselves as contributing substantially to household chores when their contributions are, in fact, negligible (Mederer 1993).

Women, of course, feel the weight of this invisible work, as one of the wives in my sample made extremely clear. She filled out the initial questionnaire, which asked about only the most fundamental household chores, such as cooking, laundry, household cleaning, and basic child care, then added a written comment on the back of her questionnaire. Her response is a dramatic statement about the invisibility of women's work (as well as a critique of quantitative methods for studying domestic labor). I reproduce it here in its entirety:

> The issue I think is missed here is that logistics, planning, contingency arrangements, etc.—all the prep work—usually fall completely to the mother. The mother secures daycare and backup daycare, evening baby-sitting, snow day school closing planning, etc. So while the father may have significant participation in doing any family tasks, the *planning* etc. is frequently all a mother's work.
>
> You don't highlight who calls the YWCA for the program schedule, who makes sure there is change each day for lunch money, who decides it is time for a dental checkup, who realizes last year's snow boots won't fit this year *before* this year's first snow, who arranges the *children's* social schedule, who plans the birthday parties, who communicates with the children's school (a real key activity in early elementary grades), who sells school fund-raising items at work, who sees that young children use the toilet before a trip in the car, who sets up the car pool for church, school, soccer, scouts, etc. All this—or

most of this—is constant, continual PLANNING. The actual execution is a cakewalk by comparison!

Clearly, the sheer number of tasks that women face in managing and caring for a family can be overwhelming, and the invisibility of this work only adds to the load that wives bear.

POWER STRUGGLES AND CONFLICT IN DIVIDING DOMESTIC LABOR

That men have not taken on domestic duties to balance their wives' economic contributions in dual-earner families suggests that housework is onerous or unpleasant—at the very least, something to be avoided. Couples often engage in open struggles over this issue; in fact, it is one of the leading causes of marital strife (Coltrane 2000; Hochschild 1989). The scenario is simple and familiar: Wives ask for help, while husbands resist or refuse. Men's ability to avoid domestic labor is seen as a reflection of their greater power in the relationship.

However, the struggle can be more subtle. We know that, in addition to performing the vast majority of household chores, wives maintain responsibility for these tasks regardless of who executes them. Wives keep track of all household details and know what needs to be done when, which sets wives up as the household experts. It also means that wives are often in the position of "supervising" their husbands as they perform household and child-care tasks. Spouses may have different ideas of what constitutes an adequate job on a particular task, and these differing expectations often lead to more conflict. For example, women complain that their husbands do not clean to their standards, and that they must often redo tasks their husbands have undertaken. Differing timetables for the completion of chores is also a source of conflict between spouses. Women report that it is difficult to get husbands to complete chores on a timely basis, and wives find themselves nagging their husbands. Or men purposely drag their feet or feign helplessness as a kind of passive resistance through which they can avoid domestic labor without having to confront their wives directly (Hochschild 1989). These tactics often succeed. With all the extra effort required to get husbands to contribute more around the house, wives often conclude that it is easier to just do the task themselves and avoid the argument.

Carrying the domestic labor burden can have negative consequences for women. The continued gap between the number of hours spouses devote to household responsibilities means that wives pay higher personal costs to maintain the family than men do. For example, women have much less time than their husbands have to devote to leisure activities, which increases the level of stress wives experience and can be detrimental to their mental health (Berk 1985; Cockburn 1991; Geerken and Gove 1983; Pahl 1989; Pleck 1985; Shelton 1992). Perhaps most alarming is that women often try to meet the demands placed on them by sacrificing such basic necessities as exercise and adequate sleep (Hochschild 1989).

Carrying this load can also harm the marital relationship, as the symbolic issues associated with caring work come to the fore. If a husband refuses to help out at home, a wife may come to believe that he sees his time as more valuable than hers. Having to do it all can make a wife feel like a servant or slave rather than a partner or lover, as the burden she carries becomes a statement of her lesser worth in the relationship. The struggle over domestic labor can become a measure of her husband's affection—"If you really loved me, you'd help me." In short, wives may see their husbands' attempts to get out of housework as "not caring" about them or their needs (Erickson 1993).

However, other symbolic issues associated with domestic labor may undercut the potential conflict over housework. Since domestic labor is so tied to caring, wives who struggle with their husbands may see themselves as not caring about their families and consequently as bad wives and mothers (DeVault 1991; Finch and Groves 1983). This is especially true in the case of child care. What kind of mother fights over who has to put the children to bed or spend an afternoon with them? To be a good wife is to care for a husband, home, and children. A wife's desire to fulfill these caring obligations may discourage her from pushing for a greater household-labor contribution from her husband.

Wives may also avoid conflict over domestic labor to preserve marital harmony. Struggles over housework and child care can set an unpleasant tone for a marriage. Trying to share chores equally can mean rules, regulations, and schedules, in addition to conflict (Thompson 1991). Women may decide that a comfortable, companionate marriage is more important than equality in household labor (Bolak 1997; Branner and Moss 1987;

Foa et al. 1993). If this is the case, then domestic labor has as much to do with affirming one's sense of personal and marital well-being as it does with accomplishing the necessary tasks of daily living—particularly for women. In other words, the symbolic issues associated with household chores and child care may be more important than the actual division of that labor, and couples may be more willing to live with the inequities of the status quo than weather the storms that challenging the gender structure would certainly bring.

Couples with higher-earning wives organize their lives amid these same symbolic issues and power struggles. Like other employed wives, these women are burdened with the bulk of the domestic labor in their families. Like other employed wives, they often struggle to increase their husbands' participation. Like other employed wives, they feel the load they are carrying, and the stress takes its toll—on them and their relationships. In short, couples with higher-earning wives exhibit domestic labor patterns that are strikingly similar to those of other dual-income couples.

CONTINUED INEQUALITY FOR HIGHER-EARNING WIVES

Money does not drive the division of domestic labor in couples with higher-earning wives. That is, these women are not able to trade their substantial incomes for a corresponding reduction in their domestic labor burden. However, higher-earning wives get a little more relief than do comparison wives. This is especially true for the five wives in my sample who are the nearly sole breadwinners for their families. In each of these cases, the husband performs the majority of the household labor and child care. Of the seventeen remaining couples with higher-earning wives, only 41 percent of husbands perform a substantial portion of the domestic labor (from one-third to, in one case, nearly one-half). Among comparison couples, 25 percent of husbands contribute at this level. All remaining husbands in both groups contribute less than one-third of the domestic labor. This speaks for the ability of higher-earning wives to buy some additional relief from household labor, but the picture should not be painted too optimistically. These are women who earn a great deal more than their husbands, enjoy substantially higher status, or both. Yet, even in the best of circumstances, they are not able to trade these resources for a similarly substantial reduction in their burden of domestic labor.

Surprisingly, few couples employed outside help with household chores. Only three couples with higher-earning wives and two comparison couples used paid housecleaners on a regular basis, and in all five cases, the wives performed most of the remaining household chores.

Higher-earning wives are more like than unlike other employed wives, in that they face the same inequities at home and carry most of the household-labor burden. Higher-earning wives also confront the familiar problems of trying to share domestic labor. First, they have to ask for help; their husbands do not tend to jump right into household chores. Second, these wives struggle with differing standards of cleanliness, reporting that they have to redo chores that their husbands did not perform well enough. And finally, there are differing timetables for performing chores, with husbands frequently putting off tasks that their wives consider more urgent. All these issues can generate conflict in these marriages.

For example, Cindy is a higher-earning wife married to Don. They have three young sons and have lived in a variety of economic circumstances in their ten-year marriage. Each has supported the other through some schooling (she received her master's degree, he received his associate's degree), each has worked part-time at some point, and each has been the primary parent at home for a period of time. Now both spouses work full time. Cindy made the move back to full-time work this past year, and she and Don have had conversations about sharing the household chores more equitably. Don has made an effort to share more tasks, but Cindy says the plan works only because she has been willing to both praise her husband for his efforts and lower her standards:

> Usually during the school year, he'll have two or three nights a week that he'll cook, I have two or three nights a week that I'll cook, and then the other nights are leftovers and that sort of thing. And we're pretty good about sticking to that. The only thing is, when he cooks, it means it's spaghetti, with maybe some French bread on the side. It's not like there's a fruit and a vegetable, you know? [She laughs.] But, if you're going to try and share things like this, you've also got to be willing to lower your standards somewhat; otherwise, it doesn't work out.

Cindy also talks about her frustrations when it is Don's turn to do the laundry. The clothes are clean, but they rarely get folded and put away. Her sons have to go fishing through the laundry baskets to find outfits to wear, and they end up with wrinkled clothes. Cindy has tried talking to Don about this, but nothing has changed. She has decided that if it does not bother him that the boys have to go looking for clean clothes, she has to try not to let it bother her.

In addition, higher-earning wives are still primarily responsible for doing "the things that nobody sees," in the words of one husband. Some couples seem to be aware that the wives carry this extra load. Even if they think they work well together as a team, they recognize that there is something significant about what the wives do. For example, this husband with a higher-earning wife says:

> To me, it doesn't make sense to say, "Who is more essential?" For us, we're both essential, and each would be sorely missed by the other. [Pause.] But Joyce could replace me with money—hire people to do what I do. I would have more trouble doing what she does because you can't replace it with money. It's the planning, looking for daycare programs for the girls, arranging outings on the weekends, buying their clothes, getting them into outfits on time, getting them into the shower, out of the shower, into bed without fighting—all of those things.

That he could not "replace his wife with money" is a powerful statement about both the significance and the value of what women typically do at home. Women's work is so specialized, intimate, and all-encompassing that the average family could not pay someone to do it. On the other hand, that one cannot put a fair market price on these services often means that they are devalued or taken for granted. In fact, this work often becomes invisible—even to the women themselves, like the higher-earning wife quoted next. She claims that her husband is responsible for getting their two young daughters to day care every morning, but her description of what she and her husband do each morning tells a more complex story:

> He does the basics, whereas I do the other little extra things, like laying their clothes out. I try to have everything ready for him in the morning 'cause he's not real good at functioning in the morning. I try to have everything laid out. The diaper bag's packed. Basically,

really, all you would need to do is give the baby a bottle and change her diaper and put her clothes on. And it is still a lot, and I appreciate him doing that.

It is striking that she places such value on his contributions and discounts her own. This demonstrates how much of what these wives do is still invisible and therefore not always recognized or defined as work; this means that women do not always get credit for performing it, which disadvantages them in the struggle for equity. This quote also highlights how tricky it can be to assess how domestic labor is divided in a particular household. I initially asked this wife, "Who is responsible for getting the children to day care?" She responded that her husband was, but this simple answer hides all the preparatory work she does to make the job easier for him. More importantly, it is quite probably her willingness to do all the background work that ensures his continued willingness to perform the task of taking their children to day care.

That higher-earning wives are working full time and shouldering the lion's share of labor and organizational responsibilities at home means that they carry the same heavy load that other employed wives do. Their lives exist in a "delicate balance," in the words of one wife. The woman quoted next is a physician with a complicated weekly schedule, including half days, long days, and one day off per week, to try to accommodate the needs of the house and her two young sons. Maintaining a balance between work and family is a constant challenge:

Right now I feel like things are in a pretty delicate balance between the family and the demands of work. And if something goes wrong, it's pretty stressful. I'd like to get a little more cushion in my life. [She laughs.] . . . It's very stressful when things are running late at work, and there's another patient to see, or a patient arrives late, and you know you have to be out at an exact time to pick your child up at nursery school. And if you're five minutes late to the nursery school, they get very upset with you and you feel terribly guilty. [She laughs.] And working on that kind of tight schedule is stressful.

This tight scheduling and trying to do it all leaves little or no time for the women themselves. That is, higher-earning wives face the same leisure gap other employed women face. When asked if she enjoyed any leisure activities, one higher-earning wife speaks for many when she says:

> Actually, no. At this point, I don't. I used to like to paint, but I don't have the time to paint anymore. I really don't feel like I have the time to do much of anything anymore. . . . . [My husband's] got lots of hobbies. He's got plenty of time to do it all.

For their part, most husbands with higher-earning wives recognize the inequities in their marriages. They are also aware that their wives would often like them to take on more responsibility. But like other husbands, they resist this pressure. They even talk about their "laziness" lightheartedly. The following is a typical justification for not doing more at home:

> I look at a room and say, "Eh, it's not that dirty." [We laugh.] . . . One of my biggest vices is that I love to watch sports. And it just so happens that sports fall on the weekends, when you should be doing things around the house, like cutting the lawn and raking the leaves. But those doggone sports things are on. I get so wrapped up in those sometimes.

Or, as this husband simply puts it: "I could probably do more [around the house], but when it comes to the choice of doing laundry or watching VH1, VH1 wins."

Wives do not express the same sense of humor when it comes to the inequities they face in housework and child care, but they are certainly aware of the ironies in their circumstances. This is evident in an anecdote relayed by one higher-earning wife, Joyce. She told me about a co-worker who got a call from her child-care provider one morning to say that she would be at work that day, but that she was going to be deported that night. The co-worker was understandably distraught and worried about what she would do with her children the following day. As her husband left for work that morning, he told his wife to "have a good day." Joyce says her co-worker "went ballistic. 'Have a good day?' Child care is being deported tonight! How could those words come out of the man's mouth?" Joyce and her friends try to laugh about the strains of working full time and being responsible for a family:

Right now, at this moment in your life, if you have multiple kids, you tend to have multiple child-care arrangements. If one person is gonna exit unannounced, it's gotta be the husband! [We laugh.] Because you can cry by yourself in your bed, and that's not a problem. But if a child care [worker] leaves unannounced, it's a major disruption in your life.

And while this woman was laughing as she told me this story, she was not entirely joking. Because of the burdens they face, and their husbands' unwillingness to lighten this load, these wives may be starting to see their husbands as expendable.

Important Work

While higher-earning wives are not able to use their substantial incomes to negotiate equally substantial reductions in their household burden, in some cases their husbands contribute a larger portion (roughly 30 to 40 percent) of the domestic labor than do other husbands. Status and income differences do not explain this variability in patterns of sharing; earning more money does not automatically guarantee wives relief from domestic labor. Stated gender ideology, such as beliefs about a woman's right to pursue employment or a man's obligation to contribute to domestic labor when his wife works outside the home, also does not match actual sharing behavior in any systematic way. Similarly, relative time demands, as reflected in the number of hours spent at work, commuting, working overtime, and traveling, do not seem to drive the division of domestic labor for these couples. To assess the more subtle dynamics between spouses, I explored whether couples give one of their jobs priority over the other by examining the opportunities for advancement for each spouse, including the possibility of relocating for those opportunities; whether one spouse's work tends to define the family's daily schedule; whether spouses discuss each other's work; and how much respect each spouse seems to have for the other's work. Examining these issues revealed a subtle calculation that goes on within each relationship. Most couples seem to have a sense that one spouse's job is more important than the other's, and the spouse doing the important work is allowed to contribute less at home. In a few cases, spouses do not see either job as more important, and this situation also leads to more equitable sharing of domestic labor. I present six cases that contrast the experiences of couples with higher-earning wives and comparison couples. These cases demonstrate how couples decide whose work is more important, and how this calculation affects the division of domestic labor for both types of couples.

Joyce and Evan

Joyce and Evan have been married for ten years. They have two daughters in elementary school and live in a large, beautifully decorated home in a prestigious suburban neighborhood. Joyce works for a large company marketing computer networks to government agencies. Evan is a fairly high-ranking official in the federal government (he is one promotion away from the senior executive corps). Evan is working in a higher-status job, but Joyce makes $90,000 to his $60,000. She also carries the load at home. Joyce says that she gets some satisfaction from her work, but that it is just a job. She stays in it for the flexible hours and the great pay. If she wins the lotto, she says, "I'm outta there yesterday." She is not interested in pursuing different career opportunities within her company, and she does not want any more job-related responsibilities. She thinks of her work as a career, but she is not "saving lives or negotiating treaties." When I ask her if either career is more important, she asks, "Is it more important that I remain in a high-paying career? Yeah, because Evan's 'more important' job, in terms of subject matter and impact on life, pays government rates." She recognizes that the family needs her salary, but she sees Evan's work as more important in a larger sense.

Evan seems to agree that his work is more important than his wife's, although he is reluctant to say so outright. He has considerable responsibility and autonomy in his position, and his work gives him a great deal of satisfaction. He can pick up the paper and read about the impact his work is having on the world. He admits that he has more influence in his organization than Joyce has in hers. He also says he is very committed to his job, whereas Joyce is "not at all committed" to hers.

Given the large income difference, we might expect the family to try to maximize Joyce's career and earning potential by allocating more family responsibilities to Evan and allowing her to specialize in the marketplace (Becker 1981). That does not happen for this couple. Joyce overwhelmingly carries the burden at home; what is more, she is very upset by it.

> I get *completely* frustrated by [the work at home]. It is unrelenting. It is never ending. You just do laundry this week to do the laundry next week. Evan laid the hardwood floor and people will admire it forever, and he'll never have to do another hardwood floor. So that's not fair, you see [she laughs], because I have to do the laundry next week. So I am *resentful* of the fact that, starting about two or three weeks ago, in the back of my mind, if I end up going on that [business] trip to Florida next week, I have to do this and this and this and this and this. Whereas Evan has, on numerous occasions, blown out of the country on a business trip on minimal notice, and the most he's had to do is remember to pack his socks. . . . [VT: Do you think this responsibility gives you more control or influence around the house?] No, because where is my control or influence that I have to do all this stuff so I can go out of town on business? . . . I can control whether or not I can make Evan die by *not* ironing his shirts, *not* telling him [what to expect while I'm gone], and seeing what he does, which I have threatened him numerous times on this trip. . . . "I will just walk out of here like you do, *then* you'll miss me! You'll be *miserable!*"

Joyce wants more help from Evan at home, but she has not gotten it. She has thought about cutting down her load by sending his shirts to the cleaners, for example, but then that would be one more thing for her to remember to do at a certain time. She can always iron his shirts on Sunday night, but she cannot pick up his laundered shirts then because the cleaners are not open. Evan agrees that his wife carries the load at home. He says, simply, that their household arrangements have evolved by "slough off—I slough off whenever I see an opportunity." They have recently hired a cleaning service to come in twice a month. That way, Joyce says, the house never reaches "the breaking point." This has taken some of the pressure off Evan to contribute more at home. However, Joyce still feels burdened by both the workload and the responsibility she has for running the household. Joyce is the wife who wrote on the back of her questionnaire the extended comment about the burden of planning for and organizing the household. The cleaning service does not lighten her load in this area.

Monica and Sam

Sam and Monica have been married for nine years. They have two daughters, a six-year-old and a five-month-old. They live in a newly remodeled single-family home on a quiet suburban street. Sam is a computer technician, and Monica is a telecommunications project manager. He makes $36,000 to her $54,000. When I specifically ask her, Monica reluctantly admits that she sees a difference in status between what they each do for a living: "A little bit. I really don't think of it that much, to tell the truth, but you're asking, so I say, 'Okay, I *do* have a better job than he does'." At another point in the interview, she expresses her dissatisfaction with what Sam does for a living:

> He's been workin' for the same company, *almost* in the same position, for twelve years. And sometimes I feel like he needs a little more ambition to try to, um, advance himself in the company. . . . And because he's been at the same position for twelve years, he'll write a memo and I'll look at it and I'll completely redo the whole thing. I'll say, "You can submit *this* [his version] or *this* [her version]." But he has no writing skills, no management skills whatsoever.

Not only is she unhappy with what she sees as Sam's lack of ambition, but also she criticizes his office skills. It struck me as an unfair criticism, because he does not have an office job. He is a technician who is out in the field all day repairing computers. He must write memos very infrequently. Her criticism is an expression of her dissatisfaction with the kind of work he is doing. It is blue collar, and she would like to see him in a higher-status (office) job. She seems to realize how hard she is being on him because she quickly qualifies her criticism: "And it's because he's never tried to use them [office skills]. I'm sure if he had to use them, or tried to use them, he'd be better at it. It takes a while."

Sam and Monica split the household labor more equitably than do most couples—about sixty-forty. As Monica and I talked in their basement, we could hear Sam moving around upstairs in the kitchen: "See?

He's doing the dishes. A lot of men wouldn't do that." Monica says Sam takes care of all the household repairs, remodels, cuts the grass, takes care of the trash.

> I don't do trash. He does his *share* of the housework. He'll mop the kitchen floor. I never mop, either. Of course, it's usually dirty. He doesn't mop *enough,* but he does mop. I give him that. He'll sweep, too. And he'll vacuum. He does all the vacuuming, too. See that? He's getting more and more tasks. [We laugh.] And he does all his own laundry.

She concludes that the labor is not split equally because she still does more cleaning and child care than Sam does, and the current division of labor has come about relatively recently. Sam has just started taking on more tasks within the last year or so, about the time Monica started in her current position.

When I ask Sam about their jobs, he readily agrees that his wife's work is more important. "Oh, yeah. She's got a much better, more prominent-type position. She's management, and I'm still basically a high-level grunt, so to speak." There is no apparent animosity as he acknowledges the status difference in their jobs. His tone is matter of fact and he seems to accept it.

Sam's description of what he does around the household agrees with Monica's. He contributes a great deal:

> I've pretty much taken on the basic things, I guess. It sounds kind of, you know, I do like all the trash, 90 percent of the time—typical macho stuff, I guess. I sweep the floor every night in the hallway, kitchen, and [family room]. I usually put the dishes in the dishwasher, rinse 'em off, and get 'em goin'. Not always, but usually. If Monica's home, she cooks, because nobody likes my cooking, exactly. . . . Everybody would rather eat Monica's. [We laugh.] So I usually end up starting the meals, and she'll usually end up finishing them—making 'em palatable.

Sam has not always been this involved in the household. In the past, Monica did 90 percent of the cleaning and child care. She is not sure why he has taken on a larger share of the load at home. Her current job requires some travel, but only once or twice a month. The remainder of the time she works only thirty hours a week, and a portion of that is from her computer at home. It would be easy for them to see her as largely available to handle the bulk of the household chores.

Sam links his increased involvement in the household to the birth of their second child five months ago:

> Well, since the second baby, since the second kid was born, it's just a matter of necessity. We never talked about it. . . . It just had to be done. I got home first. I started the meals. If she gets home first, she'll start the meals. It's just that I usually get home first. And, um, actually, we've never really talked about it. We just do it.

Though he feels the added load of another child drew him into greater household participation, there is a sense here that he too is unsure exactly how it all happened. It was not a conscious decision on their part; they "never really talked about it." It is interesting to note that they have hired a live-in nanny since the birth of their second child. With this new member of the household available to take on some of the domestic burden, Sam may have been able to argue, at least to himself, that his help was not needed. It is also important to remember that, by Monica's account, his increased participation predates the birth of their second child and coincides with her promotion to her current position.

What makes the domestic labor arrangements of this couple interesting is the way the power dynamics play out in other aspects of their relationship. They both hold quite traditional expectations with regard to a husband's authority, and Sam regularly exercises it. He "lets" Monica do the bills, because they are no big deal—they just have to be paid. However, he takes care of all their investments. He "lets" her make decisions for the house because she cares about decorating more than he does, but he reserves the right to say, "No, I can't live with that." She needed a new car, and he told her what kind of car she was going to buy. It "irritated" her that he would do that, but she did not put up a fight (more on these dynamics in Chapter 5). Though Sam exercises substantial authority, and his household contributions do not equal Monica's, Sam was pulled into greater participation at home, and with little effort. He is not an egalitarian husband motivated by a commitment to changing or challenging the traditional division of labor at home. He appears, instead, to have responded to a shift in the relative importance of their jobs.

Of further interest in this case is that Sam's perceptions seem to matter more. Monica only reluctantly acknowledges that she has a better job and even refers to Sam as "the provider" in the family at one point in the interview (more on this in Chapter 6). He readily refers to her position as "management" and to his as a "high-level grunt." This seems to be the greatest factor in determining the division of household labor. If the husband thinks his wife's work is in some sense more important, he will contribute more around the house, regardless of her perceptions. Conversely, a man who feels that his job is more important will not contribute significantly to household labor, again regardless of his wife's perceptions. Two brief examples provide further evidence of this pattern.

Sandy and Dick

Sandy and Dick have been married for ten years and have a three-year-old son. They recently bought their dream house in a middle-class neighborhood and have been working on remodeling and redecorating. Dick is a technical writer/trainer; Sandy works in employee development. He does not see a difference in the status of their jobs: She does human-resources training, he does technical training. To him, neither job is more important, but Sandy sees it differently. She runs an employee-development program for midlevel managers in a federal government agency. Because of her "exposure, visibility, and freedom," she thinks her job has higher status. She works with managers and does more leading than following. She thinks the reverse is true for her husband. Further, Sandy is not comfortable with the work Dick does. Her dissatisfaction surfaces when I ask if there have been any disappointments in their relationship. She chooses her words carefully:

> The jobs he's had since [he was in the Marine Corps] have not seemed to make *him* as happy as I've been able [pause]—he hasn't been able to get as much out of the jobs that I've been able to. And so that's been hard for me to understand—how he could be happy. And he hasn't always seemed to be. I know he hasn't been. So that's frustrating. So that's disappointing, I guess.

As for the household chores, Dick reports that they "used to kind of share cleaning." Now their division of labor is motivated by "who can't stand it anymore" and by their likes and dislikes. He says he sometimes wishes his wife did less around the house, especially when she is feeling motivated and he wants to "be a vegetable." He feels they have "divided responsibilities" for the household. Sandy feels she is responsible for the household. Things happen because she pushes or schedules them. She would like to do some of the work involved in remodeling their home but has backed away from taking on household projects to keep from doing everything. She says she is responsible for the household largely because she is more active and likes to get things done. She says it would be easier for her to do most things herself, but it does not seem right that she should do it all.

Sandy sees her work as more important than Dick's, but he does not. Consequently, she carries the load at home, and Dick has so far successfully resisted Sandy's efforts to get him to take on more responsibility for household chores.

Lily and Butch

Lily and Butch have been married for three years and have a nine-month-old daughter. The family lives in a small, well-kept house in a working-class neighborhood. Lily is a nurse; Butch works in maintenance for an apartment complex. Lily loves her work and is very good at it. She knows that her husband, however, is miserable in his job and she would like to see him find something to do that would make him happier. Despite the different levels of attachment that these spouses have to their work, Lily does not feel either job is more important. She says Butch's job is "important to the people there, and they depend on him. I think that they depend on him there as much as the patients depend on me at the hospital." Butch confirms that he is miserable in his current position. He says his work "will be a job until the day I die. A career is something you *like* to do." But he is proud of his wife's work. He says Lily likes what she does, and "there's no better person for it." He sees her job as more important than his because "she saves and preserves lives."

Though Lily performs more household labor overall, the spouses agree that they are both responsible for the house. Lily tries to give the house the "once-over" on her days off. She is responsible for the bathrooms and does most of the sweeping and mopping. She cooks more; Butch does dishes more. He also takes care of the laundry, vacuuming, and all outside chores and repair work. Lily sees herself as the primary caretaker of their daughter, but Butch feels that, now that Lily is no longer breastfeeding, they care for their daughter equally. Butch: "We both know when something needs to be done around here. . . . I have no problems with [doing] it."

These last two couples highlight the significance of the husband's perceptions in the calculation of whose work is more important. In the case of Sandy and Dick, she thinks her work is more important; he disagrees and does very little around the house. In the case of Lily and Butch, Lily does not see either job as more important. Butch thinks her work is more important, so he helps out substantially at home. So while the division of domestic labor is driven by a calculation of whose work is more important, where there is disagreement, the husband's perceptions are paramount. That is, he steps in to take on a greater share of household chores only when he thinks his wife's work is more important than his.

Comparison couples also engage in the "important work" calculation. The following two cases demonstrate the similarity between the dynamics of couples with higher-earning wives and comparison couples in determining the division of domestic labor.

Maggie and Jim

Jim and Maggie live in a beautiful Cape Cod–style home in one of the area's most exclusive neighborhoods. They have been married for four years and have an eighteen-month-old daughter. They are interesting because they have nearly identical incomes (in the low seventies), work-related time demands, commuting distances, and occupational status. Jim is an oncologist at a major research center; Maggie is a senior vice-president for a large national corporation. Both report working fifty to fifty-five hours a week and traveling about once a month for two to three days at a time. She commutes one mile to work; he commutes one and a half miles. They have the most substantial paid help of any couple I interviewed, a nanny who cares for their daughter from 8:00 A.M. to 6:00 P.M. five days a week. She performs all the household chores, including their laundry. The only tasks left are after-hours child care, cooking, grocery shopping, and errands. The last item they tackle together on the weekends; the rest are Maggie's responsibility. Again, the driving force behind this arrangement seems to be a shared sense that Jim's work is more important.

Maggie has had a great deal of success in her current position as a strategic planner, but it is not her first choice of work. It is a position she took when she was "reorganized" out of the marketing division two years ago. Taking this position was not the ideal career move for her, but it was the best alternative at the time. Maggie has little to say about her work and looks forward to moving on to something else. By contrast, when asked how she feels about the work Jim does, her pride and enthusiasm are obvious:

> I wish I did something so significant for a living. . . . I try to convince people to eat in restaurants, and Jim cures people of cancer. [We laugh.] . . . I think that's outstanding. Jim is such a wonderful person. . . . I know that there's very sick people out there that are getting very heartfelt care because my husband is in oncology, and I think that's great.

Jim is just as enthusiastic; he loves his work. He feels challenged and he thinks he is making an important contribution to medicine and to the world. At the time of the interviews, the family was getting ready to move across the country for an ideal next position for him. Luckily, his new company helped Maggie get interviews, and she has found a good position as well. Jim says Maggie was not satisfied in her current work but thinks that this new position will be great—"a logical next step for her."

> That avoided what could have been a real difficult time—if one felt they were giving up a lot and the other's career was the preemptive one. But we've avoided that. I don't know if we'll be able to avoid it always, but I don't really anticipate making a lot of moves.

Jim demonstrates great concern for, and pride in, Maggie's work and is clearly relieved that they will both benefit from the upcoming move, which was initiated by a wonderful opportunity for him. However, his concern does not extend to equity in the remaining household burden. Jim describes a typical workday evening:

> For me, when we come home, I sit down and relax. Maggie will be preparing dinner, and Kim [their daughter] wants to be with Maggie. It's hard to watch Kim and prepare dinner, and Maggie says, "Jim, can you help out?" I'll take Kim, and we'll sit down and read a book, and she'll say, "Mommy? Help? Kitchen?" and I say, "Maggie, what

can I do? I can't tie her up. She wants to be with you." So she says, "Well, you can at least be here helping out with her in the kitchen." So I have to get up from watching the news or something and go into the kitchen. But that works out okay. . . . It gets stressful at times, but I think really it's a phase.

Jim describes the child-care burden that Maggie faces as a "phase" that Kim is going through. His view may be partly true, but it is also an easy way for Jim to explain his willingness to allow Maggie to continue to carry the burden of child care. He enjoys being able to simply relax when he gets home, perhaps even feels entitled to this privilege, and only reluctantly joins Maggie and Kim in the preparation of the evening meal. It has apparently not occurred to the couple to have Jim cook while Maggie watches their daughter.

Interestingly, Maggie does not fault Jim for his lack of help. In the past she has asked for more help with child care, but she has come to accept the current situation with no apparent animosity:

There are things we always assume—about what the other will do. I always assume that Jim will walk the dog at night. He assumes that I will take care of Kim when we get home at night, unless she wants to play with him. I'm the default parameter on the baby, because she always wants to play with me. I have to tell Jim to go occupy her if I need to do something else. . . . I periodically sit down and tell him that I'm doing too much of the baby care, and he says, "Well, you never walk the dog." [We laugh.] And he's right. I don't.

Period. The dog and the child are "morally equivalent" (Hochschild 1989). Maggie seems to accept Jim's logic—as well as his right to avoid a greater share of the domestic labor.

Amanda and Joe

Amanda and Joe live in a one-bedroom apartment on one of the area's busiest thoroughfares. They are so cramped for space that their twenty-month-old son sleeps in a crib in their living room. Amanda and Joe are financially strapped and describe the occasional dinner at Burger King as a luxury that "gets budgeted under mental health." Joe is a research technician in a laboratory; Amanda is a secretary/receptionist for an accountant. Their salaries are nearly identical (in the low twenties), and they have similar work demands. They agree that neither job is more important. They both provide to the best of their ability. As Amanda put it: "We basically bring home the same thing, and we both bust our butt for it. We respect each other for it." Joe and Amanda both tell a story of shared responsibility for the household. Joe says:

> The longer we've lived with each other, the more we've gotten to know who's better at what, or who's more efficient at what, and that's sort of how the housework and child work has evolved. . . . It's just necessary. If you don't have a maid, or however rich people handle it, that's what you do. . . . Sometimes I feel I should do more. I always feel I could do better. I sometimes feel *she* should do more. It goes with the territory of a relationship.

Joe feels neither is the primary parent of their son, Danny. They are both available to meet his needs. Amanda tells a similar story of shared responsibility:

> I consider him "the wife" in *this* household. I really do. He functions more as that part. . . . Generally, I cook and he cleans. I hate to wash dishes. I told him that a long time ago and he's accepted that. . . . I just don't do them—that's how we got one of them taken care of. . . . The rest of the chores, we just do. We don't divide them. There's no structure. They're done. I'm here in the morning, so I take care of Danny, whatever needs to be done. There's no choice. It's just done. If I'm sick, then he'll cook *and* clean up. That's why I probably say he does more household chores than I do, because a lot of nights he'll do both. . . . If he's doing the dishes, I'll change Danny's diaper, 'cause it needs to be done. It's not a question of who changes Danny's diaper. It doesn't matter at all.

No matter what, she says, someone has to be with their son, so they are both always busy. Amanda says that neither is the primary parent: "He doesn't just go 'Mom, Mom, Mom.' He goes, 'Mom, Dad, Mom, Dad.' Most families aren't like that." Amanda feels that she and Joe work as a team: "We just do the job together, man. It's a job. It's a job. And the fact that we just do it all together, . . . I just appreciate that so much."

Despite the large discrepancy in family incomes, these two couples demonstrate how the question of whose job is more important can tip the scales of domestic labor equity. In both cases, the income, status, and work demands of each spouse are nearly identical. In the case of Maggie and Jim, that his job is seen by both spouses as the more important seems to translate into a much smaller share of the domestic labor burden for him. In the case of Amanda and Joe, there is little or no inequity on the domestic front. There is also no sense that one spouse's work is more important than the other's.

Her Marital Contract: How the Bargain Works When He's at Home

In five cases, the wives earn nearly all the family's income; the husbands earn just a few thousand dollars a year at various part-time jobs. These couples cover the economic spectrum, with two families living on incomes of less than $40,000 (one of these was a family of five with a baby on the way), two families with incomes in the $50,000–$60,000 range, and the last family having an income of $114,000. In four of the five cases, the men are at home because both spouses agree that they do not want their children in day care, and at the time they made this decision, the economic prospects for the wives were greater than those for their husbands. In the fifth case, the husband is at home on disability as a result of a DWI accident several years ago.

Despite the great variation in their circumstances, the husbands have responded in remarkably similar ways. Most importantly, they have taken on the bulk of the domestic labor as a fair trade for the income their wives provide. Most of the husbands describe themselves as being responsible for the household and as the primary caretaker of their children. They do not particularly enjoy the household chores, but they like being so important in the lives of their children. They describe their domestic responsibilities quite simply; as this husband (who has been home with his three boys for seven years) puts it when I ask how he feels about his role at home:

> It's hard to say. I don't know. Keeping the house up is just something I do. It's [pause]—I don't know. I've always, when I was a kid, our parents taught us to "clean up your room." Well, this is my "room" now. I straighten up after the boys, and the laundry and all that are just part of it. It's second nature. I don't even think about it. If something spills, you just fix it. That's all there is to it.

Two of these wives agree that their husbands are responsible for the household, and they seem to enjoy being relieved of this burden. In fact, they sound like the husbands quoted earlier in the chapter who consciously enjoy getting out of household chores. As one wife said: "He lets me slough off. [She laughs.] . . . I feel guilty sometimes that I don't help out as much as I could, and sometimes that motivates me to do things and sometimes it doesn't. I just feel guilty and don't do anything. [We laugh.]" She says she tries to help on weekends, but generally she's happy to let her husband retain responsibility for the household chores.

The other three wives see themselves as sharing responsibility for the household, even if they perform a smaller portion of the labor. They often spend substantial time on weekends helping out with chores. One of these wives feels it is her "mission in life" to keep the four toilets and bathrooms in her house clean—a tough job with three boys under the age of seven. Still, these wives concede that their husbands probably have greater responsibility for the household because they are home more. As one wife said: "He's great. He basically tries to free me from all my responsibilities, our responsibilities, so I just spend my time with [our son] and on work. He tries to set it up so that I don't have to worry about *anything* else."

In these cases, wives have been able to strike the bargain that is at the heart of the conventional marital contract. While the number of cases here is very small, these results show that wives *can* trade their income for domestic labor if the spouses negotiate an explicit deal. At the heart of this deal is these spouses' apparent recognition that both elements of the marital contract—breadwinning and domestic labor—are important. Wives give husbands a great deal of credit for taking on the load at home, and husbands appreciate the burdens their wives carry by providing for their families. In short, respecting each other's contributions to the relationship seems to lead to exchanges between spouses that are more equitable.

DOMESTIC RESPONSIBILITIES AS EMPOWERING?

This link between whose work is more important and the division of domestic labor rests on the assumption that housework and at least some aspects of child care are chores to avoid, and that those who do important work outside the home can get out of the unpleasant work inside the home. While the evidence suggests that this is true for many (perhaps most) spouses, this model has been criticized (see, for example, Ferree 1990; Wilkie, Ferree, and Ratcliff 1998). Research on family power has emphasized conflict resolution and the power advantages of resources acquired outside the family (such as income), while ignoring women's power that is rooted in their roles as mothers. Raising the next generation of healthy, autonomous individuals has to be seen as a position of power (Hartsock 1983; Kranichfeld 1987). As primary caregivers, women have a dominant role in shaping the values and behaviors of the next generation. This is important, powerful work.

But parenting is not the only source of power in domestic labor. Part of mothering is creating a warm, stable living environment in which children can grow and thrive. Through their efforts to cook and clean, women "create family" symbolically. They orchestrate family dinners, celebrate the important moments in family life, and pass on rituals, all of which give women a great deal of control in their homes (Daniels 1987; DeVault 1991).

While this conceptualization of domestic labor is appealing because it values much of the invisible labor that women perform, this way of thinking made sense to only a few of my respondents. Still, for these spouses, most of them women, domestic labor (especially child care) offers tremendous rewards and opportunities to exercise control. The following example demonstrates how this desire for control over the household can override even important work considerations.

Rita and Alan

Rita and Alan have been married for four years and have a seven-month-old son. Alan is a journalist for a wire service; Rita is an assistant editor for a travel magazine. I considered them a comparison couple because they both have incomes in the low twenties and there is no great difference in their occupational status. There is, however, a difference in the importance of their jobs in the context of this couple. Alan does not see a difference in status between their jobs,

> but there is a question of professional standards. I don't respect what she's doing, but that's just within the journalism world. Travel magazines are considered "puff journalism." Not much of it is worth respecting. Whereas what I do is much more respected as serious work.

Still, he says her work is more important because it is a "dream job" for her. They have made "a lot of concessions" for her job by staying in the area when Alan had job opportunities elsewhere: "It wasn't the income, though. It was the job itself, for her. It was the once-in-a-lifetime job."

Rita agrees with Alan's assessment of her work and says she has been able to "call the shots" for them professionally:

> I told him I would only move for him if the job that he was getting offered would more than cover what we were both earning, or close to it, and that there would be opportunities in that area for me to find a job. But I told him that when I was earning more money than he was. And it didn't seem that he would ever get a job that would compensate for both of us. [She laughs.]

Rita's attempt to control his options is not lost on Alan. He confirms that she said she would move for a "dream job" for him, but he does not think there is a job out there that would meet her definition of that term.

Given that both spouses see Rita's job as more important, we would expect Alan to shoulder substantial domestic duties. However, Rita says that she is responsible for the house and is the primary caretaker of their seven-month-old son. And despite her busy schedule, she does not feel burdened at all by this responsibility:

> I guess in a way I like the control, 'cause I can say, "This is *my* house; this is the way *I* want it done." And every once in a while he'll come back and say, "Well, this is my house, too. Why can't we do it this way?" And then I always shoot back, "Because I've always done it this way, and I'm the one who takes care of the house!" [Her tone becomes increasingly sharp.] So I guess control is part of it. As an only child you pretty much get used to having things your own way.

She sometimes feels that Alan should do more around the house, but only the things she does not like to do, such as taking out the trash or emptying the diaper pail. Later in the interview, she refers to herself as "the warden of the household—the . . . the . . . the chatelaine." For his part, Alan feels they both take responsibility for "certain aspects" of the household. He takes responsibility for the dishes, and he helps out in other areas. The chores he performs feel like a burden to him, and he often wishes Rita did more until he stops and thinks about all she does.

It appears that Rita's desire to maintain control over "her" house overrides the considerations of whose work is more important that might otherwise drive the division of labor in the relationship. But more importantly, Rita's comments suggest that we need to question the common conceptualization of performing housework as aversive and indicative of powerlessness.

Rita is not alone in equating domestic responsibilities with a certain measure of power. Lily, a higher-earning wife, also does not see household responsibilities as a burden:

> I take pride in it, in my house, because it was quite an accomplishment for us to have been able to buy it. So I really feel privileged to be here, because it was something that I could only dream about. . . . I can't wait to start decorating it nicely. I love my home. I love having a clean home. I think better when it's clean.

Among the wives, only these two women enthusiastically embrace the responsibility for household chores. Some women "don't mind" shouldering these responsibilities (more in Chapter 6), but most comparison wives and about half the higher-earning wives actively sought to reduce their domestic labor burden.

Several other women saw power as rooted in being a mother, in terms of the ability to have a strong impact on their children. Again, there is Cindy, who struggled with her husband, Don, over performing household chores. If she is unhappy carrying the bulk of the domestic labor, she seems very happy to be the primary parent:

> I love being a mom. I love having kids. I think, within that framework, I provide a lot of the family dinners we have. And I make *huge* deals of the children's birthdays, and I firmly believe that childhood should be very happy. And it should be a time that they'll remember with mostly good memories, and so I try to provide that.

A few wives felt that their importance lay in activities they were involved in outside the home, especially as those activities had an impact on the quality of their children's lives (see Sokoloff 1980 for a similar argument). The power potential in these endeavors resonated with Phyllis, a comparison wife. She is a former academic who is now primarily at home but also has a part-time clinical psychology practice. She has three children under the age of seven and is very involved in both the school and the community. She says that she loves being at home with her children:

> [VT: So you see being a mom as a powerful position?] Oh, absolutely! Absolutely! One thing that changed my whole paradigm shift, I guess you'd call it, was when my dad died. He had been a big man in the community—chief of staff at the local hospital—and everyone made a big fuss. And after he died, I started to watch the things my mom was doing, and I came to the realization that my mom made more of an impact on that community than my dad—in her housewife role—through volunteer activities and all these traditional women's things. And I realized that my mom's made more of an impact on the future of the world. And that was more important to me. Because I never worked for money, until now. That wasn't what was important to me. I wanted to make a difference. Somehow I saw "out there" as a more important way to make a difference. . . . But of course, that *pales* in comparison to the power you have over your children.

Phyllis left full-time work in academia several years ago to be home with her children. Since the beginning of her marriage, she had "bought into the dual-career model of success-equals-recognition-by-strangers," but now she has backed away from that. She quit her full-time academic position two years ago, "making my strongest feminist statement ever." She felt she was being a "bad mom" by leaving her children in day care twelve hours a day, and it was not in her nature to do anything poorly. By placing a priority on domestic work and parenting, she felt she was disrupting the male model of career success and affirming the value of conventionally feminine activities.

Interestingly, Phyllis has spent a great deal of her fifteen-year marriage to Mitch struggling over domestic labor issues. She has always wanted a house as neat and orderly as the one her homemaker mother kept in the 1950s, and she has expected Mitch to carry 50 percent of the labor required to meet that standard. Disagreements over this issue helped send them into therapy early in their marriage. In the past, they have had housekeeping help. Now Phyllis does most of it herself. Now, she says, "we just do what seems to work. And I'm around more, and it's more important to me." She found some of the categories on the questionnaire I asked her to fill out "frustrating, because I would check 'mostly me' or 'almost always me,' unless I'm not home, and then Mitch does it. Whoever is the primary parent at the time does it, and that's just usually me."

That is exactly the point; it is usually she who does the work. That is the reality. This last comment shows her discomfort with her current situation. She carries the domestic labor burden, and she made a conscious decision to stay home, which she does not regret, but seeing in black and white how unequal the division of labor is seems to go against her grain. She wants to see her husband as contributing more equally to the household because that is still her ideal. She seems to be feeling contradictory pulls: one toward valuing the responsibilities at home, and one toward equality, which subtly communicates that shouldering a larger share of these responsibilities is unpleasant and, more importantly, unfair.

The idea of women's responsibility for the household, or even for parenting, as "powerful" did not represent the experiences of most of the women in my sample. Only six women seemed to see these responsibilities as a way to exercise control or influence, and it is difficult to say what sets them apart. Half are higher-earning wives; half are comparison wives. They have varied personal backgrounds in terms of the kinds of families they grew up in and the amount of education they have received. The one common thread is their inability to "let go" of the home, even in cases where they are actively seeking greater involvement by their husbands. They see themselves as somehow better qualified to run the household and care for their children.

A few of their husbands complain about the control their wives seem to have. For example, Stan, a husband with a higher-earning wife, feels his wife does not treat him as an equal parent:

> Here's a big one on child raising. Linda gives me the impression that she thinks she's the final authority on our daughter. It makes me mad when she asks my opinion and never follows through with it. Not that she *has* to, but it seems like she *never* does. It seems she asks my opinion just as a courtesy. [We laugh.] And that no matter what I say, Linda's the mother and she gets the final say. So I told her, "Don't ask my opinion anymore." [We laugh.]

Four of the husbands of the six women who saw domestic duties as powerful complained about being shut out in some way, and yet, like Stan, they seemed resigned to a lesser role in the domestic sphere. It was not always a question of wanting to do more at home; the longing seemed to be of a symbolic nature—wanting to be more a part of the decisions affecting the children and, in some cases, the household. Yet none of these men mounted a serious challenge to their wives' authority in these matters; they accepted their wives' right to have the final say as "the mom."

The evidence from research on whether women's responsibilities at home are, or can be, powerful underscores the tensions we see in these couples. A few women are reluctant to give up control at home, even if it means performing the bulk of the domestic labor themselves. Still others may become gatekeepers of their husbands' involvement with their children. Wives can then exercise considerable (if hidden) power in the family through their involvement with their children, by making their husbands more peripheral members of the family (Backett 1987; Benokraitis 1985; Kimball 1988). However, it can also be argued that women's responsibilities at home offer very little in the way of real power. For example, in child rearing, men may delegate daily decision-making to their wives but reserve the authority to make the decisions they consider important. This means that women have control only over issues that men feel are not worth their time.

Additionally, women's power within the home is limited, because to exert influence, a woman must be seen as a "giver," sacrificing her own interests for those of her family (Lips 1981; Polatnik 1973). We have already seen how this level of service to the family often depletes women both physically and emotionally. Under these circumstances, it is hard to characterize such labor as a source of power.

And finally this attempt to explore the power in women's roles underscores that there is an ideological tension in caring work; it is simultaneously revered and devalued—noble labor and central to womanhood, but still a potential burden and source of conflict. It is unclear, then, how much power women can exercise by maintaining control over the household. In fact, for these women, guarding control over the household and children may be less about maintaining control and more about maintaining gender boundaries, a topic that will be addressed in Chapter 6.

GENDERED LABOR AND POWER

The results presented in this chapter provide further evidence that resource and exchange models are inadequate to explain the division of domestic labor when wives earn more than their husbands do.

Higher-earning wives are unable to trade their substantial incomes for equally substantial reductions in their domestic labor burden. These wives are performing the bulk of domestic labor in addition to bringing home the lion's share of the family income.

However, there is some variation in patterns among couples. The wives earning nearly all the family's income have rather successfully traded their incomes for domestic labor performed by their husbands. Although their income and occupational responsibilities do not entitle them to completely wash their hands of domestic duties, their husbands do perform the bulk of the household and child-care tasks in these families. While these results are encouraging because they are among the most equitable in the sample, they are by no means guaranteed. Other research reports that men who are unemployed, or severely underemployed, often assert their masculine identity and privilege by refusing to perform domestic labor (Bittman et al. 2003; Brines 1994; Greenstein 2000; Komarovsky 1980). Perhaps the difference in this sample is that four of the five husbands in these circumstances consciously chose to exit the workforce to be home with their children. It was a priority for these couples to have one parent primarily at home, and in each case, the earning potential for the wives was greater at the time the decision was made. Operating under the assumptions of the conventional marital contract, these spouses have struck an explicit bargain to maintain a largely conventional arrangement of trading breadwinning for domestic labor, even if the spouses performing these duties are not the conventional ones.

Other higher-earning wives seem to benefit from the calculation of whose work is more important. When couples agree that the wife's work is more important, or even if only the husband thinks so, women get more relief from the burden of housework and child care. The contributions of the husbands in these marriages are greater than those of other husbands—they shoulder approximately 30 to 40 percent of the domestic labor burden. Interestingly, this calculation of worth driving the division of domestic labor in these couples seems to be largely unconscious. None of these spouses come out and say that who does what at home is related to whose work is more important. In fact, most spouses are reluctant to engage in that kind of calculation, even when explicitly asked to do so. They can be proud of each other, brag about each other's accomplishments, and be supportive of each other, all indicating that they are equals. Yet these couples retain an underlying sense that one spouse's work matters more. One job might be more important because of the income it commands, or because it is deeply meaningful to the individual who performs it. Or one job might be more important in a larger societal sense—in terms of the impact it has on other people. Though many spouses claim they do not think about these issues, their perceptions of the differences in what they do for a living helps to account for the differences in what they do at home—more than income earned, occupational status, or relative time demands. And it is what the husband thinks that really matters.

However, while some higher-earning wives get more relief from domestic labor than do employed wives more generally, this was true for only half the women in this sample. And remember that, with the exception of the five wives who are nearly the sole earners in their families, these women are still performing more than half the household chores and child care. In other words, a wife's earning two-thirds of the family income in no case translated into a husband's performing two-thirds of the domestic labor. This means that the most important finding is the continued inequity at home, even for women with substantial income and occupational resources at their disposal.

These results demonstrate that all the patterns of sharing domestic labor among couples with higher-earning wives are still influenced by gender. First, the vast majority of wives continue to perform the bulk of household chores and child care, despite their substantial incomes. Second, while doing important work may lessen the load somewhat for wives, husbands still seem to benefit more from this calculation. Men doing important work have wives performing 80 to 90 percent of the domestic labor, whereas women doing important work get, at best, a 30 to 40 percent contribution from their husbands. In other words, wives still contribute much more, in terms of both income and domestic labor, no matter what their circumstances.

That men are able to evade housework and child care despite their lesser incomes demonstrates that the gender structure exerts an independent influence on the dynamics of these couples. Husbands' continued ability to limit their household-labor contributions means that they enjoy this privilege as *men,* rather than as *providers.* The cultural expectation that women are responsible for and perform domestic labor undercuts whatever power might be available in the greater incomes these wives earn. This explains why even higher-earning wives are unable to get a fair trade for their money.

In this chapter I have focused on the effects of the gender structure at the institutional level—the assumption embedded in the conventional marital contract that money is exchanged for domestic labor—to see if this equation works when women are the major earners. I have postponed discussion of the effects of the gender structure at the interactional and individual levels on the division of domestic labor until Chapter 6. There, we will see how the gender structure—specifically conventional gendered identities of men as breadwinners and wives as mothers/home-makers—affects women's willingness to take on, and men's ability to avoid, household responsibilities.

CHAPTER 4

Dollar Rich and Power Poor

WHY WIVES DO NOT CONTROL
THE MONEY

THIS CHAPTER ASSESSES WHETHER earning the bulk of the family's money translates neatly into controlling that money. This equation has worked for men; being the sole or major breadwinner has been used to legitimate men's greater control over the marital purse. But is this financial privilege available to higher-earning wives?

THE LINK BETWEEN MONEY AND POWER
IN MARRIAGE

The ability to control the family's financial resources has long been thought to reflect one's power within marriage. As the sole breadwinners, men have typically been able to dictate how financial resources should be spent, act as gatekeepers, and control other family members' access to their income (Hertz 1986). Some husbands have kept strict control by managing the money themselves. Others have delegated money management to their wives, turning over the bulk of their pay to be used at her discretion for running the household. However, even in these cases, men typically hold back a portion of their income for their own use. Men often feel entitled to this kind of control, the logic being, "I make the money, I'll decide how to spend it." In this way, their role as breadwinner has legitimated men's control over the marital purse strings (Blumberg and Coleman 1989; Ferree 1990).

Historically, women's income has not translated into the same kind of control because women's money has been viewed differently than men's (Pyke, 1994; Zelizer 1989). In the early to mid–twentieth century, many married, middle-class women worked only part-time for "pin money," that is, to pay for extras for themselves or their children. In other cases, wives worked to finance particular family expenditures, such as a family vacation or a child's college education (Whyte 1990). This kind of employment did little to alter the balance of financial power in marriage (Blood and Wolfe 1960). Husbands provided the family's real income; wives' financial contributions were seen as nonessential and were accorded lesser significance. Even the wages of poor and working-class women, many of whom worked full time and whose earnings were essential to their families' survival, did not entitle them to any great measure of financial control in their marriages (Blumberg 1991; Rubin 1976).

In the last three decades, married women have moved into the workforce as more substantial providers. Their incomes have been essential to maintain their families' standard of living, ensuring middle-class status in some cases and economic survival in others. However, earning incomes that are important to the family has not translated into much greater economic power for wives. Control over the family's finances still seems to reside with the man, as the major breadwinner (Blumberg 1991; Blumstein and Schwartz 1983, 1991; Pahl 1989; Sexton and Perlman 1989), even when wives have incomes approaching those of their husbands (Whyte 1990). Men in dual-earner families still seem to enjoy a financial edge.

The link between money and power in marriage appears to be quite strong. This link has historically worked to men's advantage, but there is some research that suggests that women whose earnings are on par with their husbands' enjoy increased power in the marital relationship (see, for example, Blumstein and Schwartz 1983; Huber and Spitze 1983; Pahl 1989; Vannoy-Hiller and Philliber 1989). However, there is also a great deal of evidence suggesting that money and power are much more likely to be linked for men than for women. For example, Blumstein and Schwartz (1983) found that money establishes the balance of power for both heterosexual and gay couples. While this might suggest that money and power can be linked without gender operating as a factor, I argue that these results demonstrate that the opposite is true. That is, they suggest that money translates into power only for men. In the case of heterosexual couples, men are far more likely to outearn their partners, so it is easy to argue that men have more financial power because they "happen" to make more money. Gay men, as men, are also used to equating money with power. Lesbians seem to stand alone against this link, suggesting that women are not accustomed to seeing their income as a source of power. In short, the money-equals-power equation appears to be gendered, since money does not seem to translate as easily into increased power for women (this is true cross-culturally as well; see Blumberg 1984).

These findings do not mean that women have nothing to gain by having an independent income, just that the advantages are not always straightforward; simply earning an income is not sufficient to give wives greater financial control in their relationships. To assess women's economic power within their families, we need to look at several factors: a wife's absolute earnings; the husband/wife earning ratio; a wife's independent control over earnings; and a wife's access to the family surplus, if any (Blumberg and Coleman 1989). In other words, the higher the wife's earnings, the greater her earnings in relation to her husband's, and the more control she has over the family's surplus, the greater her economic power. In this case, wives in my sample have at least the first two factors working in their favor, since they earn high wages—especially relative to their husbands'.

But absolute income and earnings ratios do not tell the whole story. Gendered norms and expectations also have a large impact on the relative financial power of spouses. For example, expectations for men's dominance often keep women from exerting what feels like too much control in their relationships (Blumberg and Coleman 1989; Zelizer 1989). Wives may make significant incomes but also feel that they cannot (or should not) use this economic advantage to assert a right to dominate financial decisions. They are also less likely than their husbands to feel "entitled" to control the family purse or spend money as they please. This gendered expectation for men's financial dominance constrains even higher-earning wives as they attempt to negotiate for financial power in their marriages.

Issues in Assessing Financial Power

While men's typically larger incomes have guaranteed them a great deal of financial power, the way household funds are organized is also critical in determining the relative control spouses enjoy. Money can be separate, joint (or "pooled"), or some combination of the two. Substantial pooling is the most common form of financial organization among married couples and is particularly common among co-providing spouses (Hood 1986; Treas 1993). Pooling is associated with greater equality in decision making, and wife-controlled pooling often translates into more power for wives in decision making. Conversely, separate money and husband-controlled pooling (where wives often receive an "allowance") are associated with husband dominance in decision making (Pahl 1989; Whyte 1990).

It is also important to examine couples' justifications for their financial arrangements. Couples give a variety of reasons for organizing their finances the way they do. Some are practical reasons, as when one spouse manages the money because she or he can get to the bank, knows what household members need, knows what food to buy, and so forth. Others are psychological, as when one spouse is seen as being more careful with money or more levelheaded, and the couple decides that the more financially savvy spouse should have greater control. In some cases, money-organization patterns are related to the proportion of income earned by each spouse—the spouse who has the gold makes the rules (Pahl 1989). Since husbands typically outearn their wives, this last pattern tends to work in men's favor.

Deciding what constitutes financial power is a tricky issue. Assessing who has meaningful control requires exploring the structure of financial accounts and decisions made by individual couples, and these money systems can be very complex. There may be individual and joint accounts, accounts for business or tax purposes, accounts for investment and retirement purposes, and accounts for children's education. The entire financial web of the couple must be examined. Simply asking who pays the bills or who controls the checkbook does not assess whether there are any real decisions to be made in these activities. Especially if money is tight, paying the bills may not be powerful at all; it may be an added burden or stressor for a spouse—something to be avoided.

This means that there is a distinction between money responsibility (paying the bills, worrying about money) and money privilege (spending money freely on oneself) (Pahl 1989). While enjoying money privilege is an indicator of power, being saddled with money responsibility may not be. It is important to assess whether there is any financial surplus in the relationship, and if so, who has access to it and under what circumstances. Access to and control over discretionary income is perhaps the strongest indicator of relative power.

Compiling a complete financial picture for a couple means addressing three distinct questions: Who manages the money on a daily basis, and does this role lead to greater control over financial decisions? How do spouses make joint financial decisions? How does each spouse get what she or he wants? (That is, are spouses free to act on their own or do they have to convince their partners to go along with their wishes?) Addressing these issues gives a comprehensive picture of how financial power operates in these marriages.

CONTROLLING THE CHECKBOOK: WIVES WITH THE UPPER HAND

While managing the checkbook and taking responsibility for paying the bills are not always powerful tasks, they certainly can be. This is especially true if all marital assets are pooled and the family has some surplus funds to spend each month. Under these circumstances, the spouse who holds the checkbook and pays the monthly bills may be able to act as a gatekeeper of the family's money. Familiarity with the family's monthly income and financial obligations becomes important information in other discussions and purchase decisions.

In my sample, women tended to be responsible for paying the family's bills. This was true for 77 percent of the higher-earning wives and 63 percent of comparison wives. However, in many of these marriages, husbands have separate money. Therefore, only 41 percent of higher-earning wives and 25 percent of comparison wives control a checkbook that also contains the family's surplus. In these households where all money is pooled, women who pay the bills often enjoy a great deal of control, regardless of the relative income earned by spouses.

For example, Jean is a critical care nurse making $45,000, married to Mike, an opthalmic technician making $25,000. Mike refers to Jean as the "money manager" in their relationship. She organizes the bills and makes sure they get paid. This seems to give her a great deal of financial control. Given Jean's role in managing the family finances, Mike describes how he goes about getting something he wants:

> If there's something I want to buy, as a general rule, the first thing I do is say, "Look at this. I'd like to have this because [pause]—I like it, because it looks good, or I just want it because it would be fun." As

a general rule, if I promote that kind of argument, her first return is, "Okay, how much money do we have?" and "Well, it costs too much." And that is usually derived from, "Well, we've got this much money, and payday's coming then, and we have this many things that have to go out, so yeah, we can afford it." Or "No, we'll have to wait for a while." That's pretty much how it works.

I ask Mike if he feels he has enough control over how the money is spent, since Jean is the one who takes care of the bills.

> [Deep sigh.] I think control is a hard word to equate with that. [VT: Input?] I'm sure I can always input. It doesn't mean it always gets paid attention to. She has the idea [pause]—I would say because she tends to organize the box [of bills] that she's more conscious of the priorities probably than I am.

This couple has had some relatively serious financial difficulties in the past. Three years ago, they got into trouble with credit cards, so they cut them up. Two years ago, they gave up their checking account because "checks were too easy to write." Now they deal strictly in cash, because it is easy to see how much they have, and when it's gone, it's gone.

Still, it is hard to let go of material desires. From Jean's perspective, Mike is always trying to figure out how to get more of the things he wants, and she says that generates conflicts at times. I ask her how they resolve them:

> I open the bankbook. [We laugh.] The number's right there, ya know? He thinks I can make it grow on trees. We're kind of going through that right now. There's a lot of things that we want but we can't have. And he will keep looking, and pressing, and trying to find a way. And I'm like, "Back off a little. It's not something you *need*, it's a *want*."

I ask Jean if she feels she has enough control over how the money is spent: "Oh, yeah, you bet. It spends most of its time in my wallet, so [pause]—the thing about not having a checking account and not having credit cards [is], he who has the cash has the last word." Jean is clearly the gatekeeper of the family's money, and that seems to give her a great deal of power, especially since the couple cannot use checks or credit cards to make impulse purchases. At the very least, she can make determinations about what the family can and cannot afford, which gives her a way to keep Mike's desires in check.

Other women who manage the checkbook report having similar power in their relationships. Another higher-earning wife, Sandy, describes how she and her husband work out disagreements relating to financial matters. She says she tries to reason things out with him by saying:

> "We can't afford it," or "We can't do it because of this." And that, perhaps unfortunately, can be real effective when I have that [pause]— resource at my disposal. I know the details of what we've got planned when, and where our money is. It's a lot easier for me to control the discussion.

Like Mike, many husbands in these situations seem to accept their wives' greater control over financial decisions. Sandy's husband, Dick, agrees that he has a lesser role in their decision-making process: "I see it more as a partnership. Although I guess I have a slightly diminished [pause]—but I chose to give that up when I agreed that Sandy would take care of the finances." Husbands are not always happy about the control their wives have, but they often seem resigned to it. Witness the response of this husband with a higher-earning wife when I ask him if he feels he has enough control over how the money is spent:

> Yes. It's enough, but it's not the same. But that's because she's better with money anyway. Sometimes I'll want to take money out of savings to buy something, and she'll say, "Let's wait 'til we get to a certain point, and then do it, so we'll still be above a certain amount." Even though I don't want to, I'll still go along with it because I know she's better at money management.

Because wives tend to control the checkbooks in these marriages, husbands recognize that they do not always have a good sense of the overall financial picture in their relationships. Therefore, they are often willing to defer to their wives' judgments when there is disagreement about financial matters.

In the cases of the two comparison couples in which all money is pooled and wives pay the bills, the spouses seem to work much more as partners in financial matters. The husbands are more aware of the family's financial arrangements and take a more active role in making money decisions. With such small numbers, it is difficult to draw any larger conclusions from these data.

Separate Money: Men's Stash

While the wives just described seem to enjoy opportunities to exercise financial control, they are in the minority. Remember that two-thirds of higher-earning wives control the family checkbook. However, less than one-half of higher-earning wives actually act as gatekeepers of the family's money. As I examined more closely the couples in which wives manage the checkbook, I realized that one-third of husbands with higher-earning wives had carved out some separate money for themselves.

Mick and Maria demonstrate the impact this practice can have on the balance of financial power in the relationship. Maria makes $47,000 to Mick's $27,000 each year. Maria is responsible for paying the family's bills and reports that their money system is a point of contention in their marriage. They have a joint checking account, but only her check is deposited into it. Everything gets paid out of that account except the mortgage and the two car payments; Mick pays those out of his individual account. Though Mick has a separate account, Maria says, "There's no 'your money/my money' because there's never anything left over."

While Maria is responsible for paying most of the family's bills, she does not feel this gives her much control over the money, because there are no choices to be made and there is no money leftover:

> I don't think he appreciates the money [I make]. I mean, that's the one thing that [pause]—I just think he should accept more responsibility, and I shouldn't have to be the one to, you know, fill in all the cracks. And there just seem to be more and more cracks. [She laughs.] I tend to be very resentful of that, and I don't think he realizes.

She "fills in the cracks" by paying everything beyond the mortgage and car payments. That makes bill paying stressful for her: "We have to keep putting out a hundred dollars for this each month, a hundred dollars for that, and I say, '*Where* is it coming from? It's certainly not coming from *you*.' And I say, 'I can only work so hard,' you know?"

Mick has little to say about how the bills are paid, though his account of who pays for what agrees with Maria's. He reports that though money is tight, they both have a little money left over to spend as they please, while Maria reports that there is nothing left for her once the bills are paid. She has been trying to get Mick to take over the checkbook, but he has refused. This system of separate money, which limits his obligations to a fixed amount each month and leaves her to "fill in the cracks," means that he can count on having some money left over each payday; she cannot. There is no reason for him to take responsibility for the other monthly bills to gain some financial control or opportunities for discretionary spending. Paying the bills would just be another headache for him, one that he has avoided.

Mick is not alone in viewing bill paying as a chore (rather than a position of power), nor is he the only husband who has avoided this responsibility. Another husband of a higher-earning wife talks about his role in the family's finances since his wife is responsible for paying for the bills:

> We decided it was best that she handle all that, and that I be kept ignorant. But with that comes a lot of the ability to see where the household money is spent, and where you can economize, or where, you know, things are out of line. So I'm largely involved only in the additional purchases—new furnishings, or upgrades of appliances, carpet, and so forth. I have very little interest in routine bills, I guess, at this point.

This husband is relieved to be out of the nitty-gritty details of the family's finances. This is because he does not need to do the bill paying in order to enjoy some financial control or autonomy. Later in the interview, he explains that he has a portion of his income set aside each payday in a separate account. He felt he needed to have five or six hundred dollars at his disposal so he could go "splurge" on something if he wanted to:

> When I did my own accounting, I would tend to allocate, even in a single checking account, I would have in my mind so much set aside for this, and so much set aside for that. Here, it just goes into this gaping maw and never gets reallocated for anything. So I've dealt with that in a, I think, modest and pernicious way.

Both of these husbands have extra money that they can call their own. Neither of their wives have anything similar; in fact, the wife of the man just quoted is unaware of his extra money, reporting that "we've never had separate accounts. I'm amused by friends who have all kinds of accounts. Life's too short. Besides, it would just be another account for me to balance." Both of these husbands are relieved, and quite content, to have their wives take care of (and worry about meeting) the bills.

One-third of comparison husbands also have separate money, and they exhibit patterns similar to husbands of higher-earning wives. For example, Paul's circumstances are similar to Mick's. When his family purchased their new home, Paul set up a separate account in his name only. Part of his paycheck is deposited in this account, and then the mortgage payment is automatically deducted from the balance. "That way, there's no mistakes," Paul says. When I ask if he had any extra money in that account, Paul replies, "Of course." He also reports that his wife was unhappy with this arrangement, but he says simply, "Hey, it's *my* account," implying that he did as he pleased despite his wife's objections. This system means that he has plenty of discretionary money and is happy to let his wife manage the rest of the bills.

In my own mind, I have referred to the extra money that these husbands have as their "stash," a term that connotes a certain amount of secrecy and even selfishness that seems justified by their reports. The husbands get their cut off the top, so to speak, and are quite unconcerned about whether their wives are able to do the same. Most wives are unaware that their husbands have this extra money, or are unaware how much money their husbands have at their disposal. This means that they are not in a position to effectively protest this arrangement.

In a couple of cases, wives are aware that their husbands have extra money, but they do not seem to resent it. Rather, they seem to view it as natural, or at least normal, as the following example illustrates. Steve and Rhonda are a comparison couple in which he has extra money, she doesn't, and neither seems to view this circumstance as problematic. She does all the bills; she likes to do them and he "lets" her. Steve makes twice Rhonda's income, but his income advantage is exacerbated by the fact that their money system makes her income invisible. Her paycheck goes almost entirely into an account for the college education of their two young sons. There is very little left to go into their joint checking account (this allocation of her income is all done electronically). Steve always cashes his paycheck in person, taking out whatever cash he feels he will need until the next payday. He likes to walk around with at least a hundred dollars in his wallet, whereas he says Rhonda can carry five dollars and be happy. In addition to this pocket money, Steve keeps a considerable amount of cash in his bedroom that he uses for additional spending on collectibles and memorabilia, among other things. He also saves that money for projects that he wants to complete around the house. Right now, he is saving for a new deck and has about a thousand dollars in his dresser drawer.

Rhonda is not very happy about all the money Steve spends independently, but she seems to have little to say about it since he takes the money off the top and makes purchase decisions without her. He also at times works long, extra hours for the money, so she seems to feel he can make a legitimate claim to keeping and controlling it. This financial system gives Steve all the spending money and financial freedom he wants. At the same time, it hides Rhonda's money and makes her dependent on "his." Steve describes how his wife gets what she wants, using a recent landscaping project as an example:

> I had money laid aside for the deck when her parents came up to visit. Rhonda was out there working her tail off, digging up the lawn. I thought, "Why not get it all done in one day?" I asked her what she needed to do this—stones, this, that. I didn't know what it would cost exactly, but I figured it would be a couple hundred dollars. I said, "Here, I have the money. We'll go out and get the stuff," and that was pretty much it. The money was just sitting around anyway. I'd either spend it on food or it would just sit up in the room.

The money was there for her landscaping project, but it was held and controlled by him. It was money that would otherwise have been in their joint checking account, where she could access it and potentially make decisions about its use.

Rhonda does not seem to seriously object to Steve's having money set aside for his own use. In fact, she sees Steve as "generous." When I ask her if she sees a link between money and power in her relationship, she says, "As far as being the breadwinner, yes, he does make more income than I do, but he's very generous with his money." She seems to accept that the money is his to control.

Fully one-third of the men in this sample, in both groups, have separate money. For a few of them, it is a habit left over from their single days—an account they never closed into which they put a few dollars every payday. But for most, these accounts represent a conscious attempt to get something for themselves when it seemed to them that they were putting everything they had into the common pot and there was never anything left over for them. Their wives are more or less stuck with paying the bills without gaining any measure of control over the family surplus. At the same time that these husbands are siphoning off spending money, they drain the family checkbook of its potential power.

It is interesting to note that of the eight men who regularly paid the family's bills (five with higher-earning wives, three comparison husbands), none have separate money for personal spending. Apparently, there is no need for it. These men are able to exercise the same kind of control as wives who handle the checkbook. This husband with a higher-earning wife describes how he gets what he wants:

> I spent a thousand bucks on an electronic air cleaner for our house. . . .
> First I discussed it with [my wife], and she thought it was too much
> money, and then I just went and did it, and, uh, you know, she kind
> of winced a little bit. But, you know, I paid the bill, and she didn't
> have to see it or think about it, so it just kind of went through the
> system.

Apparently, handling the checkbook gives these men all the financial control they need. And, in contrast to the sense of entitlement felt by many men, no woman talks about being entitled to some spending money off the top. None of the wives whose husbands controlled the checkbook has money stashed away for her personal use.

Paying the Bills as a
Bookkeeping Function

Though controlling the checkbook can give a spouse the opportunity to exercise some financial control, in this sample, paying the bills is not always viewed as a powerful job. About half the couples with higher-earning wives and three-fourths of the comparison couples describe paying the bills as a bookkeeping task—not terribly powerful, and something spouses would rather avoid. In fact, for many of these couples, the largest financial struggle is trying to evade responsibility for paying the bills. This happens for several reasons. In most cases, money is tight for the family and doing the bills is a monthly reminder that, despite having two incomes and working hard for them, they are barely making it. Even in more affluent families, bill paying can be a chore; since there is plenty of discretionary money available, there is no reason to take on the added task of paying the bills to gain access to extra funds. Where men have been able to squirrel away funds for their own use, doing the bills each month is one more household chore to avoid. In a very small minority of families (one couple with a higher-earning wife, one comparison couple), spouses sit down together each month to pay the bills. They prefer this arrangement because then each spouse is aware of the family's financial situation and is able to have input into financial decisions. Under this system, neither spouse is burdened with sole responsibility for this household task, and both spouses feel they have adequate control over financial decisions.

THE GENDERED LINK BETWEEN MONEY AND POWER

Earning at least 50 percent more than their husbands does not automatically translate into greater control in financial matters for wives. In fact, most of the couples in this sample manage to subvert the link between money and power for wives, while maintaining at least the possibility of such a link for husbands. This means that these wives make no greater claim to power based on their higher incomes, but that the door is still open for their husbands to do so if circumstances change.

I asked spouses several questions designed to encourage them to reflect on the possible link between money and power in their relationships. Most completely dismiss the idea that such a link exists for them. Typical is this wife's response: "There's not a *strong* one, like this one's in charge, and this one says, 'Yes, okay, fine.' There's always an equality. . . . I definitely bring home almost twice what he does, but that doesn't make me the right one, or the one that makes the rules. There's no rules." In fact, couples with higher-earning wives seem particularly uncomfortable with the idea of linking the wife's income advantage to greater power in the relationship.

There is, however, an underlying sense that husbands could still exchange money for power. For example, Don and Cindy, whom we met in the preceding chapter, both work full time. Don, a welding technician, reflects on the link between money and power in their marriage:

> I think, as a general rule, it's been very mutual, although there's been times, where I've been earning more money, I've *felt* like I should have more say. Whether I actually did, or actually *demanded* that I did, there were times that I felt like, "I earn all the money. I should be able to decide what to do with it."

By contrast, Cindy "hopes" that, over the course of their relationship, they made a conscious effort to view all assets as "our money," regardless of who earned it. She now earns more than Don does and describes a fight they had less than a year ago.

> He just got all upset and flew off the handle. I was gonna go out and buy the kids some new school clothes, right before school begins. And he said we couldn't afford it. I said, "I'll charge it. I don't want our kids going to school in old clothes." It wasn't like I was going to go out and buy hundreds of dollars' worth. And he just blew off the handle and threw something, just screamed and yelled. . . . At that point I said to him, "You know, I make more money than you. If I wanna spend money, I will." Oooooooo! He had a fit.

For Don, bringing in more money means a legitimate claim to more control for him but not for his wife. Cindy's attempt to assert such a claim precipitated what she describes as one of their worst fights.

Jill, a midlevel bank manager married to a car salesperson, tells a similar story:

> I've brought in more money, and I don't feel like I had more power. . . . I try not to mention the fact that I make more money, because that's just a taboo thing. It would send him through the roof. If I'm even anywhere close to that subject, it's dangerous. [She laughs nervously.] I think in his mind, money is power, and he thinks he'll be a much better husband the more money he makes.

Higher-earning wives, as the main income earners, do not demand extra authority over how the money is spent. They do not say, "I make more money; I'll decide where it goes" (though several comparison husbands made such statements). These women who bring home more money, some of whom are nearly sole providers, are careful to say that all their marital assets are joint. They can share what they have, but they eschew any attempt to paint themselves as superior to their husbands, or as staking some claim to an extra measure of control over the family's money. Of course, as we have seen, some wives do enjoy great control, but they do not assert a right to this as the major breadwinner. However, wives seem to realize that their husbands could still claim this right. That is, if their husbands were the primary breadwinners, they would have greater financial control automatically, and this seems unproblematic for these wives. At least, they describe it in a matter-of-fact way. For example, Bonnie is a corporate attorney whose husband, Wayne, is primarily at home with their six-year-old son. She recognizes that money seems to translate into power, but only for her husband:

> I think there *is* a link [between money and power], but only the other way. If Wayne were making all the money, I'd be resentful because I'd feel as if I had less of a say in how it was spent, regardless of what he thought. But if I'm the only one making the money, we've tried all along to make sure that all the money and assets that we have are clearly joint, regardless of where it all came from. [VT: So you don't think *he* feels the way you think *you* would feel?] Correct. I mean, he's out there buying all these toys, these treadmills and [thousand-dollar] vacuum cleaners, whereas I think if I were, if the situation were reversed, and I was at home, I mean, I'd be even more of a penny-pincher.

Gendered expectations for men's dominance play a role in how spouses see themselves and their ability, or right, to exercise financial power in their marriages. Most higher-earning wives would not dream of demanding greater control over the finances. Husbands share these expectations and would not allow their wives to make a claim to financial control based on their income advantage. The only possible exceptions to this trend in the sample are the three wives featured next, who exercise a great deal of financial control for various reasons. However, this control is not necessarily absolute and is not based solely on their greater incomes. And at least two of the three wives talk about checks on their ability to control the family's money.

WIVES WITH THE MOST CONTROL

The three couples presented in this section represent the cases in which wives were able to exercise the most financial control in their relationships. In all three cases, the wives were nearly the sole breadwinners in their families.

Rachel and Kurt

Rachel is a claims adjuster making $23,000 a year. She is married to Kurt, who has been recuperating at home for the last several years from two debilitating automobile accidents (he formerly worked as a self-employed house painter). Kurt receives a small disability check each month, which he turns over to Rachel: "I don't think anybody would be as generous with her as I am, as far as money goes. When I get some, I give her all of it, because I know she does what's right with it." Rachel handles all financial matters in their home. All the money they have goes into an account in her name only because Rachel does not trust Kurt with money. He has a history of substance abuse, though he has been clean and sober for almost two years. Interestingly, she has a similar history of drinking and drug abuse. When they met nine years ago, she says, that they could both "party pretty hard" is what drew them together. But she has been clean and sober as long as he has and has always handled the money.

Despite the financial control that Rachel has, Kurt feels that he gets what he needs:

> My main concern is to take care of the house, then give to [our daughter] and Rachel so they can buy something to look good at school and work. . . . If I need something, I'll get it. If Rachel wants something, she buys it. She doesn't just waste money; she uses her head. . . . I'm secure with the way she handles the money.

Rachel agrees that she has a great deal of money control and explains that this is deliberate:

I really gatekeep the money. He really doesn't ask for a lot, but like once recently, he said he needed some pants, and I bought them for him. I don't have a problem with that. I don't make a big deal out of it. I have a hard time just giving him money for nothing. I've got to know what it's for. He asks me for an accounting, too. If I don't have any money, he wants to know what I did with it. If there's something I want, I just get it, really.

Rachel reports that Kurt does question her, at times, about what she has spent. For example, when he hears how much a week's worth of groceries cost, he sometimes gets upset that she spent so much, but she says, "Once he sees what I got, he agrees that that's what we needed." Though Kurt asks her for an accounting of the money, it is not clear whether he is in a position to challenge her control, since she has sole access to their money, and his most recent accident has left him unable to drive. This makes him quite dependent on Rachel, who uses this control to her advantage. She does not give him "money for nothing." Although she trusts that he is clean and sober, she says he has a tendency to gamble, and they cannot afford to let any money slip away. "I put my foot down. I'm more like a—I don't want to use this word—'mother.' Not that I'm Kurt's mother, but I'm like a mother would be." She says she takes this strong role to keep the household on solid financial ground.

Jackie and Carl

Jackie is a customer-service representative for a large company and makes $38,000 per year. Her husband, Carl, has been home with their three children for five years. He earns income sporadically by providing child care for families in their neighborhood. Of the three wives presented here, Jackie seems to have the strongest sense of entitlement to financial control. She handles all the finances: "I kind of do whatever I want in that respect." As with the previous couple, Jackie's and Carl's money goes into an account in Jackie's name only. Money has always been tight for them, and it has been too tempting for Carl to write checks or take money out of an ATM. He grew up quite poor and always wants to be able to spend more money. Jackie finally agreed to let him have twenty dollars a week to spend. She knows he needs to have that freedom. She says, "Things go better when I'm not so tight with my money."

The family is clear about who has ultimate control over the money. Jackie says:

> The kids are told, "Mommy's the boss of the money, and Daddy's the boss of the—" . . . I forgot what he's the boss of. [We laugh.] He's the boss of something, and I'm the boss of the money. So if anything needs to be talked about, it always has to go through Mommy if it involves money.

Carl agrees with Jackie's account of how the finances are managed. He also agrees that she needs to be in control of the checkbook because he is too frivolous, money is very tight, and they just "can't afford to waste a penny." But he also says that he is always wishing he had more; he admits to going into his wife's purse occasionally to take ten dollars for something he wants. But, by and large, he reports, Jackie makes the financial decisions in their household: "I'll pretty much say, 'Whatever you decide, I'll agree with,' because I trust that she won't make a decision that will adversely affect our household or our relationship. . . . I'll give my input . . . but I've almost been submissive in that respect."

The straightforward control that Rachel and Jackie seem to be able to exert in their relationships contrasts with that of the next wife, Annie, who seems to defer to her husband as the authority figure in the household to compensate for the financial control she enjoys.

Annie and Tom

Annie is a nurse practitioner making $50,000 per year. Her husband, Tom, has been at home with their three children for nearly seven years. He began a network marketing business eighteen months ago. So far it has brought in very little money, but Tom plans to be "living off of a six-figure residual income" in the next three to five years. This will allow Annie to stay at home with their boys. Annie is excited about Tom's new venture, but as time has worn on she has become quite impatient with his lack of progress in the business. He has been working at it for a year and a half and she feels he should be making more money by now. She is concerned that he will not be able to make a go of it, and that she will continue to be responsible for the family financially. She can hardly wait to be relieved of this responsibility so she can be at home with her children.

Yet her position as the nearly sole breadwinner and keeper of the family checkbook gives her opportunities to exercise financial control that her husband does not share. She reveals this when I ask how she goes about getting something she wants:

> I'd say if it was [pause]—three hundred dollars or below, I pretty much do what I want . . . and that's not reciprocal, because Tom won't do that. He won't arbitrarily spend that much money without asking me about it, but I will. . . . I just don't think he feels like it's his money to spend [pause]—whereas I *do* feel that it's my money, and I *will* spend it on things that are not that expensive, like a dress, or shoes, or whatever. He will always ask me, if it's something that has some value to it.

Annie says Tom has very little input into how the money is spent each month, and he accepts that. Annie pays the bills: "Once I've done the bills, I'll say, 'This is how much you have,' and then he's free to do whatever he wants around the household on a day-to-day basis with that." Most importantly, she says, "He doesn't see the details, just the end result," so she has ample opportunity to hide her discretionary purchases, if she chooses.

Tom feels they have "equal input" into how the money is spent. He describes them as "taking turns" getting the things they want with what is left over after they pay for what they need. Tom claims there is no link between who earns the money and who controls it. He says, "She's never held her income over my head" or demanded greater control. They both know where the money is going, so they both know what they can afford. He does not feel there is ever "enough" left over to spend as he pleases, but he says, "There's no separate ideas about how the money should be spent at this point." He is apparently unaware that Annie feels free to spend several hundred dollars without his input.

Though Annie seems to feel entitled to a certain amount of financial autonomy, she does not use her income advantage to assert dominance in other areas. She is careful to say that Tom is the head of the household:

> Tom runs the house. He's the boss, as far as I'm concerned. It just so happens that I bring home more money. It works best in our house when he's the boss. Children have no idea who's makin' money and who's not makin' money, where it comes into the house, or that they

can get things because of it. They still perceive Tom as the head of the household, even though he's in the household every day. And that's what we choose. I'm happier with it that way.

In other words, while Annie enjoys the greater financial control her income affords her, she does not want to look too powerful or undermine Tom's authority as the head of the household. It seems that gender norms can be pushed but not completely subverted.

With such small numbers and the unusual circumstances of these couples, it is difficult to argue that being nearly the sole breadwinner means greater financial power for a wife. The other two women in this category do not have such power, and the three couples featured here have some complex dynamics that will be explored in later chapters. However, these three women do exercise a level of financial control that stands out in contrast to the milder gatekeeping power that other higher-earning wives report having. The complex dynamics displayed by Annie and Tom set the stage for the next chapter, in which I explore how wives often defer to their husbands in decision making to preserve their authority or dominance in the home.

Gendered Money and Power

In general, higher-earning wives do not use their income advantage to make systematic claims to greater financial power in their relationships. While they often gain some measure of financial control by managing the family checkbook and gatekeeping the money, they do not enjoy the kind of financial privileges that conventional male breadwinners have. More significantly, wives' financial power is undercut by their husbands' ability to carve out extra money for themselves. Remember that one-third of the husbands are able to set aside money for their own use, which drains assets from the common pot; wives in this sample do not have separate money and are therefore at an economic disadvantage. That these wives do not claim a right to greater financial control contrasts with the long-standing ability of conventional male breadwinners to use their greater earning power to justify their financial power at home.

Among couples with higher-earning wives, we see a continuation of the cultural convention that entitles men to spend money much more freely than their wives do. Whether they control the common pot or simply appropriate money for their own use, men are better able to make independent purchases. Having control over discretionary funds means that they can buy things privately, without having to convince their wives to go along with their wishes, or even without their wives' knowledge. Without separate funds, wives' purchases become more public, which gives husbands more opportunities to control their wives' spending.

But perhaps most importantly, even couples with higher-earning wives maintain a sense that money equals power for husbands, but not for wives. Historically, this equation of money with power was rooted in men's greater economic contribution to the household. However, if this entitlement to power were simply a function of the breadwinning role, we would expect higher-earning wives to enjoy similar privileges. Since they do not, it is clear that regardless of their economic circumstances, couples are influenced primarily by expectations for men's dominance. In other words, in financial matters, the money-equals-power equation is gendered—automatic for men, problematic for women.

Here we see the independent effect of the gender structure on the power dynamics of these couples. It shapes the beliefs of these husbands and wives in ways that reproduce men's overall dominance of financial affairs. We can see this most clearly in the cases where husbands and wives talk, in a very matter-of-fact way, about how the link between money and power exists (or would exist) for husbands but not for wives. By disrupting this link for wives, couples preserve men's economic power—even in the absence of their economic dominance.

We can also see how the gender structure shapes the dynamics relating to money and power for these couples at all three levels of analysis. At the institutional level, the expectation that men should exert control over the family finances constrains spouses as they interact over money matters. Even wives who managed the checkbook and were able to gatekeep the money exerted that extra measure of control by referring to their knowledge of the account's current balance or upcoming financial commitments. In no case did a wife say, "It's my money. I'll decide what to do with it." The one wife who did try to exert a claim to spend money based on her greater income instigated the worst fight in her ten-year marriage. Significantly, she reports that she has not made any similar claims since.

At the individual level, we see how both men and women embrace expectations for men's financial dominance, even when husbands earn so much less than their wives. One-third of husbands take money off the top to meet their own needs; wives do not. Husbands also seem to retain the expectation that, should the family's income ratio shift in their favor, they would be entitled to an extra measure of control as the major earner. Wives seem to share this expectation. These results make clear that, in terms of relative financial control, the gender structure remains largely unchallenged despite the dramatically unconventional circumstances of these couples.

CHAPTER 5

Calling the Shots

WHY WIVES HAVE LIMITED
DECISION-MAKING POWER

EARNING SUBSTANTIALLY MORE money has not helped women bargain successfully for greater equity in the division of domestic labor, or given them greater control over the family's finances. In fact, the results of the previous chapters speak forcefully for the ability of conventional gendered expectations to disrupt the link between money and power as couples divide household chores and negotiate control over the family purse. This chapter examines the third standard indicator of marital power by exploring whether these wives' income advantage translates into more influence in decision making within their relationships.

ASSESSING POWER IN DECISION MAKING

Decision making has been the most obvious and oft-used indicator of the balance of power in marriages. Most typically, research (beginning with Blood and Wolfe 1960) has asked spouses about a wide array of decisions, ranging from where the family should live, to what kind of car to buy, to which doctor to see when someone is ill. The object is to determine which spouse has more "say" in each of these areas, or who makes the "final" decisions on these issues in the relationship. As evidenced by the literature on this topic, men typically exercise more control over a wide variety of decisions in their marriages (see Blumberg 1984; Blumberg and Coleman 1989; Blumstein and Schwartz 1983, 1991; Fox and Murry 2000; Hertz 1989; Hochschild 1989; Whyte 1990).

This blanket control or authority is legitimated at the institutional level of the gender structure. Men have had more power in marriage because history and culture support men's dominance in general. Men's authority within marriage can be seen as an extension of the power they exercise in the economic and political realms of the larger society. However, within marriage, men's decision-making power has been further legitimated by their usually greater earnings; of all the resources spouses contribute, the man's income has been the most highly valued, and this has been used to justify men's position as "head of the household" and final authority (Bernard 1981).

Feminists and scholars assumed that women's moving into the workforce and becoming important co-breadwinners would increase their power in the family—especially in terms of control over money management and decision making. However, the marital power literature over the last several decades has not borne this assumption out. Women's power in decision making has increased somewhat, but not to a degree commensurate with the level of income many of them have been earning. In short, their income does not seem to buy them the same right to decision-making power that men have typically enjoyed.

Exploring the relationship between income and decision-making power in couples with higher-earning wives requires that we move beyond a simple examination of decision-making outcomes among these couples. The customary focus on outcomes obscures the more subtle, and often more revealing, power dynamics of the decision-making process. At the interactional level, we can see that decision-making processes are gendered—men and women approach them differently. "Doing gender" typically requires men to be dominant and women to be submissive or deferential (Berk 1985). This may sound overstated, and many would argue that this is no longer the primary dynamic of heterosexual love relationships. However, the results presented in this chapter demonstrate that the cultural residue of these conservative gender imperatives lingers and continues to influence marital dynamics.

Further, the gender structure organizes the resources, both cultural and practical, on which men and women can draw in their efforts to influence decision making in their relationships. For example, since men are invested with greater authority in the home, it is easier for men than for women to issue orders to a spouse; women need to rely on more subtle means of influencing the decision-making process to avoid the appearance of trying to dominate their husbands (England and Kilbourne 1990; Gottman and Notarius 2000; Zronkovic, Schmiege, and Hall 1994).

(Potential) Power in Organizing
the Household

As we have seen, that women are generally responsible for the household means that, even when they do not perform the labor themselves, it is their job to make sure tasks are completed. Wives are therefore in charge of coordinating a wide range of household activities, which include overseeing (and performing) chores and errands, keeping track of administrative details (such as household maintenance, doctor's appointments, and homework), and managing the schedules of all family members. While these responsibilities can be overwhelming at times, this role as organizer of the home also holds potential power. For example, if wives handle the bulk of the everyday decisions, they may be able to push their own priorities to the top of the list and exercise a great deal of control: They can make dates to socialize with the friends they prefer; they can create a household environment that pleases them through a variety of consumption decisions (from food to home furnishings); they can set the very pace of family life by taking on or refusing to participate in particular activities. In short, if most of the details of family life are left to women, the decisions they make may reflect their own preferences, rather than their husbands'.

Being responsible for these kinds of household decisions has not been painted as particularly powerful in the bulk of the work on marital power, though the women who carry these responsibilities—including stay-at-home wives and mothers—often relish the control they exert through their domestic activities (see Kranichfeld 1987). My results further underscore that some women see these activities as powerful. For example, Ginny, a higher-earning wife, says: "I probably have a little more power in the day-to-day things—focusing on getting money into the account, that type of thing." The day-to-day things she refers to sound like simple, mundane errands, yet she sees them as powerful. She sees the control she has over daily activities as the ability to make things happen or not happen, as she sees fit. For example, making sure that paychecks get deposited quickly means that she and her husband will always have money on hand and never bounce a check. These kinds of activities are important enough that she wants to take charge of them, and she sees this responsibility as giving her a measure of control within the household.

Other women similarly characterized the role of household organizer as a powerful one. In fact, nearly half the higher-earning wives interviewed see their role as family organizer as giving them a measure of control in their relationships. One-fourth of the comparison women make this link as well. Being so familiar with the details of the household and the needs of its members gives women a perspective and special knowledge that other family members often do not have. Women most often know who needs a new coat, who is having trouble at school, when it is time for yearly checkups, and how fast the tires are balding on the family car. Managing this information puts them in a position to plan the family's life and prioritize purchases. It also gives them control over myriad mundane decisions: It is more than a cliché that fathers often respond to a child's request with "I don't know—go ask your mother."

When it comes time to make decisions on issues outside this realm of everyday knowledge, women's role as the household organizer can give them an edge, too. Wives are more likely than husbands to do the legwork of decision making, such as making phone calls and gathering information. While this can be onerous and time-consuming work, all this knowledge can give women the upper hand in decision making. In short, this information gives them power. Sometimes they feel free to collect the information and make decisions on their own. For example, Barbara says: "I'm the prod. I get things done. I'm the one who thought we should move [out here], buy this house. I picked out [our daughter's] school." These wives see themselves as initiating action in their relationships, and this initiative enables them to shape the final decision; husbands simply go along with the ideas their wives generate.

We met Phyllis and Mitch, a comparison couple, in the last chapter. Phyllis is the clinical psychologist who quit a high-powered academic job to be home with her three young children and now has a part-time counseling practice. When it comes to making decisions, Phyllis is the initiator and Mitch largely seems to agree with whatever she wants to do. Phyllis says: "A friend of mine is fighting with her husband about furniture. She asked me what kind of style Mitch likes. I say, 'The "yes, dear" style.' I'll ask him, 'Do you like this?' and he'll say, 'Yes, dear.' I like his style. [She laughs.]"

Phyllis sees herself as "strong-willed, so if I say something will happen, it will happen, unless we discuss it and decide it's *not* gonna happen."

She describes how she and Mitch make decisions using an example of a recent purchase:

> Generally, I plan things, check with him, and he generally says, "Fine." I'm usually the initiator of things. . . . Because I manage the house, most of the stuff I come up with that I want tends not to be for me; it's for the kids or the house. Like when [our daughter] was growing out of her crib. [I said,] "We need new furniture. I'm not gonna spend a fortune. Let me put an ad in the paper and see what I can come up with." The day I found the bedroom furniture, I called him at work and told him it was a great deal. He said, "Great, go get it." I just wanted to check with him first.

She decided it was time to move their daughter from a crib to a bed, made the calls, gathered the information, found what she was looking for, and simply checked in with her husband before acting on her plan.

Cindy, a higher-earning wife married to Don, thinks her role as social organizer gives her control over the pace and flavor of family life:

> I read all the newspapers and see everything that's going on all over the area, so I always have ideas of neat things we can go and do that are generally free. We were yesterday at the fireworks, and the day before we were at the baseball game downtown, and the day before that we were at the library. We're always going and taking tastes of life everywhere we go, which like I say, for Don, coming from a family where they usually have a week and a half notice before they do things like that, may be a bit frazzled at times. . . . I also like to entertain, so that means having a lot of friends over. . . . I think that he probably gets frustrated—well, I *know* he gets frustrated—with the constant doing things, and having people over, and the whirl.

This busy, active life is the kind that Cindy prefers and wants to provide for her children. She takes control of the family's social life by researching and planning events. And though she knows her husband is frustrated by the choices she makes, she continues to organize family activities to suit her tastes rather than his.

The power available in organizing the household can be particularly potent when the wife is also responsible for managing the family's finances. In the previous chapter, we saw how women in this circumstance often have the opportunity to act as gatekeepers of the common pot. Knowing where the money is and what the family's commitments are can be an effective tool in negotiations and decision making. Sandy is both the household organizer and the keeper of the family checkbook, and she speaks convincingly about the combined power in these roles. When I ask how her husband, Dick, goes about getting something he wants, she responds:

> He probably has to go through me—always. . . . In terms of money, and time too, because I do tend to organize more what we're going to do. If we've made plans, *I've* written them down and remembered them. So even if it's not money and it's going to play games one night, it's like, "Are we doing anything?" So I end up being the keeper of all those things.

She feels that these organizing responsibilities give her "an edge" when they disagree. She tries to "reason things out" with her husband by saying,

> "We can't afford it," or "We can't do it because of this." And that, perhaps unfortunately, can be real effective when I have that resource at my disposal. I know the details of what we've got planned when, and where our money is. It's a lot easier for me to control the discussion.

At the end of the interview, I ask if Sandy thinks either she or Dick has more power or control or influence in the relationship. She replies:

> I would say I do. [VT: Why?] Because of thinking of [things] ahead of time and being prepared. Spending more time thinking about the options and doing that, so if I've made a choice in my own mind, it's easy. If the only case on the table is what *I'm* going to put out, it will happen.

Most of the literature on marital decision making has not viewed these kinds of responsibilities as powerful. Activities such as running errands, making phone calls, and gathering information are typically seen as chores delegated to the wife by the husband, with the latter reserving the right to make the final decision, and this may be true in many cases. However, fully half these wives see these activities as giving them at least some measure of power in their relationships. As wives gather information in preparation for having some kind of discussion, they often form opinions about what would be "best," or at least what they would prefer to see happen. They are then free to present the information they have collected in a way that makes what they want to do seem like the best, most logical, or most reasonable course of action. In this way, access to information can give wives opportunities to influence the decision-making process and can give them a measure of power in their relationships. After all, motivating someone to pursue your plan of action is exercising power.

These results suggest that information is an important source of power in these relationships. While women carry a tremendous burden in terms of managing household responsibilities, that work is not without its compensations. It gives women access to knowledge that either gives them direct control or sometimes allows them an extra measure of influence in joint decision making. Most important is that women are often completely aware of this power and use it consciously to their advantage.

EXECUTIVE ORDERS AND VETO POWER:
HOW HUSBANDS MAINTAIN CONTROL

Having this ability to shape the decision-making process is an advantage for wives over the long term only if we assume equality between spouses. If couples sit down as equals to make decisions, women's greater knowledge gives them an edge every time. However, men and women do not approach the marital bargaining table as equals; they face different cultural constraints. History and convention give husbands authority over their wives in marriage, and part of that authority is the husband's "right" to issue orders or to have the last word—"veto power"—in any matter, large or small. This may mean that women exercise only the level of control in their relationships that their husbands allow them to have.

The term "veto power" calls up visions of patriarchs towering over family members and bellowing orders. It is negatively associated with such cultural images as Archie Bunker—a rather comical and unappealing symbol of conventional masculinity that most men today would eschew. However, men need not resort to such heavy-handed power displays to gain the upper hand in their relationships. In fact, controlling decisions is often a subtle and complex process and can coexist alongside egalitarian tendencies. In other words, even men who exhibit relatively modern gender behavior claim veto power in certain areas or on certain occasions.

A substantial portion of the husbands and wives interviewed openly acknowledged that the men exercised some veto power over decisions (20 to 25 percent of husbands in both groups). In these cases, husbands are described as "putting their foot down" or reserving the right to have the final say, at least in some circumstances. These men typically see themselves as modern in their views of gender, or as largely egalitarian, and often demonstrate a great deal of concern for their wives and their well-being. They may contribute meaningfully to household labor and put substantial energy into caring for their children, but they still claim an extra measure of control over decision making. Two examples show how the traditional prerogative of the husband's veto can coexist alongside more modern gender tendencies in a relationship.

Bob and Barbara

Bob is a telecommunications technician married to Barbara, a project manager for a large government research project. They live in a modest, three-bedroom townhouse and have two daughters, ages six months and six years. They seem to have a very warm relationship and to genuinely appreciate each other. In fact, Barbara talks in glowing terms about the emotional support Bob gives her and what a difference that makes to her in terms of coping with the demands of both the household and her job. She thinks he is very in tune with her needs and says, "If there is such a thing as one person on this planet who is meant for me, Bob is it." Bob also describes himself as very attentive to Barbara's needs; he tries to monitor her emotional health and to be sure she takes care of herself. He knows that she is particularly vulnerable to stress, and that meditation helps her manage this stress. So when he feels she is struggling to cope, he tries to make sure she has quiet time for herself.

Barbara carries most of the domestic labor burden at home and always has. However, Bob has been somewhat responsive to her recent pleas for more help. Barbara's job responsibilities have increased in the last few months and she has been putting ten to twenty more hours per week into her work. The stress associated with this change had been unbearable for her. She told Bob, "Given your level of participation, I'm not gonna be able to do this. Something's gotta change, and that something is your level of participation." As a result, Bob has agreed to be "completely and forever" responsible for doing the dishes. This makes it easier for Barbara to relax a bit after dinner and to devote her energies to her daughters. While she still carries the bulk of the household load, she is pleased to be relieved of this responsibility and feels it has made a difference in her ability to manage her life.

Bob is a caring, responsive husband and is more involved in the work at home than are many other husbands in this sample. Still, he hangs on to some prerogatives that husbands have traditionally enjoyed, such as making individual decisions without consulting Barbara and reserving the right to have the final word on some issues. As they talk about how they make decisions, it is clear that Barbara and Bob approach this process differently. Barbara describes herself as seeking Bob's input into her decisions or ideas, whereas Bob seems to act more independently, even in matters that affect her. Barbara describes how they each handle decisions:

> For example, I spent a week in Texas with the kids without him, but I talked to him about it beforehand. I want him to think about it with me, though I usually end up making the decisions. I'm not sure if it just makes me feel better to have someone to talk to about it, or if he really contributes to my decision making. But he will make plans to go watch football with someone and not tell me until the day before. That bothers me because it affects me. I think he forgets that it affects me.

Barbara thinks she consults Bob on decisions more, whereas he tends to make more decisions on his own. He seems to agree with her analysis of the process: "She'd come to me and say, . . . 'I'd like to take a vacation at this period of time, is this going to work?' She's a lot better at it than I am. I keep my thoughts to myself until they're formulated, and she thinks out loud more." He describes his tendency to make his own decisions, or to act without consulting her, as a difference in communication styles rather than acknowledging that he feels freer than she to make decisions on his own.

Later in the interview, Bob reports that he exercises some veto power in the area of finances. He says that one of his strengths in the relationship is that he is "the one who puts the brakes on when they need to be put on." In this case, he is referring to Barbara's efforts to pay off their credit-card debt quickly, so she can return to school full time in pursuit of her master's degree. He thinks she is not leaving enough discretionary money for them to live on, so he cuts back on the payments she wants to make. He says this gives them more breathing room on a monthly basis, and he is happier that way. In both subtle and overt ways, then, Bob exercises gender privilege. He feels free to act independently in a way that Barbara does not. He also has the power to override her desires in major financial decisions.

Sam and Monica

Sam and Monica were introduced in the chapter on domestic labor, in the section on important work. Sam is a computer technician and Monica is a telecommunications project manager. Sam contributes substantially to the household labor, making him more egalitarian, in terms of his domestic labor activity, than are most husbands in the sample, but he explicitly reserves the right to control what he feels to be important decisions. For example, Sam "lets" Monica do the bills each month, but he makes all investment decisions; he "lets" her do whatever she wants to the house, but he reserves the right to say, "No, I can't live with that." Sam also has the last word on most major decisions, such as purchasing a car. When Monica needed a new vehicle for work, she says, Sam told her what kind of car to buy:

> He decided what kind of car I was gonna get. That kind of made me a little bit mad. I mean, I liked the Camry. I liked the Camry. I *did* like it. But he said, "You can either have a Honda Accord or a Toyota Camry." And, I don't know that I would've *disagreed,* but I would've liked to have been [her voice trails off]. . . . It was just kind of irritating that he would tell me what kind of car I was gonna buy. . . . It's not like I would do that to him.

Sam tells a similar story about this purchase. He reports that there are a couple of areas where

> I put my foot down. . . . Like when it came to cars. I told her she was either buyin' a Camry or a Honda. [He laughs.] She had no choice. [VT: How come?] 'Cause they're good cars, and [pause]—I like to buy quality. It costs a little bit more, but I think it pays off in the end.

Even though Monica makes 50 percent more than her husband makes
and the car was for her use, she was unwilling to challenge his right to
make this purchase decision for her.

This sense of entitlement in making important decisions is not limited to financial concerns. Men claim control of other aspects of the family's life as well. Sam and Monica are currently embroiled in a more
serious dispute largely because, in this case, she is resisting his attempt to
have the final word. Monica is Episcopalian; Sam is Catholic. She married
him with the understanding that she did not agree to raise their children
in the Catholic faith. Six years ago, they fought over where to baptize
their oldest daughter. Monica's mother encouraged her to go along with
Sam: "What does is matter, as long as she's Christian?" So Monica agreed
to a baptism in the Catholic church. Their second daughter is now five
months old, and they are facing the issue again. In fact, the conflict
heated up just a week before the interviews. Monica's voice is very quiet
as she describes their struggle:

> No, I'm not going to baptize her Catholic, and I'm not going to raise
> her Catholic. And he's saying, "Yes, you are." And he's adamant, and
> I'm adamant. [She laughs nervously] . . . It's gonna be a real problem
> because neither of us wants to give in. And he's convinced he's gonna
> get me to give in, and I'm not giving in. So there. Take that. [We
> laugh.] You might be coming back next year for our divorce.

Monica tries to make light of this struggle, but the seriousness of the
rift comes out later in the interview, when I ask if she has ever considered
separation or divorce: "Right now. [She laughs nervously.] I've threatened
it to him. I don't think he thinks I'm serious, but I really [pause]—I think
that that would be the last resort. He's so adamant that that's 'period, end
of discussion.' Well it's *not* 'period, end of discussion.' " She has tried to
compromise, saying that she will baptize their daughter Catholic if Sam
agrees to raise her in the Episcopal church, but he has refused. She
believes he is holding out because he thinks he will eventually get his
way, especially since she gave in with their first child. From Monica's perspective, this conflict has shaken the very core of their relationship.

Sam takes a much more lighthearted tone when discussing this problem: "Everybody says us Catholics are [pause]—we're too righteous.
That's what I always hear. 'We're the only good religion and nobody else

matters'—which is true. [He laughs.]" He makes a joke of it. I do not get the same sense of heart-wrenching struggle from Sam that I do from Monica. He may feel that the subject is too personal, or painful, to talk about at length. But given their history and his ability to control other major decisions, it is more likely he thinks (as Monica suspects) that this is just a temporary dispute, and that he will ultimately prevail. This means that he can ignore both her protests and the potential damage this conflict is doing to their relationship.

No other couple was currently facing an issue this hotly contested, and in no other couple did the husband exercise such an obvious right to the last word in decision making. It is interesting that Monica would take such a stand, given her history of allowing Sam the final say on such a broad range of issues. In the past, she seemed to see him as exercising legitimate authority and to feel she had an obligation to comply with his wishes. However, in some cases, to use power is to lose it (Blau 1964). A wife may accept her husband's authority as legitimate and comply regularly and predictably with his wishes. But if he crosses a line—a line that asks too high a price from her on whatever level—she may refuse to submit. And after all, short of violence or the threat of violence, it is largely a wife's willingness to submit to her husband's authority that perpetuates that authority daily.

But in some cases, conflict can introduce a new dialectic into a relationship. As people struggle, they become open to the raising of their consciousness about the power dynamics of their relationship. This awareness, in turn, can empower people to engage in further struggle (Fairclough 1989). Whatever the dynamic, it is clear that this most recent exercise of power has decreased the attractiveness of the relationship for Monica and has made her bolder about resisting Sam's right to have the last word. She is no longer willing to consent to his authority, at least not on this issue. And though she has said it would be a "last resort," she has considered separating over this issue. She has even threatened Sam with a divorce. Despite all this, Sam seems confident that he will once again have his way, and he did not express any concerns about the future of their relationship. Unfortunately, I never learned who prevailed on this issue.

Sam and Monica exemplify a larger pattern in the data. While women apparently control a great many everyday decisions, this control is ceded to them by their husbands. The men seem happy to allow their wives to take charge of the daily life of the family because, as we saw earlier, the price for this control is a great deal of responsibility, both for organizing the household and for carrying out the tasks of daily living. Instead of controlling all these details, these men simply reserve the right to have the final word in the circumstances that matter most to them.

This form of power—putting one's foot down—appears to be available to all husbands, even those who rarely use it. One husband put it this way:

> I've never felt it's really important for me to exert my power as the husband, because the fact of the matter is that we are fairly equal in terms of our earnings and in terms of our responsibilities, in our own way, and I like that. I think that [my wife] is, in every sense of the word, a partner in this relationship.

Though he sees their relationship as substantially equal, he recognizes that there is power rooted in being a husband—power that he could call on if he chose. This means that even men who take relatively modern views toward gender can (and do) claim traditional power prerogatives.

CAN SHE PUT HER FOOT DOWN?

Having access to substantially greater financial resources might allow these wives to exercise control similar to their husbands' vetoes. This logic would apply most obviously to financial decisions: "I make the money, so I'll make the final decision on how it's spent." However, in this sample, only one wife talked about exercising something like veto power. Rachel in the previous chapter was the breadwinning wife who exerted a great deal of financial control in her marriage. She handles all the finances and monitors her husband, Kurt's, access to discretionary money to check his tendency to gamble; perhaps she is able to exercise this kind of control on moral grounds. Still, her ability to restrain him in this way does not parallel the veto power that husbands seem to have. Recall that though Rachel had substantial freedom in managing the family's money, Kurt often called for an accounting of how she had spent the money, wondering why there was so little left at the end of the month.

While wives, unlike husbands, do not have the right to the final word, they are able to exert influence in spheres related to their specific expertise. Again, this influence does not operate with the institutional force of the husband's veto but is linked to women's personal qualities, experiences, or education. Wives with a master's degree in business administration may be able to exert more influence over the family budget or investments. Wives in real estate may have more say in decisions about where and when the family should move. However, this kind of control is situation specific and rarely absolute. Husbands still seem to reserve the right to challenge even acknowledged forms of expertise.

Sharon is an example of a wife with considerable financial knowledge and expertise. The comptroller of a small company, she is working to become a CPA so she can go into business for herself. Her husband, Lyle, writes and edits educational texts for a branch of the federal government. She handles all the family's finances because both spouses see her as more capable in this area. Still, Lyle seems uncomfortable with turning this responsibility over to her completely. Sharon reports that each year at tax time, after she has spent hours working on their return, Lyle hesitates before signing it, asking, "Are you *sure* it's right?" to which she responds, "*You* wanna do it?" Lyle always signs it without further ado. He is happy to delegate a great deal of the burden of managing their finances to Sharon, but he seems to be nervous about giving up that control.

Though Lyle readily acknowledges Sharon's financial expertise, he does not give her carte blanche in financial decision making. Sharon says she has to convince Lyle to go along with her plans and ideas:

> The best approach with Lyle is the logical approach. [VT: Can you think of any examples?] Oh, yeah. Shortly after we got married, I had a townhouse and he moved in there. Then the interest rate dropped and I said, "It's time to move." And he said, "Why? We've got a three-bedroom townhouse that we're not even beginning to fill." I said interest rates were down. This is a good time to look. We'll qualify for a lot more. We can move into a house. The time is right, and we should do it. And we did it.

Other wives have expertise in the area of interpersonal relationships in the family, or in parenting. Cindy has a master's degree in special education and early childhood development and works in a local school district. Her husband, Don, is a welding technician. They have three boys, ages nine, five, and fourteen months, and they struggle over parenting issues. Cindy says:

> Well, I think because I have the education background, and I know perhaps from an intellectual point of view—an educated point of view—how the kids should be disciplined. I'm more consistent. Don is very easygoing and then suddenly he'll snap. And I think because of that, the kids know when I say no, I mean no. . . . They *do* misbehave more for him. And he does [pause]—he does say things, like he'll say, "If you do that, you'll be grounded for an entire month!" And I'll say, "Don, you can't ground them for an entire month." I know that in some families they just let the person hash out discipline, and they never say anything in front of each other, and they present a united front. We don't do that.

In his interview, I asked Don how they resolve differences of opinion about what to do with the children:

> And we do [have differences of opinion]. Frequently. [We laugh.] Well, you know, Cindy's got a master's degree in early childhood and special education and stuff, so you know. She does not tell me how to fix a car. We have arguments about it, but in the long run, I figure she's probably right and knows what she's talking about. . . . I would probably ground the kids more than she would. And I'm more excitable about it. I get more pissed off and frustrated easier with the kids than she does. 'Cause she usually calms me down—"Of course, the kid can't stay in his room for six years!"

Don acknowledges Cindy as the expert in early childhood and education, yet he resists her efforts to make decisions rooted in this expertise. Eventually he "figures she's probably right," but this realization does not come without a struggle. Cindy is not saying, "I'm the expert on children here, what I say *goes*." She tries to "calm him down" and get him to see that her way of handling the situation is the reasonable approach.

What is striking about these descriptions of Sharon's and Cindy's experiences is that these wives do not have the same veto power husbands seem to have. Women are more likely to refer to their personal credibility in attempts to influence their husbands than to try to dictate what will happen in a direct way (Sexton and Perlman 1989). Even with their acknowledged expertise, these wives still must make their case to their husbands—convince them that their idea is more reasonable or better in some way. This kind of persuasion is more palatable because it has an egalitarian underpinning, since each participant in the dialogue is equally free to attempt to persuade the other. This means that persuasion is often not seen as power at all. Logic and persuasion are particularly effective ways for women to win their points, because husbands can (eventually) be moved by reason to a change in position without a loss of face; ultimatums and vetoes do not allow for this and are therefore not part of a woman's power arsenal.

Interestingly, these findings seem to be related to patterns of money management. The men who most regularly exercised their right to the last word lived in families where all money was pooled and managed by their wives. Only one husband with separate money talked about using veto power. Perhaps the man's "stash" (money he has set aside for himself, as described in the previous chapter) and his veto are merely different means to the same end. Both depend upon the cultural notion of a man's prerogative to control the family's money and decisions. In the absence of independent control over at least a portion of the family's finances, a substantial number of husbands in this sample managed to gain the upper hand in decision making by claiming the right to have the last word.

We have seen that one-third of the men in this sample have separate money, and that one-quarter exercise straightforward veto power (only one husband fits both these descriptions). This means that more than half the husbands use one of these two methods to try to gain control through traditional forms of men's power. This represents the vast majority of couples in which wives manage the family finances. Men's stashes, their ability to veto decisions, or both undercut women's ability to gatekeep the family's money or control the decision-making process, that is, to use control over the checkbook to gain more control in the relationship. More importantly, these forms of power that give husbands control require relatively little effort. That is, women in these relationships exercise some decision-making power, but with it comes responsibility and work; men can exercise veto power or issue orders without lifting a finger.

POWER PERFORMANCES IN DECISION
MAKING: EXERTING DOMINANCE AND
DEMONSTRATING DEFERENCE

Issuing orders and vetoing decisions are obvious indicators of
decision-making power, but men also enjoy hidden power advantages. It
is important to remember that men and women do not approach the
marital relationship as cultural equals. Women are at a power disadvantage
in their relationships with men. Part of being a member of the less powerful group is developing the ability to anticipate the needs and desires of
those in power. Wives cannot simply please themselves; they need to keep
in mind what their husbands are likely to see as reasonable and therefore
to go along with. Just as a parent pays a price for refusing to accommodate a child's food aversion, a wife could pay a price for neglecting to
consider her husband's preferences when she makes household decisions.
A chronically displeased husband could question the importance of the
relationship and ultimately decide to leave. This possibility leads some
women to adopt strategies in decision making that strengthen the relationship, even if they weaken the women's relative position of power
(Johnson and Huston 1998; Knudson-Martin and Mahoney 1998). In the
following section, I describe some of these strategies. It is through these
more subtle interactive processes that men's power is most commonly
preserved in these relationships.

Though a minority of couples reported that husbands make a formal
claim to the right to have the last word, couples often put a substantial
amount of energy into preserving men's dominance in the marriage in
subtle, often hidden, ways. As they describe their decision-making practices, couples reveal that wives often do not challenge their husbands
when they claim the right to make certain decisions. Even wives who
perceive this power as illegitimate seem reluctant to resist their husbands'
wishes or to make their own feelings more clearly known.

We saw that Monica was unwilling to challenge her husband, Sam's,
right to decide what kind of car she should buy. Though she was upset by
his efforts to control this decision, she seemed to acquiesce to his wishes
rather readily. We can think of this interaction as a "power performance"
in which Sam issued an order to control the decision-making process.
This performance is "gendered" because husband and wife have different

parts to play. Sam issued the order because this kind of power is culturally available to a man. For her part, Monica displayed the appropriately
feminine deference that enabled Sam to exercise power so neatly and
cleanly.

This kind of gendered power performance is common among couples with higher-earning wives, though the dynamics are often more
subtle. Donna and Rusty represent a striking example of how power can
be hidden in interactions and the decision-making process. This couple
lives in a small three-bedroom townhouse on a quiet suburban street.
They moved into this home just four months before our interviews after
renting a two-bedroom apartment for several years. They are excited
about having a place of their own, but the transition has been stressful;
the move, and the higher monthly payment that comes with it, have
stretched their finances considerably, leaving them very little extra money
each month.

Donna works as a buyer for a large department-store chain and is
nearly the sole provider for the family. Rusty stays home with their two-
year-old daughter and manages the bulk of the everyday domestic chores
(for example, shopping, cooking, and laundry). He is also trying to form
a partnership to start a methadone treatment clinic in the area, but he is
still in the early stages and has not had much success getting it off the
ground. He is currently looking for financial backing for the project. He
works at a friend's barbecue restaurant on occasional weekends for extra
money.

Donna has a great deal of formal control over the couple's finances.
The bank accounts are in her name only, and she takes care of all the bills.
The two agree to this arrangement because money has always been tight
for them. They also say Rusty is not to be trusted with money because he
is too "irresponsible." Rusty is a recovering addict. He has been clean for
nearly seven years and was drug free for two years before he and Donna
met and began to date. Still, they both seem to feel that his compulsions
could get the better of him and put them in serious financial difficulty.
Donna thinks having everything in her name gives her a great deal of
control over the money, as well as power in decision making:

> Yeah, well, I probably have a lot more power 'cause I have all the
> money. But if we had more money, where I was not so nervous about

it, then it might not be so. If there was more discretionary spending, I probably would not hold such a tight rein on the money, and therefore take all the decision-making process, you know?

In reality, Donna does not seem to control the decision-making process. Rusty is often able to prevail—especially in major decisions, such as cars, homes, and vacations. Donna may initially argue that they cannot afford something, but Rusty finds a way to make things happen on his timetable. I ask Donna how Rusty goes about getting something he wants.

> He wheedles me into it. [We laugh.] [VT: Can you think of any examples?] Oh, Lord, any amount of things. . . . He wanted the van. He *had* to have the van. He goes out and finds the van, then calls me up on the phone and says, "I've found the perfect car!" He goes to my mother and gets her to give him the down payment for the car. Which is okay [her voice has a mixture of incredulity and irritation that makes it sound not okay]. But that's the type of thing he does. This house, the same thing. It was his friend's house. He goes and finds a house and says, "So-and-so's ready to give up the house," then goes and talks my mother into the down payment, and then says, "Here it is." It's a fait accompli. [We laugh.] "You do like the house, don't you." [Her inflection, as she imitates him, makes this a statement rather than a question.] [We laugh.] But it was not like we went out shopping for a house or a car.

Rusty agrees with Donna's account of how these decisions are made. He feels he gets what he wants, even though Donna formally controls the money:

> I don't think she wanted to buy the van, but I wanted the van because I knew that that was the best thing for us to have. . . . Donna brings in the money, but I pretty much—I mean, this is a friend of mine's house that we bought. We bought the car that *I* thought we should have. There's a point where I let her do everything, but then when something that I think is very important—or I'll fight to, you know—and I do not think a woman in my—you know, if it were switched, I don't think it would work that way. [VT: So you think you're able to do that because you're a man—a woman

would not be able to?] Probably not, because a woman is just not known for having expertise in the mechanical field or, you know, in how houses are built, or things like that. Not because they're the weak female. But I think cars are something I think most women go to a man for advice on.

It is unclear that Rusty's prevailing in these decisions was based on mechanical or building expertise, as he claims. For example, he wanted the van because they are thinking of having another child and he felt they need more room. He did not argue that the van was more structurally sound than the sports car Donna had been driving. Similarly, he wanted to buy the townhouse because he was tired of throwing money away on renting. Essentially, he got what he wanted when he wanted it.

It is tempting to equate Rusty with wives who have found ways to "get around" their husbands by manipulating circumstances to meet their own needs or desires, and there may indeed be some parallels. For example, a stay-at-home wife may go out shopping with a realtor for a new house and then present her husband with the choice she has made. However, her husband would likely retain the right to veto her choice of house, or even her desire to move at all—especially if, like Donna, he did not think the family could afford to make the move. Donna does not seem to exercise this kind of power, despite her belief that neither purchase decision was a good idea at the time. Rusty controls the most important financial decisions the couple makes, and does so over the objections of his partner. Remember that Donna has complete formal control over the money, and as the partner with the steady income, she could certainly refuse to sign a bank note for a new car or house that she did not think the family needed or could afford. In the end, Donna does not seem to seriously resist Rusty's attempts to control these decisions, which gives him a great deal of latitude in making them.

There is also a sense of gender imbalance in these accounts. Rusty exerts great influence over major decisions in a way that a similarly situated woman would not. In other words, he is very clear that he is exercising some authority as a man. A woman "in his situation"—at home, raising a child, substantially responsible for domestic chores, with no formal access to the family's money—would not be able to exert the same kind of influence over such major decisions. Monica and Sam also exhibit this kind of gender asymmetry. Recall that when Monica complained about Sam's forcefully deciding what kind of car she should buy, she commented that "it's not like I would do that to him." This kind of power belongs to men and not to women.

An interesting aspect of these situations is that neither Monica nor Donna seems to feel that she has the option to protest or to resist her husband's decisions, despite being the major breadwinner in the family. Under these circumstances, we might expect them to be more effective at asserting their preferences. It is also striking that these wives know that their husbands are making these decisions unilaterally; it is not as though they are unaware of the control their husbands exercise. Assuming that both men and women would rather make decisions than take orders, we have to wonder why these wives do not more effectively resist their husbands' exercise of power. Resistance is at least a logical option. If Monica is buying a car for her use and makes so much more money than her husband does, she could simply say, "I appreciate your input, but I've decided I'd rather have a Mustang than a Camry."

But resistance can be costly. Remember that Monica is now resisting Sam's effort to dictate that their infant daughter be baptized in the Catholic church; she is torn by this conflict and worried about the future of their relationship. Similarly, Donna could resist Rusty's drive to put them into a new house and vehicle that she neither wants nor thinks they can afford. So on some level, these women recognize that they are giving away opportunities to exercise control in their relationships. The question then becomes, What is the payoff for this deference?

POWER THREATS: PRESERVING IDENTITIES AND RELATIONSHIPS

For some women, expressing or exercising power seems threatening— either to their relationships or to their gender identities. Some wives speak openly of the danger that power poses for them; they are "afraid" of being seen as powerful. For example, June is a military officer who controls a multimillion-dollar budget as part of her job. She makes twice what her enlisted husband, Adam, makes. When I ask her whether she sees a link between money and power in her relationship, she replies: "Gosh, see, I'm afraid Adam's gonna say, 'Yeah, yeah, she's got all the power 'cause she's got all the money,' and I do not see it that way. . . . I do not see myself as being in control. In fact, most of the time I feel *out of control.*"

Indeed, June seems very reluctant to exercise control in decision making. Adam senses this reluctance as he describes how they make decisions:

> If it's a thing we both agree upon, that we wanna do, she'll say, "Okay, do it if you think it's okay." And I'll go ahead and do it. If it's something that she agrees on, that I'm just making the phone calls for, and I tell her what the phone call said, she goes, "Well, what do ya think?" [He imitates them as they banter back and forth.] "I don't care, honey, it's up to you." "Well, what do *you* wanna do?" And finally I'll just say, "Okay, fine." And we'll go for it. It's weird too, because I feel like I'm makin' all the decisions, even though I'm *not* making all the decisions, and she's the one that carries the wallet in the family.

That seems to be the point. She does not want to be the one to say, "*I* think we should do *this.*" Her strategy in decision making allows him to "feel like I'm makin' all the decisions," even though she brings home substantially more money. This show of deference may be more symbolic than real, but it seems to serve its purpose.

Jill is similarly afraid of looking too powerful in her marriage. She is a midlevel bank manager married to a car salesperson. And though she has always paid the bills and managed the money throughout their relationship, she defers to her husband in much of their decision making. She describes a disagreement with her husband over the convertible he recently purchased:

> I could have more influence if I exercised it, but . . . I never pull that rank, I guess. Like when it comes to the car. If I would've said, "We're not buying that car," he wouldn't have. . . . It's like he's saying to me, "Well, if you really don't want to, we won't do it," but I won't exercise that option, because I'm afraid. [VT: Of what?] I'm afraid of being, um, afterward, being accused of being a bitch, or trying to control my husband, you know, not letting him do this or that. Or hearing about how his fellow employees think that I am controlling him. That kind of thing. So I hesitate to say, "No, you can't do that," and stay firm.

These women have the potential to exercise power in their relationships, as both they and their husbands recognize, yet using that power is too threatening. Jill is afraid of being labeled a "bitch," because a bitch is not a "wife" but is domineering, uncaring, and unlovable—someone none of these women wants to be.

Exercising power is threatening on two levels: It is a threat to these women's gender identities, and it is a potential threat to their relationships. First, it is easy to see how exercising power threatens these wives' identities as women. As we listen to them describe their interactions and their thought processes, we can see how concerned they are about how others perceive them. For example, June is afraid her husband will see her as powerful and, by implication, unwomanly. Jill is afraid to resist her husband's efforts to buy an expensive convertible because she does not want to be called a bitch, or to look to herself or others as if she is trying to control or dominate her husband. In other words, these wives manage their behavior to avoid negative sanctions for being perceived as unfeminine. They seem to defer or submit to their husbands, in part, to construct and maintain an appropriate gender identity.

Further, these women feel that exercising power could be a threat to their relationships. They assume that men do not want to be dominated by pushy wives. So instead of attempting to exert control, a wife can pointedly defer to her husband. In this way, she affirms his masculinity and supports him as the head of the household and primary decision maker. To attempt to exercise direct control over their husbands (based on income or status advantage) is to call into question the gender order, something these wives seem unwilling to do. Instead, they—often consciously—submit to the wishes of their husbands and maintain the expectation for men's dominance.

POWER PERFORMANCES AMONG COMPARISON COUPLES

These kinds of power performances also occur among the comparison couples, though to a lesser degree. Several husbands report making decisions without even discussing them with their wives. For example, Jake says:

Some things, like with the VCR we have downstairs, I just went out and bought it. [He laughs.] "What are you doing?" [He imitates his wife and demonstrates her displeasure at this purchase.] Fifteen minutes later, we're watching a movie. [VT: So she was not happy, but she got over it quick?] Yeah, she got over it quick.

The difference here is that there was no act of deference on the part of his wife. Jake felt free to act on his own, and his wife seemed to feel that there was little point in protesting after the fact.

The kind of pointed deference described among couples with higher-earning wives is hinted at in only two comparison couples, and in both cases the wives earn a few thousand more do than their husbands. Amanda and Joe are strikingly egalitarian in almost every way (we heard from them in the chapter on domestic labor). They report that they both work very hard for very little money and respect each other for that work. Consequently, they share the household and child-care labor relatively equally. In fact, Amanda feels that Joe "functions as the wife in this relationship" because he often does more than she does around the house. This sense of fairness and equality seems central to the way they handle their finances as well. Amanda and Joe are one of the two couples in the sample that sit down together each month to do the bills, rather than delegating that task to one spouse. This way, they both know what is happening each month, and neither carries the sole burden of juggling the bills. However, Joe reports that "sometimes it seems that Amanda waits for me to make the final decision, or to *authorize* our final decision." This is similar to Adam's assessment of his relationship with June, described earlier. It is a strategy that allows husbands to feel they are making the decisions and are therefore in control. Or at the very least, these wives use this symbolic show of deference to prove that they are not trying to control their husbands.

Rita and Alan are the other comparison couple in which this concern about deference appears. We first met them in the chapter on domestic labor. Remember that Rita seems to enjoy a great deal of control in the relationship. She describes herself as the "chatelaine" of her household, running it largely as she sees fit. She also exercises a great deal of financial control, managing the family's money and typically deciding what the family can afford to purchase. However, she is not entirely comfortable with this control. When I ask her if there is anything she would like to change in her life, she says: "I'd probably try not to be as dominant. I'd like him to be a little more assertive. But it would be up to him to come out and make the decisions, because if I *force* him to make the decisions, then I go right back to being aggressive." She sees herself as the dominant partner in her relationship, and she is not comfortable with it; she wants her husband to assume more of a leadership role.

This example is striking because Rita is living the scenario that most other wives fear—being the dominant partner and exercising a great deal of control. Yet she does not seem to be making decisions that her husband disagrees with. He did not express any dissatisfaction with their life or with the way she runs the household. It is possible that she has simply done an excellent job of anticipating his desires. In any case, what she perceives as a great deal of control makes her uncomfortable—a situation that most other wives are able to avoid through strategies of both real and symbolic deference in decision making.

Through these examples, we see how normative expectations for men's dominance can shape the interactions of couples with higher-earning wives and of comparison couples, though this pattern is more common and pronounced among the former. Even where opportunities to assert their preferences exist, higher-earning wives often back away from them, partly to maintain their husbands' sense of being in control—to shore up men's masculinity. But such displays are important to the wives as well, because deferring to their husbands helps these women demonstrate that they are not making claims to power over their husbands, and therefore that they are "good wives." These results link power to issues of identity, an idea we explore more thoroughly in the next chapter.

These women cede authority to their husbands in both real and symbolic terms. Practically speaking, it seems more significant if women are giving up real control in their relationships because they are relinquishing the potential power in their larger incomes. However, symbolic displays of deference are important as well. First, they preclude women from using their substantial resources to try to negotiate directly for more equal footing in their marriages. But more importantly, these symbolic displays of deference serve to reinforce the norm of men's dominance in marriage, and to allow husbands to continue to see such dominance as their right.

GENDERED AUTHORITY AND POWER

Examining the conflict-resolution strategies and decision-making practices of couples gives us another window on the balance of power in these relationships. As is the case with financial matters, decision-making patterns do not seem related to how much money each spouse earns. Wives with a higher income and occupational status do not make automatic claims to greater influence over household decisions and do not seem to prevail in decision making any more do than comparison wives.

This does not mean that wives have no opportunities for exercising control in their relationships. While they may not assert a right to make decisions based on their income advantage, wives are often in a better position than husbands to shape household decisions. This type of influence is unrelated to income and occupational variables and is reported by both groups of wives. Their ability to exert control over certain decisions is largely rooted in their role as the organizer of the household. Many wives argue that being responsible for the household, and planning for the future, means that they can direct discussions and shape final outcomes. They often see themselves as able to make things happen on their timetables and according to their preferences.

There is, however, a potential check on a wife's power: the husband's veto. Husbands report going along with their wives on most issues, but they reserve the right to put their foot down over something they just cannot live with. Here we see an asymmetry in spouses' ability to control decisions, because wives do not have veto power over their husbands. Instead, wives try to appeal to their husbands through logic and persuasion. This makes whatever influence wives are able to exercise idiosyncratic rather than systematic.

The process by which couples make decisions reveals a great deal about the hidden power in their relationships. As spouses recount examples of discussions or disagreements, we can see that preserving men's authority is a team effort in these relationships. It is not simply that men assert their authority in these decisions; in fact, wives are far more likely to quickly defer to their husbands' wishes or even urge them to make the "final" decision—even if it is an outcome that both have largely agreed to. Wives are afraid that their income advantage makes them powerful in the eyes of their husbands, so they go out of their way to conform to what Connell (1987) calls "emphasized femininity." They accommodate themselves to the interests and desires of the men in their lives (Johnson and Huston 1998; Knudson-Martin and Mahoney 1998). This strategy ensures comfortable interactions, as it preserves men's authority.

Allowing husbands greater control in decision making also has implications for the way wives see themselves. Women often defer to their husbands to prove that they are appropriately feminine and are good wives. By "doing gender" in this way, wives give up whatever power might lie in their income advantage and place control squarely in the hands of their husbands. These gendered expectations constrain women's voices and give husbands an extra, often hidden, measure of control in these relationships.

Let me be very clear here: While these results demonstrate that wives defer to their husbands in these relationships, and often in very conscious ways, I am not arguing that these wives prefer to be dominated. Rather, these women are afraid that their financial resources will make them look powerful, or that their husbands will experience their financial disadvantage as domination—or worse, emasculation. Therefore, these wives defer to their husbands to prove that they are *not* trying to dominate them (see Pyke 1994 for similar results). They do not seem to have an alternative model (a truly egalitarian one) on which to organize their marital relationships, so they reproduce conventional relations that privilege men over women.

The results presented in this chapter demonstrate what a complex undertaking it is to assess relative power in marital relationships—especially if one is guided by the central question, who has more control? Assessing who has more decision-making power in these relationships does not yield an "either/or" result—the answer is "both/and." Women *both* have extra responsibility for organizing and running their households *and* often derive some power from this responsibility. Women *both* enjoy certain opportunities to exercise control *and* are often constrained by what their husbands will "allow" them to do. Men can *both* exhibit egalitarian tendencies by taking on a little more at home and being sensitive to their wives' needs *and* reserve a traditional right to exert an extra measure of control when they see fit. The power processes surrounding decision making for these couples are subtle, complex, and often surprising. However, despite the unconventional income gap in these marriages, the men still have more resources with which to prevail.

As with the division of domestic labor and financial matters, these findings on decision making demonstrate that the gender structure exerts an influence that is independent of breadwinning or relative financial contributions. Just as women's income does not buy them either relief from domestic labor or greater financial power or autonomy, it does not buy them dominance in decision making. The pressure to enact the gendered power performances of men's dominance and women's submission undercuts women's ability or willingness to use their greater incomes to claim greater decision-making control. Similarly, their efforts to construct appropriately feminine identities require women to defer to husbands to avoid emasculating them and to prove that they are good wives. Through these dynamics, conventional gender expectations are reproduced; men still assert their authority as heads of households and enjoy a greater ability to control decision making. As these results make clear, this authority is rooted not in being the (major) breadwinner, but in being a man.

CHAPTER 6

Negotiating Identity and Power

THE THREE PREVIOUS CHAPTERS, which examined the straightforward bargain implied by the conventional marital contract, show that higher-earning wives are unable to get the same deal for their incomes that men have historically enjoyed. That is, their money does not buy them substantial relief from domestic labor or greater control over the family finances or other decisions. Instead of using income earned to determine the balance of power, spouses interact in ways that reproduce men's privilege and dominance in marriage. This chapter takes a closer look at these interactions, as well as at how attempts to construct appropriate gender identities are linked to the power dynamics in these marriages.

MAINTAINING GENDER BOUNDARIES:
MOTHERS AND BREADWINNERS

To think about gender is to focus on difference. For example, Western culture takes essentially similar human forms (male and female) and produces differently gendered bodies through various grooming practices (haircuts, shaving, and makeup) and styles of dress. These physical markers become gender boundaries—ways to distinguish between men and women and to construct them as substantially different from each other (Connell 1987).

There are, of course, innumerable other ways in which we mark men and women as different from each other. Many jobs are still typed by gender, with the vast majority of secretaries and nurses being women, and the vast majority of elected officials (particularly at the national level) being men. Men and women also confront different cultural expectations for behavior; for example, it is still more acceptable for a woman than for a man to cry in public. Maintaining these gender boundaries allows us to see women as "better suited" for particular kinds of jobs, or more "naturally" emotional than men. The nature of gender boundaries may vary across social contexts, but by maintaining such rigid distinctions and expectations for each gender, men and women are constructed as essentially different from each other.

Within marriage, the most salient gender boundaries are the gendered identities of mother/homemaker and breadwinner (Potuchek 1997). As we have seen, these boundaries prescribe appropriate activities for men and women. However, they also form the basis for constructing appropriate gender identities. To be a success as a married woman is to be a good wife and mother, providing a clean, orderly home and caring lovingly for other family members. To be a real man is to provide well for one's family by being the sole (or at least major) earner. Whatever else a man or woman might decide to do, the pull of these conventional identities remains strong (Williams 2000).

While this pull toward the conventional is largely felt at the individual level, maintaining these gender boundaries is also a team effort. Individuals want to feel that they are behaving as they should, but they also seem more comfortable when their partners more or less conform to conventional expectations (Vannoy-Hiller and Philliber 1989). That is, spouses tend to hold both themselves and each other accountable to meeting the behavioral requirements implied by the identities of mother and breadwinner.

These boundaries appear to be meaningful even to men and women in unconventional circumstances. For example, Atkinson and Boles (1984) examined married couples in which wives have the more important job or career. Husbands in these relationships take on substantial responsibility at home, and work and family life are largely organized around the wife's job or career. These women's resources seem to bring them a more equitable trade at home than other employed wives have, but there are tensions in these relationships. Wives report feeling guilty that they are not more engaged in domestic endeavors, and they worry that they are not doing enough to take care of their husbands and their children. To compensate for outshining their husbands occupationally and contributing less at home, these wives emphasize the "traditional female role" and often deliberately cater to their husbands—to prove that they are still real women and good wives.

Christopher Carrington's (1999) work on the division of domestic labor in lesbian and gay households demonstrates that these conventional gender boundaries are also meaningful to same-sex couples. Gendered beliefs that women are supposed to be interested and engaged in domestic issues/labor (and men are not) affect such couples, who work together to ensure that *both* partners at least appear to meet them. Lesbians with partners who are less involved in family work sometimes give them more credit for participating in household labor than they deserve to "cover" for the less domestic partner, that is, to demonstrate that she is reasonably engaged in domestic labor and therefore appropriately feminine. Similarly, gay men often "dump" credit on each other to avoid looking too feminine, or the partner less involved in domestic labor sometimes takes more credit for performing it to avoid having his partner look too feminine. In other words, individuals not only want to appear to conform to conventional gender expectations, but also want their partners to conform. These boundaries are meaningful to couples in a wide range of circumstances, and maintaining them is a joint enterprise.

The gender boundaries of mothering and breadwinning exist in relationship to each other, and over time, couples often renegotiate the meanings of these boundaries in their marriages (Bolak 1997; Potuchek 1997; Pyke 1994). For example, as women move into the workforce, the gender boundary of breadwinning may be relaxed: Spouses no longer hold men solely accountable for breadwinning. In other cases, having or being a wife in the workforce may feel threatening to one or both spouses, and couples may compensate by shoring up or highlighting the distinction between mothering and breadwinning: They may emphasize the man as the major provider and the woman as mother/homemaker. In other words, as spouses cross these boundaries in their behavior, they may make an extra effort to maintain them, at least symbolically.

The resiliency of these gender boundaries across various and changing social contexts is striking. The conventional identities of mother and breadwinner continue to resonate with women and men despite most wives being employed outside the home today (Williams 2000). This appears to be the case among couples with higher-earning wives as well. Instead of using their unconventional circumstances to alter the marital contract, these spouses continue to hold themselves, and each other, accountable to the conventional expectations of mothering and domestic involvement for wives and breadwinning for husbands. Maintaining these gender boundaries allows each spouse to construct an appropriate gender identity, and helps husbands and wives feel better about themselves and their marriages.

It is relatively easy for couples with higher-earning wives to maintain mothering as a gender boundary, despite the wives' role as the major breadwinners. In nearly every case, wives are still responsible for the majority of domestic labor and child-care tasks, so they are the de facto keepers of the domestic realm. However, the mothering boundary is also maintained on a symbolic level. Higher-earning wives downplay their economic contributions and emphasize the time and attention they devote to their families; in this way, they can continue to see themselves as good wives and mothers despite their substantial breadwinning activities. Husbands support wives in maintaining this gender boundary by allowing them to carry this burden and by applauding their efforts at home.

Ideologically, maintaining the masculine boundary of breadwinning is trickier for these couples. For nearly two centuries, breadwinning has been the primary way husbands have differentiated themselves from their wives in U.S. culture. Even as women have moved into the workforce, couples feel that men retain the responsibility of providing for their families (Potuchek 1997; Wilkie 1993; Wilkie et al. 1998). Breadwinning, then, becomes a crucial way to stake a claim to a masculine identity. This can be problematic for husbands with higher-earning wives. Their wives, not they, are the "breadwinners" in the conventional understanding of this term. As we will see, these couples manage to redefine what it means to be a provider to allow men a claim on this crucial component of masculine identity.

Preserving the Woman's Identity as Mother

In Chapter 3, we saw that higher-earning wives are still holding up their half of the marital contract by maintaining responsibility for organizing and performing household chores. Like other employed women, they face a second shift comprised of household labor (including invisible work) with relatively little help from their husbands. This creates a crushing load for these wives and raises the question, why would any woman carry this burden year after year? The answer: for two basic reasons—she loves her family, and she wants to be a good wife and mother.

In other words, performing domestic labor is tied up with issues of love and identity. Conceptualizing domestic labor as part of a marital contract or bargain between spouses obscures this emotional dimension of housework. This labor is not just about providing an even trade for breadwinning; for women, it is also about demonstrating care and commitment to other family members. "Good" wives keep a neat and orderly house, prepare nutritious meals, and tend to the physical and emotional needs of their husbands and children because they love them. Their labor produces not only tidy houses and well-fed children but also emotional warmth and support for their loved ones. Through their efforts, wives symbolically "create" family while they simultaneously accomplish the tasks necessary for daily living (DeVault 1991).

Providing a stable home—a "haven in a heartless world" (Lasch 1977)—is the bedrock of conventional femininity, and its pull is strong. Though gender norms and opportunities for women have expanded in the last few decades, motherhood remains a defining feature of adult womanhood, with the vast majority of women still choosing to bear children. In fact, becoming a mother is still the central way a woman can achieve an identity as a responsible, caring adult (McMahon 1995). And even the most committed career woman with a family does not want to be a bad wife or mother. Good wives and mothers love their families and give of themselves to ensure that others' needs are met, even if the effort comes at a personal cost (Lundberg and Pollak 1996). This selfless devotion is at the heart of both domesticity and femininity, and so by continuing to provide the bulk of the physical and emotional care their families require, women can assure themselves that they are good wives and mothers. In this way, performing domestic labor can be fundamental to women's identities.

Higher-earning wives are no different in this respect from other women. Despite their accomplishments in the workforce, they place a high priority on their responsibilities at home. They tend to downplay their financial contributions to their families and judge themselves by more conventionally feminine standards. They use the amount of housework they perform or time they spend with their families as the most important measures of their personal success. This tendency can be seen most clearly in the families where the wives earned nearly all the household income. After listing all that her stay-at-home husband does around the house, the mother of three young boys under the age of seven cries: "What kind of mother *am* I? I do very little around here"—despite supplying nearly all the family's income.

Another wife, a physician married to a part-time high-school sports coach, has similar difficulties evaluating her worth. When asked what she contributes to the family, she says: "I have a paycheck, which is probably only incidental. . . . I can't say I'm the strong point in the whole family, except for that paycheck, because I'm just not here often enough." Her paycheck is more than incidental, because the family would be destitute without it, but she feels that it does not compensate for not being home enough to take care of her family. In the conventional marital contract, money is exchanged for domestic labor and caring. This equation works when husbands bring the money to the table, but it is problematic for these breadwinning wives.

In addition to downplaying their economic contributions, wives who earn nearly all the family's income typically place great emphasis on the contributions their husbands are making at home. For example, Bonnie is a lawyer who makes $114,000 a year. She compares the contributions she makes to the family with those of her husband, Wayne, who is primarily at home with their six-year-old son:

> You know, it's funny. I sort of feel like I don't contribute enough. Because he's so [pause]—it sounds like he does *so much*. I mean, he does lots of things. I think, because if you try to list things at the end of the day, there's really only a number of things I do because a large category of what I do is just work, office work. And right from the morning, he'll get up, get [our son] fed and off to school, though usually I do that. Then Wayne takes him to school, and then he'll go for a run and come back and pay bills or balance the checkbook, and then he'll go to a meeting of the church finance board, and then he'll have lunch or . . . go to school and help out during recess, and then he'll come home for an hour, and then he might take a nap, but then he'll go pick up [our son]. Then he'll spend the rest of the day with him. And in the meantime, he's done three loads of wash, scrubbed down the patio chairs, vacuumed, washed the car. I don't know. There's *tons* of things to manage on the home front.

Of course, she is absolutely right, but no husband in either group spoke about his wife's domestic contributions with such awe or admiration, nor did men downplay their own economic contributions to their families to pay homage to their wives. These higher-earning wives seem to place a greater value on their gender-appropriate contributions to the household. Ten hours of office work does not "count" in their day, and their paychecks are only "incidental." When I ask them what they feel they contribute to the household, some of them have a hard time coming up with a list because they feel they are not contributing enough in conventionally feminine ways. And even their high incomes cannot make up for that.

Other higher-earning wives hold themselves to similar standards. Fully half these wives who bring home substantially more than their husbands and shoulder the majority of the household burden feel they should be doing more at home, though they are often hard-pressed to list what more they could be doing. For example, one wife, a family physician, thinks she should contribute more at home, but when I ask if there is anything specific she thinks she should be doing, she replies: "No. Just, you know. I mean [long pause]—sometimes I think [my husband] ends up having to do more dishes, more than he probably should have to. That's something. But then usually I'm putting the kids to bed at that time." She does all the cooking and most of the cleaning and child care, but she feels it is unfair for her husband to do the dishes more than half the time.

Other wives recognize that they are doing more than their share yet do not complain about it. One such wife, a midlevel personnel manager, says:

> I don't know if I wish he did more, or if he would sometimes notice or acknowledge that there are things that I pick up that he *could*. 'Cause I don't feel like I'm doing too much, but I *do* see I'm doing more. I'm not necessarily sure I want him to take any of it, but I think it would make me happier sometimes if he would occasionally acknowledge that.

She wants more credit for all that she is doing. She seems more interested in being validated for doing a good job as a wife and mother than in lightening her load at home.

By contrast, only one comparison wife, Amanda, felt she should be doing more around the house. As we saw in the chapter on domestic labor, she and her husband, Joe, have relatively equal incomes and status, and make relatively equal contributions to domestic labor, but this is not comfortable for Amanda. She feels she should do more so Joe can do less, and she can "be the wife."

Rather than taking pride in their ability to support their families so well, these higher-earning wives emphasize the amount of care they can offer their families. This seems to be a way to affirm themselves as good wives and mothers. And wives seem to be holding themselves to this standard; husbands do not judge them as harshly as the wives themselves do. A few husbands feel their wives should do more at home, but most feel their wives do "plenty" or should do less around the house (though husbands rarely talk about doing more to make up for their wives' doing less). However, husbands play at least a subtle role in this process; after all, couples have negotiated, or perhaps fallen into, these domestic arrangements. This means that husbands help hold their wives accountable to the gender boundary of mothering/caring either by resisting domestic chores or by supporting their wives' "preference" for a taking on a larger share of the load at home.

Husbands also help support their wives' constructions of themselves as "good mothers," especially in the five cases where husbands considered themselves the primary caretakers of their children. Wayne is married to Bonnie, the lawyer who spoke in such glowing terms about all he does at home. Wayne is at home with their son, which makes him the primary caretaker, but he maintains that "Bonnie is extremely involved in [our son's] life, given her demands as a senior-level lawyer in a big company. She is very focused on him, very loving. They have a very close relationship, despite [her] being away eleven to twelve hours a day." Another husband at home similarly defends his wife, Donna: "Donna makes real good use of the time she *does* spend with Emma. And so that Emma *doesn't* just have my values. I think Donna has done a very good job of using the time that she has to really make an influence on Emma." These statements are short, simple, almost insistent. These women are still good mothers, despite spending so many hours away from their children.

Other husbands also defend their wives. Mark is a part-time high school sports coach married to Tina, a physician, who works long and unpredictable hours. When we discuss the division of labor in Mark's home, I remark that their questionnaire responses make it look as if he largely tends to their nine-month-old daughter, while Tina performs most of the household chores. Mark replies: "That's what it turned into. It was better. I don't know why I haven't been doing housework, but I haven't been. And the house is a mess. But that's not her fault. She just works so much." That is, Tina is not a bad wife or mother because the house is a mess. She would do more, and already does most of what gets done, if she were not working so many hours.

These results underscore that the cultural standard for being a good wife and mother is quite high—so high, in fact, that wives who are already carrying a great burden feel that they are not doing enough. Being a good mother means creating order and cooking meals as much as talking, listening, and playing with family members. It is this feeling of all-encompassing responsibility that gives motherhood its sacred character and generates such a burden for these wives (McMahon 1995).

This standard of motherhood works to men's advantage among couples with higher-earning wives, even more than for men in comparison marriages. Comparison wives do not see their domestic efforts as inadequate and so do not try to take on even more work. Perhaps higher-earning wives feel they have something to prove (their femininity), which motivates them to take on a larger burden at home. Being the main provider may threaten their sense of themselves as wives and mothers, and they may take on more domestic work to prove that, as they succeed as earners, they are not failing as women.

However, maintaining the gender boundary of mothering and home-making is a team performance, and it is also possible that wives take on this load to preserve harmony in their relationships. Wives may think that their husbands expect a certain level of domestic service and will hold them accountable for failing to meet these expectations. However, this explanation is not completely satisfactory. It would account for why wives take on the majority of the household burden, but not for why so many of these already overburdened wives feel they should take on even more. Perhaps these wives emphasize their domestic contributions to deemphasize their economic contributions and avoid embarrassing (or even emasculating) their husbands. In any case, cultural expectations of what it means to be a good wife and mother shape the domestic negotiations of these couples and produce arrangements that privilege men and further burden wives.

This effort to maintain the gender boundary of mothering has important consequences for women. First, since being a good mother means an enormous time commitment, higher-earning wives carry a heavy load. Not only are they the major breadwinners in their families, but they are also trying to meet a standard of intensive mothering that gives them no credit for the large incomes they earn and judges them solely on the physical and emotional care that they give to their families (Hays 1995). Under the weight of this load, wives struggle to feel they are doing right by their families.

However, maintaining this gender boundary gives women an identity that feels right culturally. They feel the pull of conventional gender expectations and seem to find the identity of mother both meaningful and important. They embrace the expectations that they should be there for their families and make every effort to meet the demands of conventional motherhood. Though they may be uncomfortable with being the major breadwinners, they want to feel secure that they are good wives and mothers.

Preserving the Man's Identity as Breadwinner

Just as mothering is still central to a woman's identity, breadwinning is central to a man's. In fact, breadwinning may be an even more important gender boundary for men than mothering is for women. Many women have expanded their identities to include the role of worker or professional. And though work has not been as central in defining women's identities, it has at least provided some balance for women who are also wives and mothers. Working outside the home gives women another outlet for interacting socially and demonstrating personal competence. By contrast, fewer men have sought to similarly balance their energies by becoming extensively involved in the household and child care. Work remains the primary activity for men, and thus the chief mechanism for demonstrating both masculinity and adult competence (Williams 2000).

The asymmetry in the role work plays in identity construction for men and women is also evident in the experience of job loss. While losing a job may be economically difficult—even devastating—for a woman, it is unlikely to shake her core identity. In fact, women are accustomed to moving in and out of the workforce, especially in response to changes in family demands. However, for most men, it is still true that losing a job can mean losing a part of oneself, and the despair associated with unemployment can trigger depression, substance abuse, and domestic violence (Rubin 1994).

Breadwinning, then, seems to be the primary way an adult man constructs and maintains his masculine identity. Providing for his family distinguishes a man from his wife. It is also through paid work that a provider achieves his status among other men, separating himself from more marginalized men who are unable to support a family. To be a breadwinner is to achieve adult status; to fail to provide is to fail at manhood.

Though women have begun to share the role of providing for the family financially, men tend to maintain responsibility for providing (Potuchek 1997; Wilkie 1993). The gender boundary of breadwinning is maintained by constructing men as major (rather than sole) breadwinners, while wives are often seen as helping out. These different meanings associated with the spouses' earnings preserve the symbolic primacy of men's efforts and creates a sense of difference, even though spouses are engaged in similar activities.

Maintaining breadwinning as a gender boundary is more difficult when a wife earns more than her husband does, but spouses in these relationships work together to maintain men's breadwinner status. Couples accomplish this largely by redefining what it means to be a "provider." I asked each respondent if she or he saw either spouse as the provider in the family. It is an easy answer for comparison couples. If the husband makes more money, he is considered the provider; if the spouses earn roughly the same amount, they say, "We both provide." The equation is more complex for couples with higher-earning wives. When asked if they see either spouse as the provider in the family, most spouses deny that "provider" is still a useful term—even some of those families where the wives earn nearly all the family's income. Most commonly, couples expand the notion of providing to include meeting the emotional, as well as the material, needs of the family. The key point is that spouses seem to agree that breadwinning is a man's activity and work together to maintain a sense that men are meeting this gender imperative.

Lily, a nurse, is married to Butch, who works in maintenance. They are not comfortable according provider status to Lily as the major bread-winner. Instead, they describe providing as being about more than money. Lily says:

> There are more ways than just financial. I mean, when you talk about being a "provider," I think that just maybe it's too broad a thing— emotional, physical, financial. . . . Just because my actual paycheck may be larger, that doesn't mean a darn thing. I think it means, as a person, you provide for your family in more ways than just money.

Butch emphasizes how it takes more than one income to survive in these economic times: "Now it takes two people to provide. One may make more money than the other, but it all has to come together, or it just doesn't make a difference." Butch's family could not make it on one income, which means that he is still essential to the economic well-being of his family—a provider—even though he earns substantially less than his wife.

June, a military officer married to Adam, an enlisted man, shares Lily's broader view of providing. When asked if she sees either herself or Adam as the provider for the family, she responds:

> I would say, for the family's *whole* well-being, no. [VT: It sounds like in some ways you *do* see one of you as the provider.] [She laughs.] I feel like I'm harping on the money thing. I mean, "the provider"— some people would look at a provider and say, "It's just the money," but that's not the way I look at it anyway, so . . . [Her voice trails off.] [VT: So being the provider is more than just bringing home the money?] Oh, absolutely, absolutely. I mean, without Adam, this wouldn't be a functional family, as we found out this last week when he was gone. . . . I had more time constraints, more pressure. I was feeling more pressure because I had to take care of everything [our two-year-old] needed.

June is uncomfortable using money as the sole criterion of provider status because that would deny Adam a claim to it. She emphasizes instead how important he is to the smooth functioning of the family.

When I ask Monica (the woman from previous chapters whose husband told her what kind of car to buy) if she sees either herself or her husband as the provider, despite the large disparity in their incomes she quickly identifies her husband as the provider; initially, it does not seem to occur to her that the term "provider" could apply to her:

> I'd probably say he was the provider. I don't know why I'd say that.
> [She laughs.] I don't know why, actually. I guess because I felt at one time I didn't work, and he did bring home more. Although . . . I do bring home more money than he does, but, um, so I don't know why I should've said that he's the provider. He probably likes to think of himself as the provider.

Perhaps she does as well. Or Monica may be acknowledging the bread-winning responsibility her husband has shouldered for much of their married life, since her income has only surpassed his within the last two years. Clearly, though, she does not want to deprive him of provider status.

Perhaps most dramatic is a final example, a marriage in which the income disparity is huge. Bonnie is the corporate attorney making $114,000, married to Wayne, who quit his job to be home with their son several years ago and makes a few thousand dollars a year working part-time. When asked if she sees herself as the provider, Bonnie says: "I guess so, but I don't think of it in those terms. I don't think about that at all. I sort of see our family as being 'the cause,' and Wayne and I are doing our parts to advance our family's interests. So I guess we're both providers." Her husband echoes her comments. He describes them both as working hard and aggressively at two different jobs, creating a result that is very positive for the family. Further, as financial manager of the household, Wayne feels that his careful attention to the family's finances and purchase decisions are an important way for him to contribute financially, in lieu of bringing home a paycheck. This allows him to still think of himself as "providing" for the family in a way that parallels the conventional definition of the term.

Redefining the notion of providing is a way to preserve a sense that husbands of higher-earning wives are meeting the conventional masculine obligation of breadwinning. This new definition includes meeting the physical and emotional needs of family members through performing household chores and child care. Providing also includes other financial activities, such as managing the bills on a monthly basis or tracking investments. In this way, stay-at-home fathers and husbands contributing a smaller portion of the family income are accorded a provider status that is unthinkable for women in similar circumstances. A housewife may be seen as contributing vitally to the family through her efforts at home and in the community, and these contributions may be highly valued by both spouses, but she is unlikely to be called a provider.

Similarly, women who earn significantly less than their husbands are unlikely to be called providers. They are more commonly viewed as helpers. This, in fact, is the pattern for comparison couples. Broadening the notion of providing is unique to couples with higher-earning wives and seems to be part of an overall effort to maintain the gender boundary of breadwinning and help husbands in these marriages meet this masculine imperative.

Maintaining the gender boundaries of mothering and breadwinning is important to constructing and preserving appropriate gender identities for spouses. Maintaining these boundaries also preserves a sense of fundamental difference between spouses. Doing gender in such conventional ways usually involves producing differences that maintain social divisions by sex. Spouses in couples with higher-earning wives turn unconventional difference into similarity to the same end. When faced with a dramatic difference in incomes, these couples do not accord the wife provider status, because that would be a serious blow to the husband's accomplishment of masculinity (earlier, we saw what a threat breadwinning can be to the wife's accomplishment of femininity). Instead, spouses obscure the difference in incomes by drastically altering the conventional definition of provider to include things like meeting the emotional needs of family members, or carefully managing the family's finances or investments. Couples also emphasize that one person alone cannot provide for a family today, so it makes no sense to accord provider status to the person who brings home the most money. These arguments are particularly striking in families where husbands earn only a few thousand dollars a year. Couples obscure and reconstruct the unconventional differences between them to create a sense of conventional difference that feels more comfortable.

Maintaining Gender Boundaries When the Man Is at Home

Preserving a sense that husbands and wives are engaged in gender-appropriate activities is particularly challenging for the five couples in which the wives are the nearly sole financial providers for the family and the husbands are primarily at home. Two men in this situation, Carl and Wayne, describe themselves and their situations in dramatically different terms, highlighting the struggle to construct and maintain an appropriate gender identity, as well as the potential dangers to that identity in crossing gender boundaries.

Carl

Carl has been home full time with his three children for about five years. His wife, Jackie, is a customer-service representative for a large company. They decided on this division of responsibilities because Jackie's salary was constant, and the commissions Carl made in retail sales barely paid the babysitter. He was also getting burned out on sales, so they decided, as a couple, that he should stay at home. The family of five (with one on the way) lives on an annual income of $38,000.

Carl struggles to feel good about being at home. He recognizes that he is important to his family, but his experiences have been unsettling:

> [Being at home] makes me feel important. I enjoy it because I feel like I'm important to my children. I feel like I'm filling a need that needs to be filled. I don't enjoy, as you can see [he gestures around the room], cleaning [we laugh] or the day-to-day drudgery that comes with it. . . . I can certainly sympathize with house*wives*, traditionally, now who have always said [pause]—let me preface that. Before, I had always assumed that women sat home and complained, and that was just kind of their thing: "We're housewives, nah, nah, nah." The typical answer to things. The typical "Where have you been? I kept dinner for you," and I thought that was just kind of what they do, how they play the game. I never had a full understanding of what it was, and now I do. And I find myself doing and saying the same things I've heard my mother saying before, my first wife say before, and it's almost scary. [We laugh.] I'm starting to take on a lot of the—what I used to assume were a woman's trait. I'm taking them on simply because of the job. Not that you have to be a woman to feel that way. I'm upset when I have to keep dinner and she doesn't call. Trying to juggle getting the kids to school on time,

and having breakfast set, and those kinds of things. Keeping the laundry up, and trying to keep the house at least livable, dealing with the pest-control guy, and the TV people, and the appliance repairman. I don't resent it. I just feel there's definitely a need there that needs to be fulfilled. It's not all I thought it was cracked up to be before. It's a tremendous job. It's extremely hard. If somebody said, "I'll give you twenty dollars an hour to be my housewife," I'd slap 'em. [We laugh.] It wouldn't be enough money. I can't clock out at six o'clock and say, "See ya!" It's a twenty-four-hour job.

Having performed this job for five years now, Carl feels the experience has "feminized" him in a number of ways. He describes himself as being different from the person he was before he took on these responsibilities at home, and as being different from the men friends he has now:

Sometimes I almost feel like I'm a little more effeminate in my attitudes. I don't really know how to explain it. I don't feel like the burly "get me a beer/I'm watchin' the game/don't bother me" kind of person. . . . I feel that's so unfair. I think that people aren't really giving the people that stay home, I don't feel, the kind of respect they should have for what they're doing. The myth is you lay around and eat bonbons, à la Peggy Bundy, and watch *Oprah!* all day. . . . I think I have a better understanding for what it's like—I know this sounds strange—for what it's like to be a woman in a man's world. I know that sounds strange. . . . We know couples where they both work, and when they get home, the woman—in the man's mind—is still expected to go get dinner, take care of the kids, do the laundry, get things ready for the next day, while he sits on the couch and burps. It's very unfair, I feel. But you don't say anything to people, you know, because they'll think something's wrong with you—like you're a weirdo. . . . You're almost afraid to say, "Go help your wife with the dishes! What's the matter with you? Why would you treat her like that? Don't you love her? How much did you pay for her when you married her?" I don't know why I have that attitude, but it's not comfortable around male friends because they [pause]—so I have to play that game: "Yeah, I stay home [in a deep, burly voice]." But, well, it's gotten to the point now that it can't be explained away. I stay at home because that's my job. . . . It has nothing to do with your sex. It's just a position that has to be filled.

Carl feels somewhat estranged from the men he knows. Being at home has given him a window on women's experiences, and he strongly identifies with them. This feeling is unsettling for him.

Carl also says that he has taken quite a bit of "flack" from family and friends for being at home. He has even broken off contact with some of them because he refuses to accept their message that what he is doing is useless.

A buddy of mine might come over, and I'll be sitting on the couch folding clothes or something. And it's like, "Aha, your wife's really got you whipped." And I don't even try to argue back anymore. I don't even try to justify it. I just tell 'em, basically, "You like your clothes folded?" "Yeah." "You like 'em clean?" "Yeah." "Well, so do I. If I was *single*, I'd have to do this, right?" And they go, "Yeah, well, all right." I won't allow them to play it off as a joke on me anymore, and that's toned down the amount of flack I get.

Carl demonstrates a mixture of pride and embarrassment about being at home. He is adamant that what he does is valuable, but he often labels himself as "weird" or "strange." He calls his men friends "Stone Age" and is disgusted by their attitudes toward their wives. If he suggests that his friend help his wife with the dishes, the friend will respond, "Are you kidding? That's what I married *her* for." Carl says, "You can go to the Middle East and *buy* someone to do these things for you. That's not my idea of respect or love."

Carl sees marriages fail all around him for what, to him, are obvious reasons. The men in these divorces felt that they were doing their part in the relationship, but Carl asks: "Did you ever do the laundry one week? Did you ever change a diaper?" The men always respond: "No way! That's women's work!" Carl feels that, for a marriage to succeed, each spouse has to give 100 percent: "This fifty-fifty stuff doesn't work." Before he began working at home, it would have made sense to him to divorce a woman because she would not do the dishes, but now he sees things differently.

Again and again, Carl does something no other man in my study did—he equates a man's performing household chores with loving and respecting his wife, and he is horrified that other men do not make the same connection. Other husbands in this sample who shared most significantly in the household labor seem to focus on "fairness," if anything, rather than love and respect. This association of helping with caring is common for women, but quite rare in a man. Perhaps performing these tasks daily engenders this kind of sensibility. Feminist scholars have maintained that one of the benefits for men of becoming more involved in household chores and the daily care of their children is that men would become more in tune with the full range of their emotional life (Coltrane 1996; Connell 2000; Ehrensaft 1987; Radin 1988). Perhaps this is what Carl is experiencing.

However, experiencing a more complete range of emotions is troubling for Carl. He feels that his work at home has feminized him to a degree, and this worries him. He has great empathy for women who stay at home and now sees that some of their behavior is role related, rather than gender related. However, he sees other changes in himself that worry him. He says, "I'm almost becoming too housewifey." He has started worrying about things that he thought only women worried about, like household skills. For example, he does not like the way his wife folds the clothes or loads the dishwasher, and he says that "feels weird." He thinks he has even taken on some feminine mannerisms, like crossing his legs. He has tried to develop other interests for himself, such as writing, illustrating, drawing, and painting, but he is "careful" to be sure that these do not come off as being "effeminate things." He is trying to "guard against going over the final edge," as he puts it. In his mind, he has to draw the line so he can still "function with the guys, and be mommy/daddy for the kids."

How Carl appears to others is important to him. We have seen the criticism he has received from those close to him, but he feels scrutinized by neighbors and strangers as well. He does some child care during the week, earning a little extra money for the family, and he has gotten "a lot of weird responses" to his doing it. Some people have said it would "confuse" their children, having a man at home when their own father is not. Sometimes people seem to treat him like a "pervert." There are mothers in his neighborhood who will not allow their children to play at his house, even though they are eager to have his children play in their homes. Carl interprets this lack of reciprocity as evidence that neighborhood mothers are wary of him because he is a man at home.

Remember from the chapter on finances that Carl's wife, Jackie, appears to have sole control over the money. Their incomes go into an account in her name only. They agree that this is the best way to handle the finances, because money is so tight for them, and Carl is so irresponsible with it. He readily acknowledges the control Jackie has, as well as his financial dependence on her. He does not feel he has the power to force her into anything.

> I feel she pulls the strings. In other words, I feel that she is the [pause]—if it came down to the bottom line, I would have to concede to her decision. . . . I almost always concede to her, when push comes to shove. I don't know if it's just, in the back of my mind, I know there's not a whole heck of a lot I can do about it, even if I *do* make a big show and push on it. What are you gonna be able to do anyway, so why do it? . . . I know she wouldn't do anything to purposely hurt me. We're weird. [He laughs.]

When I ask Carl if there are any changes he would like to make for the future, he says he would like to go to college:

> I don't wanna do this for the rest of my life. I wanna have some kind of value in *my* mind. [My wife] constantly says, "You have value in doing things for me. If you never have a degree, that's not important." But it's important to *me*. I need that feeling of accomplishment, that feeling of self-satisfaction, and . . . I don't know if I could do that. I don't have the confidence that I can do it right now. Again, it almost gets back to being a housewife who says, "I can't get by without him." I don't know if I can do it, and I feel that way sometimes— like, what can I do, other than the dishes and the laundry?

For now, Carl will continue in his current role. He is meeting an important need for his family, and the family will need him for another six years, because Jackie is pregnant with their fourth child.

What is most striking in this narrative is how Carl compares himself to women who are at home. He empathizes with them, certainly, but it is more fundamental than that; he feels he now thinks as they do and responds as they would. He feels he has been feminized by his experiences at home. And while he in no way would want to demean women, or what he and they do, he obviously feels that he is somehow diminished in his current situation.

This response to a role reversal is not at all uncommon. Men like Carl often struggle to assert their masculinity. Negotiating relationships outside the family is also tricky, since men may "lose face" outside the home, and can even be viewed as suspect by other mothers (Ehrensaft 1990; Fenstermaker, West, and Zimmerman 1991; Russell 1987). Carl has experienced all these challenges and is still struggling with them. Constructing an appropriately masculine self is an ongoing issue for him. For all of us, masculinity and femininity exist in tension, and each is constructed by some repression of the other. Carl feels that being at home has encouraged some feminine mannerisms and sensibilities to emerge, and he experiences this feminization as problematic for the construction of a masculine identity. Most tellingly, he is worried that he will "go over the final edge" into a place where he is no longer considered a man.

Wayne

Wayne is the stay-at-home dad married to Bonnie, the corporate attorney. They have a six-year-old son, Chase, and Wayne has been at home with him for the last two and a half years. Before making move, he was also a corporate attorney, but he was not happy in his job, and the company was pressuring him to move. He and Bonnie thought their son, who had been with a sitter full time since he was seven weeks old, "needed more parental time," so Wayne decided to move out of paid employment. Wayne has a very different view from Carl's of his life at home:

> It's been unbelievably fantastic. I keep meeting fathers who wanna do the same thing. I met a father today, at my son's Montessori school, who said he's in the Foreign Service, and in ten days he's gonna leave to go to Liberia for something like two years. He's leaving his wife and kids here, so they can have some continuity in their school life. My son has had four years at his school, which is one block away. I know all his friends. I know the parents of his friends. I know our community. I contribute to our community, and it would

take a *monumental* change in things for me to give that up. So I feel like I've invested the last two and a half years in building social capital, if you will, for our family, rather than earning money. To the great benefit of my child, my wife, and myself, as unorthodox as it might initially appear.

Wayne has built a tremendous amount of social capital. In addition to performing almost all the household chores and being available for his son and his friends, Wayne is very involved in the community: He is the "most active volunteer" at his son's school; he is a member of several local legal organizations; he is involved in several local charities; he hold offices at his church; he coaches children's sports; he writes and does research pro bono for a local organization; and finally, he works a few hours a month as an arbitrator, earning a few thousand dollars a year. No other respondent, man or woman, reported being this active in the community, and Wayne enjoys it all.

Wayne thinks there is no better child-care solution than having one parent at home.

> It's like I'm the nexus, if you will, of the family. A lot of people try and delegate the functions I do in our family, but I'm doing them directly. And the result is a higher level of quality, I think, in the result, but a much higher opportunity cost in the form of lost wages.

In addition to performing most of the household chores, Wayne is responsible for managing the family's finances. I asked if he felt these responsibilities were a burden, or an opportunity to exercise control or influence.

> As far as the financial aspect, I definitely like having direct control. As far as, say, the cleaning aspects, the laundry, I think there's no *glory* in that, it's just gotta get done. I try and do it quickly, efficiently, and get on to more stimulating things. If money were no object, I suppose I'd employ help to do that. It does trouble me, because I think it's not necessarily the best use of my time, but it does permit me to main-tain that role as nexus of the family, and very active father. . . . [VT: Why do you like having control over the finances?] Well, because I'm determined that this family be a successful economic unit. And to do that, you need to carefully watch where the money goes, and that

you achieve important objectives, that you don't have cash-flow problems, that you maintain an excellent credit rating, that you make good investment decisions, that you—particularly for this neighborhood—that you don't pay more in mortgage payments than you have to, that you acquire things inexpensively when you can. [VT: So do you feel like that's a way for you to contribute financially, in lieu of income you could be earning?] Yes. Definitely. To bring a higher level of ability, and a more thoughtful amount of decision making to financial decisions to benefit the family. Because it would be expensive to buy that service, and it would be difficult to find somebody willing to do it as enthusiastically and in as focused a way for this particular family.

The control Wayne describes here stands in sharp contrast to that of Carl, who largely submits to the decisions of his wife. In fact, Wayne seems to take the lead on most decisions. He talks about how he goes about getting what he wants:

If I were buying a new computer, I would usually at least mention it to her—*try* and get her agreement. [I laugh.] If I failed to get her agreement, I might later just do it and sort of regard our discussion as [pause]—as more or less obtaining her agreement. A recent example would be I spent a thousand bucks on an electronic air cleaner for our house, for two reasons. One, I felt it would help her get through the horrible spring pollen season—she has bad allergies. And two, I thought it would make our house a whole lot less dusty, which means a lot less work of cleaning it up. And both of those have proved, in my view, to be correct. And the way I [pause]—I decided to do that was, first I discussed it with her, and she thought it was too much money, and then I just went and did it, and, uh [pause]—you know, she kind of winced a little bit, but you know, I paid the bill, and she didn't have to see it or think about it, so it just kind of went through the system.

Wayne enjoys a great deal of financial autonomy, but Bonnie does not seem to mind his spending. She confirms, for example, that he has a lot of toys. In the area of recreation alone, he has a full-scale trampoline, a motorcycle, a touring bike, a mountain bike, and a racing bike. She would not have bought all these things for him, and she has nothing comparable, but they add so much to his enjoyment of life that she does not begrudge his having them.

Wayne does not seem to feel uncomfortable with his life at home. He describes the reactions of other fathers as positive, because they see how his efforts benefit their own children. He admits, though, that he is not sure how the legal community will view his choices when he looks for employment in a few years. Wayne has less difficulty than Carl has in maintaining his sense of self-worth, but he also has an advantage over Carl in this area: He has a professional self to draw on in his efforts to validate his current work.

> Now I describe myself as an attorney/stay-at-home father/community activist, and that's plenty to wear on my sleeve, really. . . . When people ask what I do, I say, "I wear a couple of hats." I say, "I'm a lawyer," but I also say, "For the past two and a half years I've stayed at home with my son, and I've been very involved in school and community activities, and I'll do that until he doesn't need me as much at home." So that's how I tell the story. And I say, "Prior to that, I was a corporate lawyer."

Wayne makes his professional credentials very clear; he is not relying on his current responsibilities in the home for his status.

If Carl's view of himself and his life at home emphasizes the feminine, Wayne's view of his life and himself are decidedly masculine. He describes his relationship with Bonnie and their commitment to the family, which they refer to as "the cause":

> It's sort of like, you know, we're in a boat, and we're both rowing an oar. And we have a different oar to row, but we both row steadily, and aggressively, and consistently. And we earn, together, a result that, you know, is very positive. It's just that we both do a different job.

And here, Wayne relates his feelings about being a parent. He thinks he is doing a good job, being at home with his son:

> I'm fighting against the very corrosive trends in our society for children to raise themselves, to be in institutionalized care excessively, to be forced out of childhood prematurely. Absolutely. I'm the guardian

defending at least this one child and his friends from such negative influences.

As Wayne was speaking, I could not resist picturing him in a red cape with a big *S* on his chest. Far from being feminized by these activities, Wayne speaks of his job in superhero terms; he is the defender of helpless children in a hostile world. What could be more masculine?

Admittedly, comparing Carl to Wayne is problematic, because they live in very different social worlds and under very different sets of circumstances. Carl is a man with a GED taking care of a family of five on $38,000 per year, with little access to the family's income and what appears to be only a token role in decision making. Wayne is a man with a JD and an MS taking care of a family of three on $114,000 per year, with substantial control over the family's income and a great deal of autonomy and influence in decision making. Carl is performing household chores and child-care tasks in an environment relatively hostile to his efforts; Wayne is something of a hero in his circles. All these differences have an impact on the way the two men experience essentially the same set of responsibilities.

But one key difference seems to be that, within his world, Wayne has successfully constructed these activities as masculine. He does not feel that cleaning and doing the laundry have feminized him. In fact, he barely mentions the household chores he performs. Instead, he emphasizes his role as a father and redefines caring work as an effort to guard and protect his son in a dangerous world. Wayne also emphasizes the highly visible role he plays in the community, and the ways his activities have built "social capital" for his family, in the same way that the charitable activities of upper-class women do (Ostrander 1984). The difference, again, is that casting these activities as creating social capital, rather than as volunteer work or community service, gives them an economic (and more masculine) feel.

Perhaps most importantly, Wayne is able to make a more credible claim to the symbolic components of breadwinning than Carl can. First, he does have professional degrees that he could use at any time—he just chooses not to use them at the moment. And as he said, he makes it very clear to others that he has these credentials, so he is not judged entirely by what he is doing now. Second, Wayne's handling of the family's finances gives him the kind of control that breadwinning has historically conferred on men. He seems to spend considerable sums of money, often without obtaining his wife's agreement beforehand. Wayne also believes that the careful attention he gives to all the details of the family's financial life largely compensates for whatever income he could be earning. In these ways, Wayne is able to make a symbolic claim on breadwinning and defend at least part of that gender boundary for himself in a way that Carl is not.

The experiences of the other three husbands at home fall between those of Carl and Wayne. They struggle to make sense of being a man at home but do not seem to face the crisis of identity that Carl does. For example, Tom has three sons under the age of seven and expresses his dissatisfaction with being at home for so many years:

> I can tell you I never expected to be home raising kids by myself this long. You know, when we had [our oldest], I thought I'd be workin' a job or doin' something after two years, or after he was in preschool. I didn't expect that for seven years I'd be Mr. Mom. [VT: How do you feel about that?] Um, it's rewarding, but I don't know [pause]— if I was raised with the parental skills, or if that's something you're raised with. I don't think I'm fully equipped—I don't have the maternal drive and all that. They're just like a [pause]—they're my job now.

There is a clear sense that Tom is distancing himself from the mother role. He is at home, and he is parenting, but he is *not* maternal.

Tom also tries to place distance between himself and women who are at home.

> [As a man at home] you're not fully integrated because you're not a woman, basically. When I drop one of my sons off at school and I'm standing there waiting, there's little cliques of women and you're [pause]—you're not accepted because you're not a woman. So I don't *mind* that. I understand that. It's not that you're a threat or anything. It's just that they have their things to talk about and you're not part of that.

Though there is a sense in these words that Tom feels he does not belong, there is also a sense that he is happy to be separate—or more precisely, different—from women who are at home. Instead of identifying with these women, as Carl has, he maintains that sense of being socially separate. Perhaps that allows him to feel more like a man.

Being at home is a struggle for these men. Maintaining a masculine self-identity is challenging when engaged in work that is typed as feminine. Crossing gender boundaries, then, can be perilous, and it takes a certain amount of ideological and emotional work to construct and maintain an appropriately gendered self. Wayne has been successful in his efforts to construct a masculine identity at home: He maintains financial control and sees himself as protecting his child from hostile influences in the world. Other research suggests that involving men in household chores and caring labor is more successful when it can be characterized as appropriately masculine. Scott Coltrane's (1996) work on egalitarian couples demonstrates that men become more engaged in housework when they have the "right tools" for the job, such as powerful vacuum cleaners, or can equate household chores with janitorial work. Characterizing tasks in this way gives them a more masculine, and therefore acceptable, feel. This strategy seems to help smooth construction of an appropriate gender identity, which makes crossing gender boundaries less threatening.

NEGOTIATING GENDER BOUNDARIES

As we have seen, the gender boundaries of mothering and breadwinning exist in relationship to each other. Over time, couples often renegotiate the meanings of these boundaries in their marriages and work to resolve tensions that are created when these boundaries are violated. These negotiations become even more complex for couples with higher-earning wives. I present one final case in this chapter to demonstrate how one spouse may be more interested in preserving these boundaries than the other, and how couples try to come to a common understanding of how to define the boundaries and each person's responsibilities.

Linda and Stan

Linda and Stan have one of the most equitable relationships in the sample in terms of the division of domestic labor and child rearing. They work alternating shifts to be home with their daughter as much as possible and seem to genuinely share child care. Despite their spending equal amounts of time with their daughter over the course of the week, Linda still views herself as the primary parent. In his interview, Stan expresses his frustration over their efforts to parent together. He complains that Linda "crowds me out" of child care and acts as if she is the final authority on their daughter. This upsets Stan because he is a very involved father and he has been unable to get Linda to treat him as an equal parent.

In terms of domestic labor, Linda performs more than half the household chores. Stan is willing to take on more housework but says that he and Linda have different timetables in mind. For example, he often takes mental responsibility for a task and plans to do it in a few days, only to find that Linda decided it needed to be done sooner and so has done it herself. He has told her to tell him when she thinks something needs to be done right away, and he will do it. However, Linda reports that it is easier for her to do things herself than to wait for Stan or to remind him that a particular chore needs to be done.

Linda seems to exercise a great deal of control in financial matters and decision making, but she is not entirely comfortable with it. She and Stan have a rather complex financial system. They have joint checking and savings accounts, as well as individual checking and savings accounts (left over from their single days). Linda makes 50 percent more than Stan does, but "to be fair," they contribute equal amounts to their joint accounts every payday. They use what they have left over to pay their own debts (credit cards and student loans) or for discretionary purposes. Since Linda makes so much more than Stan, she has more left over each pay period. This means she can spend more on herself, but she also uses this money to purchase items for the family that the two of them cannot agree upon as a joint purchase (for example, she recently bought a video camera with "her" money). Stan recognizes that Linda's income sometimes gives her "an edge" in purchase decisions, especially when she is free to act on her own in a way that he is not. He also reports deferring to her judgment in joint financial decisions because he sees her as being better with money than he is.

Though Linda enjoys acting independently, she seems uncomfortable with the power it gives her. As Stan reports: "I think we're pretty equal on most decisions, though there are times when Linda wants me to make decisions, to say 'This is what we're going to do.' She'll say, 'You're the boy, you decide!' " In a playful way, Linda communicates that she wants Stan, as the man, to exert an extra measure of control.

In addition to preserving the gender boundary of mothering for herself, Linda wants to maintain the masculine boundary of breadwinning for Stan. She is not happy being the primary breadwinner:

> Sometimes I feel resentful that I make more. Like I wish it was the other way around. [VT: How come?] Because I feel like . . . I can't go part-time, you know? It's like, I would like to go part-time, and stay home more with [our daughter], and do more house things, and have less stress. But I feel like I can't because I am the one that makes more.

What is striking about this couple is that they could be poised for working out a truly egalitarian relationship. Stan performs a great deal of the domestic labor, is willing to do more, and wants to be an equal partner in parenting. He also values Linda's working (she is employed at a residential facility for troubled youth) and has high ambitions for her to move on to a better position:

> I get mad at her for staying where she is because . . . she is a nurse, so she has many more opportunities to go other places, . . . just because nurses are very much in demand now. . . . She's just been doing the same thing she's been doing for eight or nine years, and she could be someplace else that's a better place to work. She could be learning more and be challenged, which she says she wants to do. But when it comes down to doing it, she won't do it. [VT: What would you like to see her do?] I'd like to see her be anyplace where she's happier, . . . in a doctor's office, hospital, whatever.

However, Linda does not seem interested in finding better employment. She has put in applications, for example, with the public health department, but has received no response and has not followed up on these possibilities. She is more concerned with moving out of full-time employment than with finding a better job. She has become focused on trying to improve Stan's chances of obtaining more lucrative employment. She is supporting him through a master's program. He will finish up in another year or so and look for a better-paying position. Then Linda will be able to cut back to part-time work.

Despite the advantages Linda enjoys in their current situation, she is uncomfortable being the primary earner in the family. Instead, she wants to preserve the conventional gender boundaries of mothering and breadwinning, reserving the former for herself and delegating the latter to Stan. At this point, he seems to have acceded to her wishes. Since he has started working on his master's degree, he is also looking forward to the time when he can move into a better-paying job. He wants to see Linda move to part-time employment, partly because he knows this is her desire, but also because he thinks it will alleviate much of the stress they have been experiencing as a dual-earner couple.

Linda and Stan demonstrate how the pull toward maintaining conventional gender boundaries can be difficult to resist (Potuchek 1997; Williams 2000). Even if one spouse is willing to cross these boundaries, power seems to lie in the inertia of the spouse who wants to maintain the status quo. These couples appear to have few role models for restructuring or renegotiating the conventional marital contract. Without such alternatives, the prevailing model is not only the most accessible, but also the most compelling.

REINFORCING THE MARITAL CONTRACT: THE LINK BETWEEN IDENTITY AND POWER

Gender is critical in identity formation, and conventional gender constructions call on women to be mothers/homemakers and men to be breadwinners. Couples with higher-earning wives hear this call as well. Though they are engaged in unconventional activities, as long as spouses are able to *perceive* women as mothers and men as breadwinners, they can maintain these boundaries and give each spouse access to the crucial component in forming the appropriate gender identity.

Maintaining these boundaries has important implications for the power dynamics in these relationships. By refusing to name wives as providers, couples relegate women to the less powerful role and deny women access to the privileges associated with being a provider. As wives continue to define themselves as mothers, they (often willingly) continue to shoulder well over half the domestic labor burden as they provide the substantial majority of the family income. And as men's position of authority as breadwinner and head of the household is preserved, they are assured the domestic services of their wives.

Exploring spouses' commitment to these conventional gender identities gives us a window into the hidden power dynamics in these relationships. There is no overt grab for power, nor is there much conflict associated with identity construction. As spouses describe how they see themselves and each other, their attachments to these conventional identities seem unproblematic. That is, they do not seem to struggle with them or question their usefulness, given their unusual situation. By embracing these identities, couples also accept the power differential embedded in them, which continues to give men an advantage in these relationships.

Again, these results point to the strength and stability of the gender structure. Conventional expectations for mothering and breadwinning at the institutional level create pressures for husbands and wives to construct identities at the individual level that conform to these expectations. At the interactional level, spouses rework the meanings attached to breadwinning to allow men to continue to construct appropriately masculine identities around this gender boundary. Similarly, spouses continue to see women as primarily responsible for mothering and domestic duties and try to ignore the potentially disturbing effects of their greater incomes.

While these couples appear to challenge the gender structure, they reproduce conventional gender expectations and the power dynamics embedded in them through their interactions and attempts to construct meaningful identities. By refusing to recognize wives as providers, they deny them the privileges associated with that role. These privileges include freedom from domestic labor, ample leisure time, and the right to make decisions based on their greater earnings. By emphasizing their domestic responsibilities, women can construct comfortable identities, but they are then firmly rooted in a less powerful role.

But maintaining these gender boundaries has important implications beyond the construction of appropriate gender identities. That is, spouses also seem to maintain these gender boundaries to preserve a sense that their marriages conform to the conventional marital contract. Having or being a higher-earning wife can be uncomfortable for couples, and spouses often work to maintain conventional gender boundaries to manage the tensions this situation creates. In fact, these couples are more interested in constructing conventional relationships, or in making their marriages seem more familiar and comfortable, than in trying to reconstruct cultural notions of what it means to be a good wife/mother and a good husband/father.

CHAPTER 7

Are They Happy?

MANAGING TENSIONS AND DISAPPOINTMENTS

THAT COUPLES WORK to preserve the gender boundaries of mothering and breadwinning does not mean that they are blind to the status and income differences between them, or that these differences do not generate a great deal of tension in these relationships. While husbands may find ways to see themselves as providers, they are still well aware that they are lesser providers vis-à-vis their wives. This awareness creates dissatisfaction that the couple must manage to ensure both the happiness of the spouses and the longevity of the relationship.

This chapter examines how couples assess their relationships, paying special attention to the dissatisfaction spouses feel and express, as well as the various strategies couples use to manage these feelings. Again, these feelings of disappointment seem to stem from the expectations embedded in the conventional marital contract; that husbands are not the main breadwinners in these relationships is at the root of much of the dissatisfaction and disappointment expressed by both husbands and wives. Efforts to manage these feelings revolve around trying to find ways to make these marriages look and feel like more conventional ones.

WHAT DOES IT MEAN TO BE "HAPPY"?

Family scholars use the terms "marital quality," "marital adjustment," and "marital satisfaction" to describe how happy people are in their relationships. These terms typically include measures of the quality or extent of communication between spouses, their feelings of affection for one another, the level of their shared interests, and other companionate aspects of marriage. More subtle measures of martial satisfaction ask spouses what (if any) changes they would like to make within their relationships, how committed they are to each other, and whether they feel they could do better elsewhere (see Becker 1981). These basic measures give a sense of the quality of the relationship, as well as how satisfied spouses are with it.

In the case of couples with higher-earning wives, other issues become important as well. For example, do spouses feel they are either "getting a good deal" or giving too much in their relationships? Their unconventional contributions, particularly in the case of higher-earning wives, may throw the exchange between spouses off balance. Spouses are more likely to see things as fair if each is meeting conventional gender expectations (Wilkie, Ferree, and Ratcliff 1998). If spouses are contributing to their relationships in unconventional ways, they may have a more difficult time recognizing and appreciating what each other has to offer.

There is disagreement in the research literature over whether a wife's status and income advantage lowers spouses' satisfaction with the relationship. Several studies find that having or being a higher-earning wife is indeed stressful for both spouses and has a negative impact on marital happiness (Heckert, Nowack, and Snyder 1998; Rogers and DeBoer 2001). Given the cultural norm for men's breadwinning, it makes sense that couples with higher-earning wives would struggle to feel good about their relationships. However, other evidence suggests that social-psychological variables are more important than socioeconomic ones when it comes to marital happiness (see White and Rogers 2000). That is, couples are happier when husbands and wives are doing what they, and their spouses, expect of them (Vannoy-Hiller and Philliber 1989).

In Chapter 6, we saw that the expectations embedded in the conventional marital contract assume that husbands are responsible for providing for the family materially, while wives are responsible for caretaking. If a wife takes over material provision by contributing the larger portion of the family income, this can be a threat to the husband's masculinity or sense of self as a man and therefore uncomfortable for him. Further, if a wife becomes more responsible for providing materially, she may be less able to provide the care she feels her family deserves, and this may be a threat to her sense of self as a woman. If spouses feel they are failing as husbands or wives, it may be difficult to be happy in their relationships. This means that the ability to construct an appropriate gender identity—to have a confident sense of oneself as a "real" man or a "good" woman—has an important impact on marital happiness.

Assessing spouses' satisfaction with their marriages requires examining their feelings about the relationship on multiple levels. Asking spouses directly about how satisfied they are in their relationships is not sufficient to assess their complex feelings toward each other. In general, most couples report being satisfied with their marriages (Geerken and Gove 1983; White and Rogers 2000; Wilkie, Ferree, and Ratcliff 1998). Getting a more complete picture of how spouses feel about their relationship requires moving beyond global measures of general satisfaction. Therefore, I asked spouses to talk about what attracted them to each other, why they decided to marry, what each contributes to the relationship, and what they continue to value and appreciate about each other. I also asked them to talk about conflicts or disappointments in the relationship. And finally, I explored threats to marital stability, both past and present, by asking spouses whether they had ever considered separation or divorce (and why), and whether they had ever discussed the possibility of separating. These questions gave me multiple windows into the way spouses view each other and their relationships, as well as how satisfied they are with them.

Appreciating Each Other

In general, across the higher-earning and comparison groups, spouses reported being satisfied in their marriages. Despite whatever dissatisfactions they reveal in the course of the interview, the vast majority begin by saying that, overall, they are satisfied. One person may give more in some areas, but spouses feel that is just the nature of relationships. Whatever ups and downs couples may experience, they see their contributions as balancing out over the long run. Witness this higher-earning wife, who says her strengths in the relationship are "keeping the organization going—operations and maintenance":

> I contribute more quantity, and Evan, again, contributes more [pause]—not quality, because that *demeans* what I do. But again, it works out fine. And that is Evan's point about it. "Why should *two* people balance the checkbook, because that's certainly a one-person task." Why should *two* people learn to wallpaper or cook, in my book. It's a one-person task. So I would say they're balancing things. [VT: How has that balance changed over time?] It hasn't changed. It's

that, again, in operations and maintenance, that workload increases geometrically with children in general, and with more than one child in particular. So it's not that he does less or I do more, it's just that with the kids, the increased workload falls with those things that are on my side of the list. Which is something else . . . talking about wanting to make sure the relationship is fifty-fifty. Well, get a roommate, not a spouse. It ain't gonna be fifty-fifty. You know, it'll be ninety-ten on some issues. It definitely won't be fifty-fifty. That's not life.

Clearly, "balancing out" does not mean equality. This wife feels that the load she carries in the relationship has increased over time because caring for the children falls on her side of the balance sheet. However, by emphasizing that both spouses contribute to the family, even if one does more than the other, they can assess their relationships more positively and report that, overall, they are satisfied with them.

While the great majority of spouses report being largely satisfied with their relationships, roughly two-thirds (fourteen of twenty-two) of the couples with higher-earning wives are unhappy with their relationships on some level. By contrast, only one comparison couple out of eight reports being dissatisfied. One of the reasons for this disparity becomes apparent when I ask spouses to reflect on what they appreciate about their partners. Spouses in the comparison couples are much more likely to speak in glowing terms of each other and the contributions they make to their relationships, and to feel that their spouses appreciate their own contributions:

> *Maggie*: He's a fabulous father. He's an even better spouse than he was a boyfriend. He's just a really good guy. The relationship has just gotten stronger over time.

> *Rita*: He is the rock—both feet on the ground. He will keep me anchored and calm, and pretty much be the backbone of the family. While I'll fly off and do this and that, and this and that, and get crushed or come back elated. And he'll always be there to keep us in a unit.

> *Mitch*: She's very well-balanced. She has a great way of thinking about things, like with the kids. I tend to get more upset than I

should, and she calms me down. She helps me get perspective. . . . She's a great listener. She's very committed to the relationship, and she's a good lover.

David: She's very supportive. We have fun together. We talk. If one of us is insensitive, it's probably me. We're married, we're lovers, we're friends. It's a lifetime commitment to make it work.

By contrast, couples with higher-earning wives often had trouble describing what attracted them to their partners, or what they appreciate about them. Indeed, these questions were often the most difficult ones for spouses answer. And typically, when spouses have trouble recognizing or expressing what they appreciate about their partners, the partners know it. Donna and Rusty, who were profiled in the chapter on decision making, demonstrate this pattern. Donna earns nearly all the family's income, and Rusty is home with their two-year-old daughter, Emma. Donna has a great deal of difficulty discussing her relationship and iden-tifying Rusty's contributions to it. Rusty senses this. He feels Donna does not appreciate all he does as a stay-at-home father. And in terms of time and energy, their daughter, not Rusty, is Donna's priority.

Donna: [VT: What would you say are his strengths?] Hm. [Long pause.] I don't know. [She laughs.] I never thought about it much. I mean, he's kind of like, you know. [Pause.] I don't know. [VT: Well, how about *your* strengths—things *you* bring to the relation-ship?] Well, I don't know that either. [Pause.] I don't know. [Long pause.] [VT: Would you like to just skip this part?] Yeah, skip it. Pass!

Rusty: I'm like, the whole role-reversal, you know? I take care of them. I cook all their meals, and I make sure they get where they're going. And I'm in charge of the things the man is supposed to do also, you know? I do all the man's chores, plus, you know, all the domestic chores. So, you know, that's not easy for a man to do. [He laughs.] [VT: What's not easy?] Both. Either one would be easy. It's doing them both that's hard.

  I'm the last on the totem pole. Emma is her first priority, then me. But Emma's not gonna be here forever. But Donna doesn't realize that. She's not looking at that at all. I mean, she's not gonna be able to follow Emma when she leaves.

Based on other information from the interviews, as well as their questionnaire responses, Rusty does not do it all. Donna does a great deal of child care in the evenings and on weekends and contributes to domestic labor as well. However, Rusty does a great deal around the house and is the primary caregiver of their daughter, so it is striking that Donna could not list a single thing that he contributes. Rusty feels neglected and unappreciated in his relationship.

We see similar dynamics among other couples with higher-earning wives. For example, I interviewed Monica, whose husband told her what kind of car to buy, before I talked with her husband, Sam, and I asked her what she thought were her strengths or the things she contributes to the relationship:

> Gee, he probably won't be able to think of *any*. [We laugh] . . . I would probably say that I take care of the kids more than he does. I cook more than he does. I clean more than he does. I pay all the bills. I take care of all the finances, except investments. He does investments. . . . I do all the grocery shopping, usually, but now that we've been going to Price Club, he helps. He likes to do that. [She laughs.] . . . [VT: Do you think he appreciates your contributions?] [Big sigh.] Mmmmmmmmmm, sometimes. [She laughs.] You'll probably find out when you ask *him* these questions. He'll probably have to stop and think about what it is I do around here. [We laugh.]

Indeed, Sam did have a difficult time answering these questions. Instead of giving me a list of contributions, after searching a bit for an answer, he said simply: "I guess I'm more practical, while she's the planner. She contributes the things that most people probably don't think of." Including him.

This contrast between the two types of couples suggests that spouses in couples with higher-earning wives have more difficulty appreciating each other. Often this is because spouses' contributions are not considered gender appropriate. Notice that the income higher-earning wives contribute is not mentioned by either spouse. It is invisible in the couple's calculation that, overall, the spouses' contributions "balance out." Given a cultural prescription for husbands to engage in breadwinning activities and for wives to engage in domestic activities, comparison couples, who conform to these expectations, seem to have an easier time appreciating each other's contributions. That is, comparison couples are living out the marital contract as it is currently written in our culture, and so they are spared the tension of contesting the norm. This means that the conventional marital contract not only is a model for how spouses should think about themselves and interact within their relationships, but also determines the value of each spouse's contributions. So while higher-earning wives contribute more in practical terms, they are still judged by only some of their contributions—those that are consistent with the role of mother and keeper of the domestic realm.

Managing the tensions created by having or being a higher-earning wife is an important part of sustaining marital happiness in these relationships. As we are about to see, couples try to construct relationships that look more like conventional ones so they can feel good about their marriages.

DEFENDING HIS HONOR: "I'M NOT THE DOCTOR'S WIFE"

Husbands of higher-earning wives are sensitive that they may be viewed as the lower-status partner in their relationships. Mark is a part-time high-school sports coach whose wife, Tina, is a physician. Though he has taken primary responsibility for their one-year-old daughter, he insists, "I'm not the doctor's wife"—a kept woman who draws her status, and reason for being, from her husband. Most husbands with higher-earning wives are similarly concerned that they not be judged as inferior to their wives. To that end, they often pointed to more lucrative occupations they could be pursuing—if they wanted to, if they were trained for them, or if their families did not need more time with them.

For example, in the preceding chapter we saw how Wayne, home full time with his son, managed to keep a sense of himself as a professional by referring to his law degree when people ask what he does. Mark, who is not the doctor's wife, similarly refers to the master's in business administration he received a few years ago. This degree acts as a safety valve against the pressure to pursue a more lucrative occupation. Mark is currently coaching high-school sports because he dreams of becoming a Division I college coach someday:

I always knew I wanted to coach, but I was never sure if I could make it or not. . . . I don't question my ability, but whether you're going to get the breaks. It's almost like the entertainment business. You could be a great singer, but that doesn't mean you're ever gonna make a dime singing. . . . That's one of the reasons I married [my wife], . . . that was the thing that put me over the edge. [He laughs.] This is true, that's really what I want to do, but for some reason I didn't think I could, you know? You'd have to be poor for like five, six, seven years before you really can get a full-time job coaching. So you really need someone there to support you emotionally, and maybe even financially at times.

Mark's wife, Tina, is happy to support him and help him pursue his dream:

I'd like to see Mark get into his career so he is happy with it and feels fulfilled by it. . . . I hope he has whatever he wants out of coaching. . . . I don't think he has great aspirations. Just as long as he's having fun, he doesn't mind coaching Little League. [She laughs.] It doesn't have to be prestigious. So I'd like to see him be able to have the time to do that.

Mark has higher aspirations for himself than Tina has for him, but also there is no pressure, at least from her. The key point here is that, along the way, Mark received his MBA. He has never used it, but both he and Tina are very aware that Mark could go out, write a résumé, and command a good salary if the family needed it. Since the family does not, he is free to pursue the less lucrative occupation of coaching.

While only Mark and Wayne among the husbands have such advanced degrees or credentials that they are not using, all but one husband with a higher-earning wife want to better themselves occupationally. Each has plans for pursuing a more advanced degree, changing jobs, or moving up in his current occupation. Many of these plans are quite detailed, though only a few of the men have taken steps toward pursuing these goals. Whatever futures these men dream about, they are clearly motivated to prove that they can keep up with, or even surpass, their wives. This may be because many of the husbands in this sample have floundered a bit occupationally, while their wives have enjoyed (often unexpected) occupational success. This husband speaks for many:

Most of our marriage, she's made significantly more than I have. Like I said, I've been catching up, and hers has been stagnating. I think with promotions and things I could potentially [his voice trails off]. . . . She had been in the workforce a little bit longer than I had, and I'd been fumbling around, doing some other things.

This husband has been looking for opportunities to move up at work but has not found many. He is now looking into pursuing a doctoral degree to improve his chances for finding a better position.

Husbands are not motivated simply by a desire to keep up with their wives occupationally, however. Many talked about wanting to improve their job prospects so that their wives could cut back at work, moving to either part-time employment or full-time homemaking. They would love to be able to do this kind of favor for their wives. The comments of these husbands are typical:

Chris, a realtor: I guess what it is, is that I feel guilty that she has to work. . . . If she wanted to quit right now, we could get by. A lot better in six months, when the money starts coming in from these sales and things. If she wanted to quit [pause]—she said she wanted to go part-time, and I said, "Fine." Whatever she wants to do.

Adam, a medical technician: I'm trying to make my work better. I'm investing more in schooling for a new career [as a physician's assistant]. I want to build my career so June can stay home, eat bonbons, and watch *The Young and the Restless* if she wants. [He laughs.]

Husbands seem to emphasize their plans for occupational change to conform more closely to the conventional marital contract. They want to be primarily responsible for breadwinning and give their wives the option to work part-time or move out of paid employment altogether.

Disappointed Wives: "He Just Could Be Doin' So Much More"

Most higher-earning wives are at least somewhat disappointed that their husbands have not been more successful occupationally. In some cases, his salary is the key to her disappointment. Money is tight for the family, and the wife feels she is pulling her weight financially, so it is up to her husband to try to improve his job situation. In other cases, wives feel that what their husbands are doing is beneath them, and they want the men to be more ambitious at work. These feelings come out when I ask wives how they feel about the work their husbands do, or whether there have been any disappointments in their relationships.

For example, Alice, a regional manager of a cosmetics company, is married to Vince, who works as a paralegal. He worked in higher-education administration when they were first married and was involved in association work several years ago but was fired. He has not been able to find a job equal in pay or status to the one he lost. At sixty-one, Vince feels he is facing age discrimination. Alice is dissatisfied with his current job, though she is happy to see him working again:

> I feel he's grossly underpaid for the talents and skills he has. He makes $6.50 an hour with no benefits. He's challenged, in that what he's doing is new, but he doesn't like it, and I'm unhappy that he's not happy. For most people, their value is still based on how much money they make. That's hard for him. But I'm glad to see him walk out of the house in the morning with a suit on. I was unhappy when he wasn't earning any money and doing something for himself.

Later, Alice admits to being angry that Vince has not found a better job. She claims he just has not tried hard enough.

> I'm mad that Vince isn't making more money. He's accused me of being mad in the past, and I denied it, but now I see that it was true. I'm especially mad that he hasn't worked harder at finding another job. He didn't go out and meet people. He just sent out résumés. . . . He's more than what he does.

Other wives express similar disappointment. Maria is a medical transcriptionist making twice what her husband, Mick, makes as a service technician. I ask her how she feels about the work he does:

> To me, Mick would be the perfect teacher. I mean, he *was* a teacher. He was teaching high school in an all-boys school. To me, Mick is the ideal elementary teacher. And he just won't hear of it. I mean, he absolutely won't hear of it. And I just think that the work he does [pause]—it's not that it's *beneath* him, but he just could be doin' so much more.

Later in the interview, I ask Maria if there have been any disappointments in her relationship with Mick:

> The only disappointment has been Mick's salary. He'd probably have a fit if I said that—if he *knew* I said that. . . . He seems perfectly happy doing what he's doing and, you know, it's a commission type of thing. And even though he works very, very hard, he just doesn't get any money for it. But, you know, he said, "At least I don't have an ulcer." I didn't know him when he was in college, but he said he had ulcers. And when he was a teacher, he didn't even make it the first year. So he's happy, and he doesn't have ulcers, so that counts for something.

Her tone in this passage says otherwise. Her voice has an impatient, droning quality as she lists Mick's reasons for not wanting to make a change in his work (he was, in fact, the only husband not expecting to make an occupational change). Maria is disappointed in what Mick does for a living and does not fully understand why he will not find something better.

Higher-earning wives want their husbands to find better jobs so that they can be proud of what their husbands do, and so that the family can enjoy a higher standard of living. But many also want their husbands to improve their job situation so that the wives can cut back on paid employment. We heard Linda make this statement in the last chapter:

> Sometimes I feel resentful that I make more. Like I wish it was the other way around. [VT: How come?] Because I feel like . . . I can't go part-time, you know? It's like, I would like to go part-time, and stay home more with [our daughter], and do more house things, and have less stress. But I feel like I can't, because I am the one that makes more.

And again, Maria: "I just really think that he needs to be makin' more money. And then I would [pause]—could relax a little bit more, and not feel that I had to make up all the difference."

This Wasn't Part of the Deal

Only six of the twenty-two couples with higher-earning wives knew when they got married that this would be their situation. The newlyweds in these six marriages were in established occupations or were about to enter them, and both spouses knew that their respective choices would mean that the wives would earn more than their husbands, work in higher-status occupations, or both, at least for the foreseeable future. In that sense, this unconventional arrangement was "part of the deal" for these six couples. However, for the majority of couples in this sample, this situation was as unexpected as it was disconcerting. Wives might have found themselves promoted very quickly at work; husbands may have floundered a bit occupationally, either because they were not entirely sure what they wanted to do, or because they had experienced a layoff or been fired. For many couples, a combination of upward mobility for the wife and occupational stagnation (or downward mobility) for the husband led to their current circumstances.

That these diverging occupational paths were not part of the deal when the couples married would seem to explain why they are so anxious to try to change this situation, or to construct relationships that at least seem more conventional. Typically, both spouses want to see husbands work harder to find better jobs, often so that wives can relax at work and begin to concentrate their efforts on domestic duties. However, it is not just about choice. Even those individuals who chose to marry knowing how unconventional their relationships would be do not envision themselves remaining in this situation permanently. Remember that only one husband had no plans to move into employment that would improve his economic and status position. Even the men who willing gave up full-time employment to be full-time dads do not envision staying at home forever. It is a temporary situation that they more or less gladly embrace, but only until their children do not need them as much.

RESOURCE AND POWER SHIFTS: THE PULL
TOWARD THE CONVENTIONAL

Constructing as temporary the experience of having or being a higher-earning wife has enormous power implications. First, it is easier to ignore large differences in income and status if they are not seen as permanent. And if these differences are not openly acknowledged by couples, it is more difficult for wives to use their resource advantage to enhance their power within their relationships. Second, whatever additional power or influence the wives might enjoy as a result of their greater resources can more easily be swept away when economic circumstances change in favor of the husbands. The following couple demonstrates how easily such shifts can occur.

Chris and Ginny are an example of a couple in which the wife has earned more over a relatively long period. For most of their six-year marriage, Ginny has made more money than Chris. Her work has also been considered more important. Consequently, as they had children, Chris picked up a very large share of the domestic labor and child-care burden; at the time of the interviews, he was contributing close to half the domestic labor. However, Chris has grown increasingly resentful of the primacy given to Ginny's work and increasingly critical of Ginny as a wife and mother. He began working as a realtor within the last year, and this has caused some profound changes in their relationship. Chris and Ginny demonstrate how, even if a wife's greater resources can work to her advantage, the power dynamics in a relationship can shift very quickly and dramatically in favor of the husband.

Ginny and Chris

Ginny is a midlevel manager making $35,000 per year in a large government agency. Chris started working as a realtor within the last year and is just starting to bring in some "real income." He made about $11,000 last year. The couple receives an additional $34,000 in income from investment property that they own, which Chris manages (he reports this income as "his" on the questionnaire he filled out). They have daughters four months and three-and-a half years old.

The birth of their second child has precipitated a crisis in the family. Ginny took several months of maternity leave and has been back at work for a month. Her load has been unbearable. The week before the interview, she began to look for a part-time position in her agency. It was a hard decision to make. She had gone back to work full time after her first daughter was born, which was difficult but manageable. With the second child, Ginny is so exhausted and so impatient with the children that working full time does not seem worth it. She thinks the family is in a good financial position so she can make this move. They had been saving to move from their townhouse into a single-family home, and that money will cushion the blow from the drop in Ginny's income.

Ginny tries to put a positive spin on making this career move. She thinks working part-time will "take the edge off," and she will have the best of both worlds since she will work three full days a week and still retain all her benefits. She is, however, concerned about the impact on her career:

> The only thing I hated to do it was 'cause I *had* done very well there, and I probably would've been promoted relatively soon after I had gotten back, and now I probably won't get a promotion for a few years. But that's okay. . . . [VT: Was there any discussion of Chris changing his schedule to be home part-time?] We talked about it originally, when I was home on maternity leave. We even talked about him working at night, and I would work during the day, and then we wouldn't even *have* to have day care. But the closer it got to the time for me to go back, he just felt it wasn't gonna work. And then he did get the job working for a developer. He's selling fourteen of his homes, so he has to work Friday, Saturday, Sunday, Monday, Tuesday.

They considered having the kids stay with Chris on Wednesdays and Thursdays, but he still has a lot to do on his days off. "And he just doesn't really *want* to do that," says Ginny.

Ginny is reluctant to give up her current job, a good one with high visibility. She has talked to her boss twice to try to convince her that she could do the job part-time or job share, but her boss has not been accommodating. Ginny has her eye on a part-time vacancy in another department that she will take if she has to. She likes what she is doing now, and she worries about being able to get "back on track" when she returns to full-time work in the future. But Ginny tries to look at the benefits of going part-time. She describes herself as career minded up to this point and realizes that she has her entire life to be involved in work; she would rather change directions for a few years and enjoy her children while they are young. In short, she is about to give up a very successful career trajectory, and work she loves, to accommodate the needs of her family.

Ginny feels she owes a great deal of her success to the support of her husband, Chris. She says she would not have made it so far, so fast, without his help. Historically, though, Ginny has not been as supportive of Chris's occupational plans. Throughout their marriage, Chris has tried to figure out a way to develop his own business, and Ginny has not been comfortable with that:

> We used to always have the discussion about him working for him-self. We used to *always* get into fights . . . slam-door type of deal. Because I feel very strongly that I need to work for some*one*, and he feels very strongly that he can do it on his own. And he has a lot of different ideas, and ways to invest money, and things like that. So we always had quite a few discussions about that, and he felt that I wasn't being supportive.

These arguments were so fierce and frequent that around the time their first daughter was born, Chris and Ginny considered separating. They went to marital counseling and discovered that "we had a lot going for us" and managed to work it out. As time went on, Ginny says, she mellowed a bit. She felt more secure, knowing that her salary could pay their mortgage, so she was more willing to let Chris give his ideas a try. Ginny says they have not fought about his work in almost two years, and she is proud of what he is doing now. She is pleased that he enjoys work-ing in real estate and that he seems to be good at it.

Chris agrees that his work has been a source of conflict for the couple:

> My biggest complaint with Ginny is that when Ginny's involved with something, like school or whatever, I try to become involved with it. She never becomes involved in anything I want to do. . . . I think that we were close to divorcing, and it was because she just did not become involved in anything I wanted. For Ginny, she would've been happy if I had stayed on at Marriott and, you know, moved up.

Chris has wanted to work for himself for a number of years and has finally made the occupational move. He is very happy working as a real-tor. He likes the autonomy:

> In this particular instance, if I make a mistake, I know it's costing me money—it's costing *me*. But if I have a hunch, and I've done my research, and I want to make a decision on what I feel is necessary for my business, I can do that. And if it succeeds, it succeeds, and I'm rewarded for it. If it fails, I learn from that and move on.

Although Ginny's attitudes have shifted in recent years and she is now supportive of Chris's working for himself, this is still an important issue for the couple and an ongoing sore spot for Chris. He is getting support from Ginny, and she is pleased and proud that he has found work that excites and challenges him. But Chris does not feel he is getting the kind of enthusiasm or involvement from her that he desires, and this is disappointing for him.

Chris is also upset about the division of household labor. He is very critical of Ginny and her contributions at home. When I ask him to list Ginny's strengths, or the things she contributes to the family, he responds: "Let me tell you her weaknesses. Then maybe her strengths will come to me." He expresses his frustration with what he sees as her inability to get the house in order:

> One of the things I have a problem with Ginny right now is, at work Ginny's a very competent person. Or that's my perception. Obviously that's other people's perception, because she's gotten promoted and awards and things. But at home, and I don't know if it's me or what. . . . I guess what it is, is that I feel guilty that she has to work. And yet, that's what she wants to do. . . . Whatever she wants to do. But yet, I still work, and I still take care of the house, and I still get the kids up in the morning, pick them up, get them dinner—things like that.

Chris compares Ginny, unfavorably, with other mothers who work outside the home—his old boss in particular: "She works ninety hours a week, has twins and another kid, a husband, and I don't know what their personal life is, but she does it all, and she never complains." Not knowing about their personal life is key in this comparison, but this lack does not alter Chris's feeling that his wife does not measure up to other women in similar (or worse) situations. Chris says: "I'm contributing what I feel to be more than 50 percent. Now Ginny does a lot. She does the little things, like shopping for clothes, which I hate to do. Things which no one ever sees . . . but she whines. [He whines, to imitate her.]" They have discussed the disorganization at home, but nothing has changed, from Chris's perspective. He has recently taken to putting all Ginny's things into boxes and putting them in her room upstairs for her to deal with. "Needless to say, there's about twenty boxes upstairs," says Chris.

Chris and Ginny seem to split the physical household labor and child care more equally than any other couple does, though Ginny still does more (especially when it comes to invisible work). There are times when Ginny wishes Chris would do things, such as taking out the trash and recycling, without having to be reminded, but overall she feels he does plenty; Ginny is one of the many wives who feels she needs to do more. What is interesting about their struggle is that Chris experiences doing less than half the household labor as a major and, more importantly, unfair burden. He also seems to underestimate all that Ginny does contribute to the household. For example, Chris describes his responsibility for taking the kids to day care each morning, but in the chapter on domestic labor Ginny describes all the prep work she does (laying out clothes, making bottles, packing the diaper bag) that makes that task much easier for him. They both seem to place a high value on what Chris contributes around the household while ignoring or minimizing what Ginny does.

Understanding Chris's hostility is important because most husbands were nowhere near as critical of their wives as he. The underlying problem for Chris seems to be that Ginny's work has historically been more important than his, and he now resents it:

> I have found that when Ginny was making more money than me, . . . I got the impression that Ginny felt her job was more important than [mine]. I don't know if it was a matter of making more money. Well, let's face it. Ginny was, and if she continues going the way she will, she'll be very successful. She'll get the executive service probably very early. And then if she wanted to move on to corporate, she'd be the equivalent of a senior VP, but that's if she wants. So yeah, in that position, her job is more important. My job is basically money; . . . her job is more important, not for the money, but because . . . of its potential for her. Where me, as a secretary, it wasn't . . . [his voice trails off]. And because of that, I assumed the roles of the one who will pick up the kids, and who will take 'em in the morning; . . . my job has taken a backseat to her job.

In this light, Chris's complaints about the household disorganization and the burden he is carrying seem to be about his work not receiving the respect or consideration he feels it deserves. Until recently, Chris had nothing that either he or Ginny would have called a "career." And as the partner with the less important work, Chris consciously assumed a more substantial portion of the burden at home. He has given Ginny quite a bit of support, but it is clear he wants to back away from that. He wants *his* work to be more important, and they seem headed in that direction; Ginny's move to part-time work is an important step in this process. Her work will still be important to her, but it will be less a career and may no longer receive first consideration by the couple.

Another shift appears to be under way between Ginny and Chris. As Chris is enjoying the freedom to make decisions in his new business, he is beginning to act autonomously when it comes to the couple's finances. He and his brother went in together on a deal just last week without Ginny's knowledge:

> I bought some real estate. Anyway, I ended up spending $800,000, and I didn't tell her, which shocked me because Ginny and I discuss everything. I think that from the questionnaire you'll see that I answered that we discussed [pause]—everything's fifty-fifty.

Given their history of making joint decisions, Chris seemed genuinely surprised by his behavior as he told the story, but not apologetic. At this point, Chris does all the bills and handles the family's considerable investments, so he enjoys a great deal of financial control. If he continues to act independently in these areas, the power shift will be complete. Work, money, and domestic labor will be restructured according to his agenda as he and Ginny move quickly and deliberately toward a more conventional marriage.

IN THE MEANTIME: HIDING AND IGNORING DIFFERENCES IN INCOME AND STATUS

In many cases, the plans that spouses have for moving their relationships in a more conventional direction will take years to come to fruition, as husbands pursue advanced degrees or try to move up at work. The task in the interim is to find ways to minimize the differences that make them uncomfortable. The following two couples demonstrate how they have accomplished this. Cindy and Don feel tension in their relationship, based largely on the educational and status differences between them. They manage this tension by living in separate social worlds generated by their separate statuses. June and Adam cannot ignore the status and income differences between them, so they work to hide June's income advantage and choose to live in a world dictated by Adam's status.

Cindy and Don

We have heard from Cindy and Don in earlier chapters. Cindy is a special education teacher with a master's in her field; Don is a welding technician. They have been married ten years and have three boys, ages nine, five, and fourteen months. Both have a varied occupational history, including periods of full- and part-time employment for each spouse, as well as time spent at home caring for the children and pursuing schooling. They met while Cindy was in college. Don was working as a messenger/delivery person. He had tried college but decided it was not for him. Shortly after they met, Don decided to go to welding school. Cindy recalls:

> When I first met Don, he was a messenger. He'd just drive around in a car and deliver things for a company. It was really, you know, a real dead-end kind of job. And I don't know if it was because I was in college, or he had just reached that time of his life, or maybe I prodded and pushed, I can't remember. But he decided to go to welding school.

Don worked as a welder for several years while Cindy worked on her master's degree. During this time, their first son was born. When their son was a toddler, Don quit his job and stayed home to be with him and complete his associate's degree in computers. He was home for three years. Don thinks this experience changed him in important ways, and he sees housework and child care differently than most men do.

> You see how hard it is to take care of a kid. It's a tremendous amount of energy to expend. Not just so much the physical, it's the mental. . . . Then there's a lot of rewards with it, too. Yeah, I would definitely say that had a lot to do with [my attitude now]. You complain about the way somebody waits on you in a store. Then you go to work at the store and find out what they have to deal with—the cash register doesn't work, and they're trying to help you with a broken cash

register—and you don't realize that as the customer. It's just being on the other side of the fence.

Since he has been on both sides of the fence, I asked Don if he preferred one over the other. He says: "I would stay home if I had the chance. I would be a homemaker. If we could afford it, I would do it; . . . you know, kids are only young for so long. Whereas you can always get a job, you can't always have a one-year-old."

Don's description of being at home sounds almost idyllic. Cindy remembers this period in their life very differently. She says Don was miserable at home and that it was the worst point in their marriage. They almost separated over it.

> I think it went so against what he had been raised seeing and it made him feel worthless, which is a shame, because I did not share that [feeling.] The way I look at it is that we're a team, and that if I'm making money or he's making money, we're making it for the good of the family, as a team. And I think he believes in that theoretically and intellectually, but emotionally, I think it's very easy to fall back to what you're used to. And possibly he even got some bad press from his family, I don't know. But it was *very* hard for him. He had *terrible* temper tantrums, where he was just impossible. Anyway, then he went to work full time, and I could see a big difference. It made him much happier.

They both report that they sought counseling to help them through this time, and that they seriously considered separating. Don blames the troubles on their being so short of money, since he was not working and Cindy was just starting out in her career. However, it is difficult to see, given Cindy's account, how Don could be happy staying at home full time again.

After Don received his associate's degree in computers, he started working full time, and Cindy worked part-time for the next several years. For the last three years, they have both worked full time. Don has never found a job in the computer field. No one would pay him more than six dollars an hour to start, and he needs to make more than that. He has been taking a class here and there in an effort to earn a bachelor's degree in computers, but he has far to go. Cindy is not sure if he will make it.

She tries to be supportive of Don, but she sees some real differences between them occupationally. When comparing their work, she sees her job as more secure and thinks she derives more satisfaction from her work than he does. I ask if his work is a "job" and hers a "career."

Yeah, I'm trying to think. I guess to some extent that is true. He is still going to college. He takes a course every semester, except for summer, and [he's] hoping that eventually he may become an engineer, or move [pause]. I guess I feel like [my work] is pretty much where I am, and I'm happy with it. And eventually it might be nice to go on and get my doctorate, and that's kind of fluff. Whereas for him, I think he looks at where he is as, what you said, a job. Although it's an area that he wants to be in. Although he *does* hope to move himself up via education. He only got the two-year degree at the time he stayed home, and he would like to go on and get the four-year degree and move into something different. But I don't know if he *really* sees himself doing that.

Cindy is disappointed that Don has struggled occupationally. This becomes clear when she talks about how she feels about the work he is doing now:

Usually I'm willing to be happy with the work that he does. His parents, especially at the time he was going to college, would say to me, "You gotta *push* Don. You gotta do this, you gotta do that." And I would say, "You know, I married Don because he's my friend. I didn't marry him because he was a brain surgeon, or because I had a desire for him to become independently wealthy." I knew all along, when I married him, that that probably would not occur. So, you know, it's very important to me that he's happy. I guess sometimes it scares me when he says he *isn't* happy with what he does, because I kind of think, "Well, God, what are his options?"

As Cindy and Don talk about their work and their feelings about what the other does, it is easy to see the distance between them occupationally. They do not discuss their work at home. Don says his wife likes her work, and he thinks that is great—it is something she has always wanted to do. Cindy says, "He works with things that work or don't work, which is something that is totally out of my frame of reference."

She adds that he "has to put in seven o'clock to four o'clock, rather than most people, it seems to me, get a half-hour lunch as part of their day. He doesn't get that." This, to her, is a signal of the lower status of his work; he does not get the same perks or benefits that "most people" do. In fact, when I ask Cindy to place them within the class system, she refers to herself as "professional" and Don as "blue-collar."

This occupational distance reflects an intellectual gulf between them. This difference becomes clear when they talk about how they make decisions. They have had heated arguments over money on many occasions, and Cindy does not feel they work well together when making decisions. If she wants something, she has to "go through the back door" with Don.

> If there's a big purchase that I want to make, like right now, I would like to buy some living-room furniture, because we've *nothing*—no furniture in our living room. And so I'll raise the fact that I'd like to, you know, look at different things. And then initially he'll say, "Oh, no, we can't afford that." And so I'll get my shackles [*sic*] up and say, "Oh? Well, then how come we can afford this, this, this, and this? This is important!" . . . We are not very good at just sitting down and directly resolving things. We both, you know, fly off the handle, and he gets very sarcastic. . . . There's also the problem, too, of not having very much time to just be alone together and talk. We're not making the time, you know? . . . We don't really, I think, sit down and discuss it in a *meaningful* way.

Cindy seems to feel that this difficulty making decisions reflects a distance between them that troubles her:

> Well, sometimes it's hard, with a relationship. Like, Don doesn't read. He doesn't read the newspaper, he looks at the ads. He doesn't read books. I think he had learning disabilities, as a special educator, that were never really looked at. When he writes, I can tell. But I think sometimes, the fact that he's not as educated as I [pause]—frustrates me. And I wonder if I had not been in a situation where I was nineteen and my parents were separating, if maybe I had dated more guys, then I would *know* for sure. Right now, I just don't know. . . . I hope to find that we have enough in common, and that we appreciate the

differences in each other, that we'll be able to stay together. But sometimes the lack of education, the lack of reading, being able to relate on that level, him—from my point of view—reacting often emotional on issues, rather than through using a base of knowledge, frustrates me.

Cindy is concerned about the relationship. Both spouses say they do not spend nearly enough time together, and they blame it on the struggle to raise three young boys. However, their lists of individual leisure and social activities suggest that something else may be going on here. Cindy has time to have lunch or dinner and go to the movies or to dance class with friends from work and college. Don spends evenings and weekends hanging out with his friends, working on cars. Don and Cindy seem to socialize with friends from their respective "worlds." There is plenty of time for individual activities, but "no time" together. They seem to have fallen into this strategy to maintain their relationship. They each avoid the distance between them by spending time with people who are like them. This is problematic for Cindy, because the time spent with friends who are "interesting and articulate," she says, makes her wonder "what have I missed" and "am I happy in this relationship." She says she knows they need to spend more time together, but she is afraid that if they do, they will discover that they do not enjoy each other's company or have much in common anymore. Living in separate worlds, then, seems to be an effort to manage the tensions created by the status difference between them. Though this strategy allows them to avoid some potentially painful and messy issues, the tensions are still palpable. For Cindy, at least, leading separate lives is not a wholly successful solution.

June and Adam

June and Adam have done a more complete job of hiding the differences between them. Adam is a medical technician in the military, making $17,000 per year. June is a military officer administrating a $144 million budget, making $36,000 per year. They have been married for two and one-half years and have a twenty-month-old son. This couple is unique in that they cannot ignore the difference in status between them. The military is very deliberate about its rank structure, and the gulf between officers and enlisted personnel is enormous. It is also difficult for this couple to separate their statuses the way Don and Cindy have, because they work in the same military hospital and know many of the same people. However, they both recognize the differences between them and work together to minimize them. To this end, they have adopted a strategy of making her work, including the income and status that accompany it, invisible.

Like other higher-earning wives, June is disappointed in her husband's work:

> He's smart at what he does, so I feel proud for him. But I have higher aspirations for him that I'm not sure if he goes along with or not. [VT: What would you like to see him do?] [She sighs.] He really has made steps toward becoming a physician's assistant, but I want him to get . . . picked up in the navy as a commissioned officer. . . . I think I want it a lot more than *he* wants it.

Though June would like to see Adam work harder at improving his career, she is grateful for the support that he gives her. Over time, she has grown to appreciate

> the fact that it doesn't bother him that [pause]—my career [pause]— seems to be important [pause]—be *very* important [pause]—be as important as his. And the fact that I make more money than him doesn't bother him a bit. And I like that, because lots of people have problems with that sort of thing.

She seems to be trying hard not to say that her work is more important than his, though she does admit to having these feelings later in the interview when I ask the question directly:

> [VT: Do you see either job as more important?] You want me to be honest? [She laughs.] Mine's more important because it brings in more income. Mine's more important because it has a bigger impact on navy medicine, to be honest. I *think* Adam would agree with that. And I take mine a lot more seriously than he does. . . . Some days I'll come home like life or death. "Something's gotta be done or it's all gonna fall apart!" And he *never* gets that wrapped around an axle.

In fact, Adam does not agree that June's job is more important than his. He is a medical technician who supervises the surgical preparations for a suite of operating rooms. It is his job to be sure that all the required instruments and materials are available in each operating room before surgery. He feels his job is more important than his wife's because he is working with people's lives. As for June's work, Adam says that she is smart, hardworking, and talented, and that she is more committed to her work than he is to his own. Still, he thinks he has it "better" at work—that he gets more respect:

> It's difficult to look at it from her being the officer and me being the enlisted person, okay? Because I probably get more respect, a lot of times, than she does, even though she deserves it more than I do. Because I've been in for so long, and I know so many people, and I have to deal with so many different ranks. . . . It's difficult for guys like me. I may not have the knowledge written down on a piece of paper somewhere, but I've got it up here [points to his head].

Several times in the course of the interview, Adam talks on the one hand about how unfair it is that he does not get the respect he deserves because he is enlisted and does not have a college degree. On the other hand, he tries to show how much respect he receives because of who he is, how long he has been in the navy, the quality of his work, and whom he knows. His discussion of their respective jobs is a reflection of his struggle to be supportive of June's work while maintaining the dignity and worth of his own.

There is another level of struggle over work in this relationship, and it is here that June's work suffers. She says:

> I don't like feeling that I always have to make a choice between whether I'm gonna do my job or whether I'm gonna come home and take care of my family. I'm sure that's something you're lookin' for [she laughs], but it's true. I mean, Adam and I have argued *many* times on the demands that I have at work, and why can't I just *drop* it. And I can't *do* that. He doesn't understand that very well.

Near the end of her interview, she comes back to the difficulty created by the demands her job places on her. "I think he really *does* understand it, but he doesn't agree with it. And he thinks it shouldn't happen, because he doesn't agree with it. And in reality, it happens."

The stress June feels in her job is largely created by the way the couple organizes child-care responsibilities. June says she cannot just punch out like an enlisted person could. Overtime is expected. It is especially stressful for her, because she has to pick their son up by the time the day-care center closes at 5:30 P.M., and that is a daily struggle. What is interesting about this struggle is that it could easily be resolved. Adam takes their son to day care, so June picks him up, "to be fair." They both leave the house at about the same time each morning, between 5:45 and 6:00 A.M., but Adam is usually home by 4:00 or 4:30. If June dropped their son off and Adam picked him up, not only would June be relieved of this end-of-the-day stress, but also their son would spend less time in day care (a priority for every other couple in this study). But, if they did this, Adam would lose the "quiet time" he enjoys in the afternoon. He also would lose his ability to control how much time his wife puts in at work.

While June and Adam are well aware of the income and status differences between them, they have done a pretty thorough job of hiding them. The money system for this couple obscures the potential power in June's greater income. Each spouse has a separate account, but June monitors all the bills. Generally, Adam is responsible for his truck payment, child support for the son from his first marriage, and the mortgage payment on the house they bought at their last duty station (the rental income they receive from that property is deposited back into his account). June pays for everything else, though occasionally she will ask Adam to pay a bill she thinks he can handle, such as the cable TV bill. June never feels she has enough money left over to spend as she pleases; the cost of living is high in this area. Adam says they both have "more than enough money left over" to do what they want, though he admits, "I do more with mine than she does with hers." He even goes to June for money if he runs short before payday. This financial arrangement hides the fact that June makes more money. Essentially, she pays all the family's bills. The things Adam pays for do not contribute to their current quality of life. June has nothing left over, but Adam has plenty to spend. She evidently conceals from him even that she has no money left over, since he is convinced that she does.

June and Adam take similar pains to hide the status difference between them. They say that they rarely associate with other officers and describe this as a choice they both make. June says they are uncomfortable in that circle. However, the following comment from June suggests that Adam is the one who is uncomfortable.

> I've always balked at the expectations that are placed on officers. . . . Officers are supposed to be better than enlisted, and that can cause dilemmas in our household. If I have officers' functions to go to, he doesn't wanna go, or he doesn't know what's expected of him. You gotta make sure you say the right things. You gotta make sure you *do* the right things.

Adam confirms that he is uncomfortable socializing with officers. He resents that June is expected to attend these functions and that he has to accompany her; he calls it all "bullshit" and pokes fun at the rules:

> When I'm at her things, . . . I'm on my best behavior. Drink out of a glass, you know, I don't pick my teeth with a toothpick. [I laugh.] She put me through spoon-and-fork school when we got married. She goes, "Okay, honey, the first thing you gotta do . . ."—she gave me a little class. "This is your salad fork, this one's for this." What the hell do you need three forks for? Just have one fork. I mean, eat your salad, eat your steak, whatever you're gonna eat, with one fork!

June says they attend only events necessary for her work. They go to her functions, she says, but "we enjoy ourselves at his." They describe this as a joint preference, but it seems to be part of the effort to manage the difference in status between them by hiding her status privilege. This statement of Adam's communicates the pressure June feels to live in his world: "I don't change. I'm the same person. If she can deal with my lifestyle and enjoy my friends, it'll work."

Both these couples demonstrate the class antagonism, or clash, that can occur in dual-income families (Collins 1991). What is interesting is the way the clash has been resolved, or managed, in these cases. In an upward-striving society such as ours, one might expect these couples to seize the highest possible status for themselves and their families. They choose instead to live in separate status worlds or the lower of the two, respectively. Allowing the wife to define the family's status appears to be too threatening. Moving in separate circles, or in a world dictated by the husband's status feels more comfortable and is a way to manage the tensions generated by having or being a wife who earns more than her husband does.

BALANCING POWER AND HAPPINESS

Maintaining a satisfying relationship can be a challenge for couples with higher-earning wives. Husbands are often defensive about their lesser occupational accomplishments, vis-à-vis their wives. Correspondingly, wives are often disappointed that their husbands have not been more successful or brought home more money. Managing the tensions created by this situation is no small task.

Some of this tension or discomfort is evident in the difficulty spouses in these couples have in appreciating the contributions each makes to the marriage. Since spouses are not always contributing to their relationships in ways that conform to conventional gendered expectations, they do not always recognize the value of these contributions. Most striking is that these wives seem to receive very little credit for the substantial income contributions they make to their families.

Given the importance of money in U.S. culture, we might expect couples to place a high premium on the incomes these wives earn. The women themselves could feel great about being able to raise the standard of living for their families so significantly, and the men could be grateful that their wives provide well enough to take some of the pressure off them. Instead, spouses tend to downplay wives' income advantage. In fact, wives' monetary contributions are often not mentioned at all. Both husbands and wives prefer to emphasize the contributions that are more gender appropriate and consistent with the identities of mother and breadwinner. Couples seem to work to fashion more conventional marriages so spouses can see and appreciate each other in ways that make sense and feel more comfortable to them.

Constructing relationships that are more conventional has enormous power implications. By hiding or minimizing these large differences in income and status, wives lose whatever chance they might have to use these resources to enhance their power within their marriages. So it is not simply that women's resources are worth less, but that they are often made invisible and therefore seem not to count at all. This helps explain why these wives are unwilling to use their greater resources to negotiate for more power in their relationships.

Finally, when couples with higher-earning wives construct their situation as temporary, they undermine the potential for this experience to transform gender constructions and the conventional marital contract. Even couples who have been living this way for years do not define it as a permanent arrangement. Instead, they cling to the conventional gender identities of mother and breadwinner. All but one husband has plans to make occupational changes, and many of the wives express a desire to cut back on their paid work to better tend to domestic responsibilities once their husbands' plans come to fruition. Constructing their current situation as temporary means that there is no need to drastically alter the conventional marital contract in response to these unusual circumstances.

More importantly, this pull toward the conventional means that women have only a tenuous hold on whatever advantages they might be able to negotiate as a result of their greater incomes. There is a cultural "place holder," if you will, for men's power. We saw a similar dynamic in Chapter 4, when spouses felt that though wives could not exchange money for power, men still could, if and when they earned more. In this chapter, we saw that Ginny was able to get Chris to take on added responsibility at home when she was working the more important job. But now her occupational star is fading, while his seems to be rising. This trend is setting in motion a profound shift whereby she will become more completely responsible for the domestic realm and he can make major financial decisions without even her knowledge. Their case underscores the power that is culturally available to men and demonstrates that whatever power shifts women are able to negotiate can be easily swept away when economic circumstances change in favor of their husbands.

CHAPTER 8

Floating Along for the Ride?

Higher-Earning Wives and the Prospects for Gender Change

While couples with higher-earning wives seem to be moving against the cultural tide, they are not making waves. Though these wives hold tremendous resource advantages over their husbands, they are unable or unwilling to use their incomes to negotiate more egalitarian power relationships in their marriages and therefore do not seem to present a serious challenge to the gender structure. In this final chapter, I highlight the central findings of this study and explore what these couples can tell us about gender and the power dynamics within marriage.

I also consider what these results can tell us about the prospects for gender change. I recognize that these findings will be disconcerting to many. In an age where women have come a long way and have the greatest range of options in history, it is disturbing to see that wives with such tremendous resources at their disposal largely conform to conventional expectations that limit their power. However, while the results presented in this book may seem regressive, couples with higher-earning wives can teach us something about the possibilities for reconstructing gender. That is, even as they conform to conventional expectations, these couples demonstrate that new gendered understandings and constructions are possible.

Gender Trumps Money in the Marital Power Equation

Higher-earning wives represent an important case for understanding marital dynamics because they pit gender and income against each other as potential sources of power within marriage. They give us the opportunity to assess whether a woman's bringing in the greater income can disrupt the cultural expectation for men's dominance within marriage. However, we have seen that these wives have not used their substantial income advantages to negotiate an equally substantial reduction in their domestic labor load, or more equal control over financial or other decisions.

This means that gender trumps money in the marital power equation. Men retain their right to domestic services from their wives and continue to exercise a great deal of control over money and decision making within these marriages. They continue to benefit *as men* from the privileges they have enjoyed under the conventional marital contract, even when they are no longer the primary breadwinners in their families. The power dynamics between the spouses in these couples have little to do with income and everything to do with gender.

Women are disadvantaged in the marital power game. That they cannot trade their incomes for the privileges men have historically enjoyed means that women's money is "worth less" culturally than men's (Blumberg and Coleman 1989; Hochschild 1989). The resources spouses bring to their relationships are gendered: Their value is based on who contributes them. Women get less credit for being the major earners in their families, and couples find ways to attach greater value to men's contributions.

However, it is not just that women's resources are worth less than men's would be under similar circumstances. Women's greater resources actually become liabilities for them in these marriages. Instead of trading their incomes for more help at home, wives take on more work to prove that they are appropriately feminine and to avoid further emasculating their husbands by pressuring them to do "woman's work." Instead of using their income advantage to negotiate more egalitarian power relationships with their husbands, wives try to compensate for it by deferring to their husbands and maintaining men's position of authority in the home. Overcoming the potentially damaging effects of their greater incomes adds to the tremendous burden that these wives already carry.

These results demonstrate that earning an income is not the ticket to equality that feminism thought it would be. Working and earning even a substantial income does not necessarily put wives on equal footing with their husbands. As we have seen, women's incomes do not automatically buy them the privileges that men have enjoyed. Their incomes do not entitle them to relief from domestic labor, or even the right to equal access to the family surplus. Having money of one's own may be a necessary condition for constructing a more egalitarian relationship, but it is not sufficient.

THE CONVENTIONAL MARITAL CONTRACT: REPRODUCING GENDER AND (HIDDEN) POWER

These results highlight the stability of the gender structure. Though these couples may represent one of the most promising options for rewriting the conventional marital contract, they seem to deliberately work to reproduce and conform to it. The spouses interact in ways that preserve men's dominance, in both real and symbolic terms, while they hold themselves and each other accountable for fulfilling the obligations associated with mothering and breadwinning. In these ways, the experiences of these couples highlight the ability of the gender structure to adapt to new and potentially anomalous social practices in ways that reproduce the status quo.

We have also seen how the gender structure shapes the power dynamics of these couples on three levels. At the institutional level, the conventional marital contract provides the beliefs and institutional arrangements upon which these couples draw. They confront a world in which men are encouraged and expected to be fully engaged in the labor market, and women, whether employed or not, are marginalized as caregivers (Williams 2000). To be a successful man is to embrace the identity of breadwinner; to be a successful woman is to embrace the identity of mother/homemaker. At the individual level, spouses in these marriages find these identities meaningful despite their unconventional circumstances, and they find ways to meet the expectations attached to these identities. At the interactional level, spouses work together to maintain conventional gender boundaries and hold each other (as well as themselves) accountable to the behaviors and expectations associated with them. Women emphasize the time and care they provide their families, rather than the large incomes they bring home. Similarly, couples find ways to continue to see men as providing for their families, even as they earn substantially less. Women also defer to their husbands in decision making to demonstrate that they are not trying to use their greater incomes to dominate their husbands. At each of these three levels, then, we find that couples with higher-earning wives reproduce, rather than challenge, the current gender structure.

By reproducing the gender boundaries embedded in the conventional marital contract, couples also reproduce the gendered power relations implied by these boundaries. By downplaying wives' substantial incomes and continuing to see men as breadwinners, husbands are able to retain and assert their dominance. By constructing wives primarily as mothers/homemakers, higher-earning wives are denied the power that might be available in their greater resources. Again, I want to highlight the important distinction I am making here: While the results demonstrate that wives defer to their husbands in these relationships, and often in very conscious ways, I am not arguing that these wives prefer to be dominated. Rather, these women are afraid that their greater resources will make them look powerful, or that their husbands will experience their resource disadvantage as domination—or worse, emasculation. Therefore, these wives defer to their husbands to prove that they are not trying to dominate them and are therefore "real" women and "good" wives.

Reinforcing the current gender structure also helps these couples feel better about their marriages. These spouses find themselves in a situation that produces a great deal of stress and tension, and they are looking for ways to make their marriages feel more comfortable and satisfying. These couples live in a culture that gives a great deal of lip service to egalitarian ideals but offers little in the way of meaningful role models to follow. Unless spouses happen to know a couple that has managed to work out a true partnership, they are largely left with a vision of marriage that no longer fits the reality of dual earners.

In this absence of alternatives, couples fall back on the wife-as-mother/husband-as-breadwinner expectations that they grew up with and that still exert a strong pull (Williams 2000). These higher-earning wives are unaccustomed to thinking of their incomes as the most important contribution they can make to their families, and so they value instead the time, attention, and care that stay-at-home moms are able to provide (Hays 1995). They judge themselves by that standard. Similarly, their husbands are unused to thinking about providing as a shared endeavor. A wife can help with this task, but husbands of higher-earning wives feel they retain the responsibility for a family's financial well-being, as evidenced by their plans to improve their employment situations so that their wives can cut back at work or stay home (Potuchek 1997; Wilkie 1993). Spouses find these conventional identities both comfortable and meaningful.

It seems very important to these spouses that they be able to see themselves and each other as meeting their conventional obligations, and there can be a great deal at stake here. For example, we know that being a breadwinner is so fundamental to a man's identity that threats to this role performance (by being un- or underemployed) can have serious repercussions on both individual men and their families—ranging from depression and strained relationships to substance abuse and violence (Rubin 1994). It should not be surprising, then, that these spouses work so hard to sustain more conventional gender boundaries and identities—especially when such identities seem so fundamental to one's sense of well-being.

However, embracing these identities has tremendous power implications. Under the conventional marital contract, the breadwinner is not just the major earner; he is also the head of the household. He enjoys the right to exert his will over other family members, as well as the right to a certain level of service from them (Bernard 1981). Being a mother, on the other hand, implies a level of selflessness and devotion that entails giving without concern for fairness or reciprocity (Hays 1995; McMahon 1995). Rather than demanding power, a mother feels a sense of obligation and gratitude to the man who supports her and her children. In short, the rights to power invested in these roles and identities are asymmetrical; the comfortable gender identities come with expectations for men's dominance. To embrace these identities, in conventional terms, is to largely accept this differential access to power.

These attachments to conventional identities provide perhaps the best example of how hidden power operates within marriage, but hidden power operates in other ways in these relationships. We have seen how wives monitor themselves and their interactions with their husbands, being very careful not to dominate them or undermine their authority. They want to avoid looking too powerful—to themselves, their husbands, and others—so they avoid displays that could be interpreted as bids for greater control. While this may not be a new task for women, it seems to take on heightened importance among these couples in which wives earn so much more. In this situation, maintaining the husband's dominance does not necessarily require him to assert a right to it but becomes a joint effort. And men's ability to command this kind of effort is another indication of the hidden power they enjoy within marriage.

These results demonstrate that the most important dynamics within marriage are often hidden—embedded in existing ideology or practices—but shape each spouse's ability to exercise power within marriage. Men continue to benefit from cultural conventions that exempt them from domestic labor and construct them as the heads of their households. While these conventions are being challenged by some, they continue to shape the lives of most married couples (Williams 2000). Perhaps most telling is that husbands' power and privilege within marriage is often preserved with the cooperation of wives. For women to participate in their own subordination, they must see it as somehow beneficial or important—the very definition of hidden power with which we began (Lukes 1976).

Above all, these couples show us that gender, not economics, is at the heart of men's privilege within marriage. This in-depth look at couples with higher-earning wives has given us a way to separate money from gender, and to examine the effects of each on marital power dynamics. Gender exerts an independent and potent influence on these dynamics. We can see how pressure to reproduce the gender structure undercuts whatever power might exist in these women's substantial incomes, and limits the ability of spouses to imagine new constructs that would alter the conventional balance of power in their marriages.

The Benefits and Costs of Reproducing the Gender Structure

To understand the choices made by these and other dual-income couples, we have to recognize that there are substantial benefits to reproducing both the conventional marital contract and the larger gender structure. Perhaps most importantly, these structures provide the stability so fundamental to basic human interaction. The gender identities of mother and breadwinner delineate responsibility for accomplishing the tasks of daily living. Only fifty years ago, this divided responsibility was widely accepted as vital to the survival of the family (Parsons and Bales 1955). While these expectations have become less determinative of behavior within individual families, they continue to exert a strong pull on couples (Williams 2000).

Resisting this pull requires a great deal of effort. One of the difficulties of trying to swim against this tide and construct an alternative or egalitarian relationship is that couples often feel that everything has to be discussed and negotiated. After all, one of the fundamental tenets of egalitarianism is not assuming that any person will take on a task or behave in a particular way based on gender. On what bases, then, *will* we decide these things? Will you cook because you are better at it? Or will I cook because I enjoy it more? Or will we pool our skills and creativity and cook together every night? Will we contribute an equal number of hours to child care each week, or a proportionate number of hours based on our work schedules? Trying to work out a fifty-fifty deal means discussions, schedules, and calendars—all of which can be a hassle. Couples often describe themselves as having "fallen into" a more traditional division of labor because it just seemed easier.

The benefits to men of a conventional arrangement are obvious. Men enjoy a clean home, hot meals, and well-adjusted, well-behaved children—all with comparatively little or no effort from them. They may participate in domestic labor, but often on the terms they choose—for example, opting to play with the children rather than wash the dishes. Husbands also claim the right to make important decisions and happily delegate responsibility for the little things that are of no consequence to them, knowing they can "put their foot down" if something displeases them.

It is important to note that this conventional arrangement offers benefits to women as well. While women are disadvantaged by the conventional marital contract overall, they enjoy privileges often unavailable to men. For example, women's paid employment is seen as an option, rather than as a duty. This means that it is easier for women to choose full-time homemaking and mothering as their life's work, with the corresponding right to be financially supported by their husbands. While this option increasingly reflects a class privilege, since fewer families can live comfortably on one income, staying at home is still an option that only wives typically enjoy.

Finally, conforming to the conventional expectations embedded in the gender structure gives both men and women a comfortable way to organize their lives and make sense of their experiences. Making the identities of mother and breadwinner central to their sense of self means that they can construct lives similar to those of their parents, siblings, friends, and neighbors. Even in the new millennium, trying to construct alternative identities often opens employed mothers up to the charge that they are pushy career women who value their own needs above their children's (Hays 1995). And men who are more involved at home—or make decisions that favor family interests over career advancement—often risk being marginalized by co-workers or charged by friends with being henpecked (Ehrensaft 1990). Good old-fashioned social disapproval (or accountability) adds another cost to swimming against the tide.

While we can easily understand the investments men and women have in the conventional gender structure, these commitments entail substantial costs. The most obvious costs are borne by women. Higher-earning wives, like other employed women, often face staggering fatigue due to overwork and lack of leisure time. In the long term, carrying this load means that resentment against husbands can build—not only because men are not doing their fair share at home, but also because they continue to disappoint their wives occupationally. Wives feel the burden of being the major breadwinners acutely and readily express their frustration and disappointment that their husbands have not been more successful or brought in more money.

Women also seem to bear the brunt of the work to maintain peace and harmony in the home. They often work to bolster their husbands' masculinity by deferring to them in the relationship and avoiding displays of power. This can entail tremendous psychic costs for women as they monitor their behavior and sensor themselves to avoid looking too powerful. Continually gauging their husbands' response to having a wife who earns more becomes another burden for these women to bear.

Beyond the marital relationship, the family obligations that women shoulder hurt them in the labor market, because wives often choose to cut back at work to manage the load at home (Williams 2000). This appears to be as true for higher-earning wives as it is for wives who are secondary earners. Remember that many of these wives wanted their husbands to earn more so they could cut back to part-time work or leave paid employment altogether. And even if every wife does not cut back at work to help manage the at-home load, that some women do leads employers to see all women as potentially less committed to their jobs, and therefore less deserving of the best positions, assignments, and compensation (Williams 2000).

In the long run, this strategy of cutting back at work to reduce work/family stress hurts women economically—in lost income, promotions, and pay raises. It can also make it difficult for women to reenter employment or "catch up" in their careers later. This may be of less concern in the context of a lifelong partnership. If a woman remains married and can rely on her husband to provide for her and her children, a strategy in which she cuts back on paid work seems sensible and can increase the family's quality of life. But today, when nearly one-half of all marriages are expected to end in divorce, it is a risky bet. In other words, embracing the gendered identities embedded in the conventional marital contract without the guarantee of the lifelong partnership implied by that contract means that a significant number of women and children will be economically vulnerable down the road.

It is tempting to see the current gender order as simply advantaging men at the expense of women. However, there are costs for men, though they are less immediately obvious. While most studies highlight the benefits for men of the gendered division of labor in the home, especially when men are able to resist women's efforts to increase their participation, there can be emotional costs for husbands. The quality of their marriages often declines when wives feel overburdened by the load at home (Coltrane 2000; Wilkie, Ferree, and Ratcliff 1998). Wives can become bitter and resentful, leading them to withdraw emotionally and sexually from their husbands (Hochschild 1989). Equally important, by refusing to share in family work, men are missing out on the enormous rewards associated with raising children. Being intimately connected to their sons and daughters can give men a more vital emotional life. The greater sensitivity and emotional expression that men develop as the result of involved fathering transfers to their relationships with their wives, strengthening the marital bond. By continuing to see themselves as breadwinners and leaving the bulk of child rearing to their wives, men are missing experiences that would greatly enrich their lives (Hawkins et al. 1993).

There is, however, a much more serious cost for men in reproducing the conventional marital contract. The story that Joyce told (Chapter 3) about a co-worker who suddenly lost her child-care provider has haunted me throughout this project. Joyce came to the chilling conclusion that, given a choice between a husband and a reliable child-care provider, the husband has to be "the one to go." Her choice points to a more significant cost on the horizon for men. In *Brave New Families*, Judith Stacey (1990) argues that, because so many fathers abdicate emotional and financial responsibility for their children postdivorce, many men are becoming "irrelevant" to their families. Joyce's story suggests that men may also face the danger of becoming irrelevant *within* their families if they continue to allow women to carry such heavy loads alone. That is, while men have been largely successful at avoiding domestic labor and child-rearing responsibilities, this success may come at a cost. Men may risk becoming expendable in the eyes of their wives and children.

FINDING A BETTER DEAL?

With the load that higher-earning wives bear, we might ask why these women do not leave their husbands for partners who would more highly value their resource contributions. Some of them have considered it, and at least one couple divorced within two years of being interviewed. But we have to recognize that the search for a man willing to share power could come at a great cost. While divorce might seem to be an easy answer, it is always an expensive endeavor, both emotionally and economically—even for women with such financial resources at their disposal. First, these families rely on two incomes to maintain their standards of living. Divorce would mean a significant financial loss for these women and their children. Second, there are personal resources that cannot be easily transferred to another relationship—loving a particular person, understanding and anticipating that individual's tastes and needs, sharing a history, and so on (England and Farkas 1986). In other words, while marriage can be described as a contract, it is distinct from a free-market exchange (Brines 1994). Spouses are not as easily interchangeable as other commodities, and it is often difficult to drive the hardest bargain possible, especially for women—even, as we have seen, for women with tremendous resources.

Additionally, advising women to increase their power by divorcing is built on an assumption that gives us another window into the hidden power advantages enjoyed by men: Men have more power to define the terms of their marital relationships. If wives look for replacements for their husbands, presumably these will be men, which means these women will confront the same gendered power relations in subsequent marriages. In other words, if a woman's best recourse in these relationships is to find another partner, this underscores the fact that women's relative power depends on men's willingness to share theirs.

Because divorce is such a potentially costly option for women, preserving these marriages and maximizing their quality becomes very important (Agarwal 1997). In this light, wives' decisions to bolster their husbands' power make sense. In the absence of good alternatives, wives need to find ways to feel good about themselves (as women), their husbands (as men), and their relationships. Constructing marriages that are more egalitarian seems unworkable, or undesirable, for these couples. Divorce would be costly. Therefore, they focus their efforts on making their unusual marriages look and feel more comfortable and conventional.

THE PROSPECTS FOR GENDER CHANGE

Family and gender scholars often say that the lives of women have changed dramatically over the last several decades, while the lives of men have changed relatively little. This disjuncture between the enormous changes in women's responsibilities and the comparatively small changes in men's has been characterized as a "stalled revolution" (Hochschild 1989). Implicit in this term is the notion that relations between men and women are changing dramatically, and that the current difficulties in balancing work, marriage, and family life are merely a temporary pothole on the road to greater equality between husbands and wives.

The results presented in this book call into question the assumption that relations between men and women are progressing steadily, inevitably toward equality. Women moved into higher education and the world of paid employment, at least in part, to enable them to stand on more equal footing with men. Though many women are now capable of commanding high salaries and have entered male-dominated occupations, these resources have done little to improve women's power in their most intimate relationships. Wives are unable to trade their incomes for a proportionate reduction in domestic labor or greater control within their marriages. The revolution is still stalled.

Even higher-earning wives seem incapable of moving the gender revolution forward. They represent a very small, privileged group of women who hold tremendous resource advantages compared to their husbands. By all rights, they should be on the cutting edge of gender change. Yet, they behave in ways that conform to many conventional expectations for women and work with their partners to reproduce men's dominance in the private sphere. Their experiences underscore the stability of the gender structure and do little to jumpstart the revolution.

Moving the Revolution Forward

We will have to look elsewhere for potential egalitarian models. Moving the revolution forward will require learning more about the experiences of a wider variety of couples, because the ability to construct alternative relationships may vary by social location. For example, the gender boundaries of mothering and breadwinning may be less salient for African Americans and Hispanics than for whites. We know that, because of economic and social discrimination, African American men have historically had a much more tenuous relationship to the occupational structure than have white men. This may mean that black husbands and wives have less ambitious or rigid expectations for men occupationally.

We also know that the experience of black women has not been dominated by the ideology of separate home/work spheres to the extent that white women's experience has. Constructions of black womanhood, especially for middle- to upper-middle-class wives, have always included a responsibility to work outside the home (Landry 2000; Williams 2000). For black women of lesser economic means, choosing not to work has rarely been an option. Consequently, African American men have more liberal attitudes toward working wives and tend to spend more time in household labor (Blee and Tickamyer 1995; Shelton and John 1993). We see similar patterns among Hispanics, with men contributing more at home and women seeing paid labor as a way to contribute to the well-being of their families (Shelton and John 1993; Segura 1994).

This means that there are good reasons to suspect that African Americans and Hispanics think about work and family responsibilities differently than do whites. More fluid constructions of the gender boundaries of mothering and breadwinning may also lead to greater sharing of power between spouses. A more complete understanding of the gendered power relations within marriage demands that we know more about the gendered constructions and practices of a wider range of couples.

Moving the revolution forward will also mean taking greater advantage of what we already know about relationships that are more equitable. While the evidence suggests that wives face an uphill battle in the quest for marital equality, we know that such relationships are possible (Coltrane 1996; Deutsch 1999; Risman and Johnson-Sumerford 1998; Schwartz 1994). However, they require concerted effort on the part of both spouses to reject the breadwinner ideology that seems so firmly rooted in most dual-earner couples. Constructing these more egalitarian relationships requires spouses to place equal importance on each of their jobs or careers, weighing occupational decisions jointly and carefully with the interests of both partners in mind. Such couples consciously undermine the assumption that men's work comes first and, in so doing, create conditions under which a more equitable sharing of all of the work associated with family life becomes more likely.

Partners in egalitarian relationships are also driven by a desire to be fair with each other. This leads them to share the load at home, ensuring that each partner is involved in the full range of responsibilities associated with caring for and raising a family. Spouses also demonstrate a commitment to treating each other as equal partners within the marriage, sharing decision-making and money-management responsibilities. In other words, successful egalitarian relationships are driven by a commitment to feminist ideals, which involve undermining the gender boundaries of mothering and breadwinning and rejecting the conventional gender arrangements that call for men's dominance and women's subordination.

While the experiences of higher-earning wives highlight the resilience of the gender structure, the available work on egalitarian couples demonstrates that new gender constructions are possible. Spouses can share responsibility for earning the family's income, and respect and appreciate each other for the labor their paychecks represent. They can share the physical and emotional labor required to maintain a home and raise children, thereby valuing that labor and ensuring that no one carries an undue portion of this burden. Treating each other as true partners undermines men's dominance in a direct and meaningful way.

However, creating a real partnership means managing the tensions between egalitarian ideology and conventional gendered practices, and these tensions can be considerable. Actively working to rewrite the marital contract often requires engaging in calculations that seem out of place in a love relationship. Efforts to be fair in child care, for example, can feel like high-level treaty negotiations. Women may be left wondering, "What kind of mother *am* I, that I'm fighting over who *has* to take care of our children tonight?" Similarly, keeping track of the time spent on domestic labor or in efforts to support the other person's work can leave spouses feeling like accountants or mercenaries rather than lovers. As we said at the beginning, What's in this for me? is a question one is not supposed to ask of marriage.

Yet, if gender change is the goal, such questions are unavoidable; equity, if not equality, demands them. They represent the only way out of the stalled revolution. It is my hope that the experiences of the couples presented in this book will help others to think through their own relationships and their personal commitments to conventional gender arrangements and identities. Couples with higher-earning wives can sensitize *all* couples to the subtle power dynamics in their relationships. Only when individuals are fully aware of their own investments in conventional gender arrangements can they actively work to undermine them.

Effectively disrupting the gender structure will require a great deal of commitment and vigilance. The gender imperatives of mothering and breadwinning are difficult to ignore. To swim against the cultural current, couples will often have to do what they know to be right, rather than what feels right. This will be awkward, even painful. Working to undermine conventional gender constructions can lead to "gender vertigo"—a dizzying state of discomfort and uncertainty (Connell 1995; Risman 1998). After all, for many of us, these changes represent an attempt to disrupt and reconstruct assumptions that lie at the core of who we think we are, or should be. But only in this way can we move closer to new gendered practices that undermine men's dominance.

The experiences of couples with higher-earning wives document the obstacles that await those who want to challenge the current gender structure. As they talk about their fears and disappointments, these couples demonstrate what other partners will have to work through; they provide a more nuanced map of how to negotiate the pitfalls of gender vertigo and move the revolution forward.

The experiences of couples with higher-earning wives are valuable for another reason. Though they do not provide a model for how to challenge the current gender structure, they highlight the potential for new gendered understandings and practices to emerge. That these breadwinning wives do not enjoy greater power in their marriages means that being the major provider does not have to translate into overall marital dominance. If it is possible for power to be separated from money when women are the major earners, it should also be possible to sever that link for men and treat dual-earners as co-providers and equal partners. Similarly, if couples can so highly value men's noneconomic contributions and use them to increase men's status in the home, it should be possible to do the same for women. That is, performing domestic labor and child care should be a source of power and status for whoever engages in these vital tasks.

Ironically then, while overall these results highlight the strength and resilience of conventional gender expectations, they also demonstrate the potential for couples to disrupt them. The experiences of couples with higher-earning wives shed light on potential cracks in the gender structure from which larger transformations become possible. However, these couples also demonstrate that without a clear vision that relations between men and women can or should be different, as well as a vigilant effort to combat the pull of the gender structure, the revolutionary potential of these new meanings will remain untapped.

Appendix A. Questionnaire

HOUSEHOLD QUESTIONNAIRE

I would like to ask you a few questions about how decisions are made and how household tasks get done in your family. Please fill out this questionnaire separately from your spouse. It should take about 15 minutes to complete. Be assured that all of your answers will be held in the strictest confidence. Thank you for your help.

The response choices are:

    husband always
    husband more than wife
    husband and wife equally
    wife more than husband
    wife always
    done by someone else
    no one/not applicable

HOUSEHOLD RESPONSIBILITIES

There are certain tasks that are done in the course of daily living. These first questions ask you how some of these tasks get done in your family. Please indicate who does the following chores in your household placing an "X" in the appropriate box:

CHORES	husband always	husband more	equal	wife more	wife always	someone else	N/A
grocery shopping							
cooks breakfast							
cooks dinner							
evening dishes							
tidies up							
mows lawn							
shovels sidewalk							

	husband always	husband more	equal	wife more	wife always	someone else	N/A
repairs things at home							
dusts furniture							
cleans bathroom							
sees to car servicing							
laundry							
takes care of money & bills							

The following items concern daily needs for children. Please indicate (as above) who does these things for them. The category "child(ren) themselves" has been added for the cases where the children usually do these things for themselves:

	husband always	husband more	equal	wife more	wife always	someone else	child(ren) themselves	N/A
makes lunch								
bathes them								
puts them to bed								
oversees their homework								
disciplines them								

Do your children ever perform any household tasks?   Yes   No

Do you have regular outside help in performing these household or childcare tasks?   Yes   No

If yes, is this paid help?   Yes   No

HOUSEHOLD DECISIONS

A couple has to make many decisions for themselves and their family. Many couples will talk over important decisions, but eventually a final decision must be made. These questions ask you to report who has the most say, or makes the final decision, in certain areas.

In your family who usually makes the final decision about . . .

	husband always	husband more	equal	wife more	wife always	N/A
what car to get?						
whether or not to buy life insurance?						
what house or apartment to take?						
what job the husband should take?						
what job the wife should take?						
how much the family can afford to spend per week on food?						
what doctor to have when someone is sick?						
where to go on a vacation?						
when to make a major purchase for the home?						
how the monthly budget will be spent?						
how to discipline the children?						
which school, daycare, or childcare arrangements will be used?						
which friends to see socially?						

Would you say that you and your spouse disagree over some of these decisions?   Yes   No

If yes, which one(s) particularly? (please list them, use back if needed)

Finally, I would like to ask a few questions about your own family background.

Date of birth _____

Racial or ethnic background _____

Father's main occupation when you were growing up _____

Mother's main occupation when you were growing up _____

Highest grade of school, training, or year of college your <u>father</u> completed:

1 2 3 4 5 6 7 8 9 10 11 12   trade   13 14 15 16 17+
    grades of school   school   years of college

Highest grade of school, training, or year of college your <u>mother</u> completed:

1 2 3 4 5 6 7 8 9 10 11 12   trade   13 14 15 16 17+
    grades of school   school   years of college

Highest grade of school, training, or year of college <u>you</u> have completed:

1 2 3 4 5 6 7 8 9 10 11 12   trade   13 14 15 16 17+
    grades of school   school   years of college

Your date of (current) marriage _____

Number of years you have worked since marriage _____

How many children do you have? _____ What are their ages? _____

Your current occupation (be as specific as possible) _____

What was your total family income for 200__? _____

How much of this was your personal income? _____

Are you the HUSBAND or WIFE   (please circle one)

Again, I remind you that all of your answers are confidential, and I appreciate your honesty. I will be contacting you soon to schedule the interview. Thank you very much for your time!

Appendix B. Interview Guide

I'll be asking you about how you manage the demands of work, marriage, and family life now, but I'm also interested in how your life as a couple has changed over time. So I'll be asking you quite a bit about your history as well.

Background Info

Place and date of birth
Parents' work/jobs
Ethnic background
Religion: growing up, and now
Siblings: how many, where are they now, what are they doing
Previous marriages, if any
Names and ages of children
Other members of the household, if any (including live-in help)
Educational background
Job/work history.

Present Occupation

How long have you been in your present job? Please describe what you do with as much detail as possible.

How closely are you supervised? Do you supervise others? If so, who and how many?

How many hours per day/week do you work? How much vacation do you get? How much sick time?

How much time do you spend commuting?

How often do work demands take you away from home? What kinds of demands take you away?

How secure is your job, given the current economic situation?

Are there opportunities for you to move up (in pay or responsibility)? Are you interested in them?

Do you think of your work as a job or career?

How do you feel about the kind of work you do? What do you like/dislike about it? Is there something else you'd rather be doing? What's keeping you from doing that?

Do you ever think about not working at all? Would you/could you make the choice to not work?

THE MARITAL RELATIONSHIP

Did you always see yourself as getting married?

What would you say are the important ingredients of a "good marriage"?

When did you meet your spouse?

What attracted you to him/her?

How did you decide to marry your spouse?

What are some of the thing you've grown to appreciate about your spouse *over time*?

What strengths, or resources, so you feel you contribute to the relationship?

What do you feel your spouse contributes? [Ask about money, if not mentioned spontaneously.]

Do you feel like your spouse appreciates your contributions?

Would you say that one of you contributes more overall?

Do you feel that one of you contributes more in some area(s)?

Has it always been this way?

How much energy would you say you put into the relationship, vs. work and other activities?

Are you satisfied with the amount of time you spend with your spouse?

Are you satisfied with the quality of time you spend with your spouse?

How do you feel about your marriage?

Would you say either partner is more committed to it?

How do you think your marriage stacks up to the list you gave me?

Decision-making: How do you go about getting something that you want?

How does your spouse get something s/he wants?

Can you think of examples?

Has this process changed over time?

Do either of you tend to gather information before a decision is made?

Some people are more concerned with some household decisions than others: which are the most important issues for you to have input?

Can you think of any recent disagreement you've had with your spouse? How did you resolve this issue?

Have there been any particular issues that have ever caused problems, or been a source of struggle in your relationship [money, relations with other family members, raising the kid(s), sex, etc]. Are these struggles ongoing?

What is the toughest problem you face now, as a couple?

Have you ever considered separation or divorce?

Have you ever discussed this possibility with your spouse?

Is there anything you'd do differently in your life, given what you know now?

FAMILY AND HOUSEHOLD MANAGEMENT

You answered some questions about household chores on the questionnaire you filled out, but I'd like to get a better picture about how things are divided up . . .

Would you tell me about the things each of you tend to do, and which things, if any, that you share?

How did this arrangement come about? Did you make a conscious decision to do things this way?

Would you say that the household is *your* responsibility? That is, are you in charge of making sure things get done?

If you are responsible, how do you feel about that? Is it a burden, or an opportunity to exercise control?

If you aren't responsible, do you feel free, or out of control?

Do you ever wish your spouse took more responsibility, or did more, at home?

Do you ever feel like *you* should be doing more?

Do you ever discuss making changes in your current system?

Children: What is your child(ren)'s daily routine?

What childcare arrangements, if any, do you have?

Do you see either of you as the primary caretaker of your children?

Does the primary caretaker seem to have more control over, or influence on, the child(ren)?

How do you feel about the job you're doing as a parent? Are you comfortable? How would you describe your experiences parenting?

How involved is your spouse in the lives/upbringing of the child(ren)?

Do you have any aspirations for your child(ren)'s future?

Is there anything about your life that you'd like to be different for your
child(ren)?

RELATIONSHIP BETWEEN WORK AND FAMILY LIFE

How does your work affect your family life? Do you bring work home,
travel, does your work tire you mentally or physically?

Is there anything about your work that puts stress on the family?

Do you discuss work with your spouse, or do you feel it should be kept
separate from family life?

Have you ever moved because of your job, or your spouse's job?

Would you move *now* for your work? For your spouse's work?

How does your spouse's work affect the family?

How do you *feel* about the work your spouse does?

How committed are each of you to your respective work?

Would you say either job is "more important"—either to the individual,
or to the family?

Do you see either job as more secure?

How would losing your job affect the family?

Would you say that either of you is "the provider" in the family?

FAMILY FINANCES

Seeing that you have two incomes coming into the house, how do you
allocate money for bills—what is your system? Do you have separate
accounts, joint accounts, or both?

Is your income used for anything in particular? Is your spouse's?

Do you have any money left over to spend as *you* please?

What would you consider to be a major purchase?

How do you decide on these purchases?

What if you disagree, how are things resolved?

How do you allow for large expenses, like a car, vacation, purchase for the
home, children's education?

How much control do you feel you have over how your income is spent?

How much control do you have over how your *spouse's* income is spent?

On the questionnaire, you listed your income as _____? Will it be the same this year?

Life Outside Work and Family

Do you belong to any clubs or organizations—political, professional, religious, hobby-related, etc.? If yes, for how long?

How much time do you devote to these activities?

If no, is there any particular reason why?

Do you have any activities you would consider individual hobbies?

Any activities you and your spouse enjoy together?

Any activities your spouse does alone?

How important are these outside activities to you?

Exploring the Link between Money, Gender, Status, and Power

In the traditional family, a husband used to earn all of the family's income, and whatever job he did had a certain status attached to it, and gave the family a place in the community, or determined the family's social class. Wives stayed at home, and remained responsible for the household and children. Part of what I'm doing is exploring how these responsibilities may be different for two-income couples.

Do you think you fulfill different responsibilities as "husband" and "wife" than the spouses in traditional families did/do?

Which social class would you say you belong to? Or don't you think of yourselves in those terms?

How does this compare with your family's status? With your spouse's family's status?

Is your position based on *your* work/income, your *spouse's*, or *both*?

Do you see a status difference between your work and your spouse's?

Do you think the types of jobs you two have affect your marriage or family in any way? Why or why not?

Men used to derive a lot of authority or power in the marriage when they brought all the money home. I'm exploring how having two incomes may affect that equation.

Do you think how much money you bring home affects how much say
you have in the marriage? Why or why not?

If it does, in what way(s)?

Some people say power, or control, is divided in their relationship—
meaning one person has more say in some areas than others. Would
you say that is true in your relationship?

If so, what area(s) does each spouse have control in?

On balance, would you say one of you tends to have more of a say in the
relationship than the other?

You've told me a lot about your past and your life now. As you look
toward the future, is there anything you're looking forward to?

Are there any changes you'd like to make?

Do you think they'll come about? Why or why not?

Appendix C. Strategies for Data Analysis

I CONDUCTED, TAPED, and transcribed all the interviews. I used a constant comparative method (Glaser and Strauss 1967) and analytic induction as tools for analysis. I first coded the interviews using rough descriptive codes derived from the basic interview questions, as well as from the issues that emerged during the interviews. Initially, I made comparisons between spouses to look for discrepancies in perceptions and reports of behavior. I then coded the interviews by pattern or theme, as part of the movement from data description to conceptual clarification and theorizing. Here, I compared wives and husbands as groups. Also at this stage, I compared couples with higher-earning wives and comparison couples. I then matched husbands and wives again, in an effort to explain why some couples seemed to fit the pattern or theme under examination and others did not.

Throughout the book, then, I make comparisons on various levels. When I am concerned with issues of equity within relationships, I compare higher-earning wives and comparison wives with their respective husbands. When I am interested in the effects of income advantage, I compare couples with higher-earning wives to comparison couples. And finally, I present variations in thinking and behavior among couples with higher-earning wives—all in an effort to tease out the relative effects of gender, income, and status on the balance of power in these marriages.

BIBLIOGRAPHY

Acker, Joan. 1992. "Gendered Institutions: From Sex Roles to Gendered Institutions." *Contemporary Sociology* 21:565–569.

Agarwal, Bina. 1997. "'Bargaining' and Gender Relations: Within and Beyond the Household." *Feminist Economics* 3:1–51.

Atkinson, Maxine, and Jacqueline Boles. 1984. "Wasp (Wives as Senior Partners)." *Journal of Marriage and the Family* 46:861–870.

Backett, Kathryn. 1987. "The Negotiation of Fatherhood." In *Reassessing Fatherhood: New Observations on Fathers and the Modern Family*, edited by Charlie Lewis and Margaret O'Brien. Beverly Hills: Sage.

Barnett, Rosalind, and Grace Baruch. 1988. "Correlates of Father's Participation in Family Work." In *Fatherhood Today: Men's Changing Role in the Family*, edited by Phyllis Bronstein and Carolyn Pape Cowan. New York: John Wiley.

Becker, Gary S. 1981. *A Treatise on the Family*. Cambridge: Harvard University Press.

Benokraitis, Nijole. 1985. "Fathers in the Dual-Earner Family." In *Dimensions of Fatherhood*, edited by Shirley Hanson and Frederick Bozett. Beverly Hills: Sage.

Berk, Richard A., and Sarah Fenstermaker Berk. 1979. *Labor and Leisure at Home: Content and Organization of the Household Day*. Beverly Hills: Sage.

Berk, Sarah Fenstermaker. 1985. *The Gender Factory: The Apportionment of Work in American Households*. New York: Plenum Press.

Bernard, Jessie. 1981. "The Good Provider Role: Its Rise and Fall." *American Psychologist* 36:1–12.

Bianchi, Susan, Melissa Milkie, Liana Sayer, and John Robinson. 2000. "Is Anyone Doing the Housework? Trends in the Gender Division of Household Labor." *Social Forces* 79:191–228.

Bittman, Michael, Paula England, Liana Sayer, Nancy Folbre, and George Matheson. 2003. "When Does Gender Trump Money? Bargaining and Time in Household Work." *American Journal of Sociology* 109:186–214.

Blau, Peter M. 1964. *Exchange and Power in Social Life*. New York: John Wiley.

Blee, Kathleen, and Ann Tickamyer. 1995. "Racial Differences in Men's Attitudes about Women's Gender Roles." *Journal of Marriage and the Family* 57:21–30.

Blood, Robert O., and Donald M. Wolfe. 1960. *Husbands and Wives*. Glencoe, Ill.: Free Press.

Blumberg, Rae Lesser. 1984. "A General Theory of Gender Stratification." In *Sociological Theory 1984*, edited by R. Collins. San Francisco: Jossey-Bass.

———. 1991. *Gender, Family, and Economy: The Triple Overlap*. Beverly Hills: Sage.

Blumberg, Rae Lesser, and Marion T. Coleman. 1989. "A Theoretical Look at the Gender Balance of Power in the American Couple." *Journal of Family Issues* 10:225–50.

Blumstein, Philip, and Pepper Schwartz. 1983. *American Couples: Money, Work, Sex.* New York: Morrow.

———. 1991. "Money and Ideology: Their Impact on Power and the Division of Household Labor." In *Gender, Family, and Economy*, edited by R. L. Blumberg. Newbury Park, Calif.: Sage.

Bolak, Hale Cihan. 1997. "When Wives Are Major Providers: Culture, Gender, and Family Work." *Gender and Society* 11:409–433.

Branner, Julia, and Peter Moss. 1987. "Father in Dual-Earner Households—Through Mother's Eyes." In *Reassessing Fatherhood: New Observations on Fathers and the Modern Family*, edited by Charlie Lewis and Margaret O'Brien. Beverly Hills: Sage.

Brayfield, April A. 1992. "Employment Resources and Housework in Canada." *Journal of Marriage and the Family* 54:19–30.

Brennan, Robert, Rosalind C. Barnett, and Karen Gareis. 2001. "When She Earns More Than He Does: A Longitudinal Study of Dual Earner Couples." *Journal of Marriage and the Family* 63:168–182.

Brewster, Karin, and Irene Padavic. 2000. "Change in Gender-Ideology, 1977–1996: The Contributions of Intracohort Change and Population Turnover." *Journal of Marriage and the Family* 62:477–487.

Brines, Julie. 1994. "Economic Dependency, Gender, and the Division of Labor at Home." *American Journal of Sociology* 100:652–688.

Carrington, Christopher. 1999. *No Place Like Home: Relationships and Family Life among Lesbians and Gay Men.* Chicago: University of Chicago Press.

Cockburn, Cynthia. 1991. *In the Way of Women: Men's Resistance to Sex Equality in Organizations.* Ithaca, N.Y.: ILR Press.

Cohen, Philip. 2004. "The Gender Division of Labor: 'Keeping House' and Occupational Segregation in the United States." *Gender and Society* 18:239–252.

Coleman, Marion T. 1991. "The Division of Household Labor: Suggestions for Future Empirical Consideration and Theoretical Development." In *Gender, Family, and Economy: The Triple Overlap*, edited by R. L. Blumberg. Beverly Hills: Sage.

Collins, Randall. 1991. "Women and Men in the Class Structure." In *Gender, Family and Economy: The Triple Overlap*, edited by R. L. Blumberg. Beverly Hills: Sage.

Coltrane, Scott. 1996. *Family Man: Fatherhood, Housework, and Gender Equity.* New York: Oxford University Press.

———. 2000. "Research on Household Labor: Modeling and Measuring the Social Embeddedness of Routine Family Work." *Journal of Marriage and the Family* 62:1208–1233.

Connell, R. W. 1987. *Gender and Power: Society, the Person, and Sexual Politics.* Stanford, Calif.: Stanford University Press.

———. 1995. *Masculinities.* Berkeley, Calif.: University of California Press.

———. 2000. *The Men and the Boys.* Cambridge: Polity.

Cowan, Carolyn Pape, and Philip A. Cowan. 1992. *When Partners Become Parents: The Big Life Change for Couples.* New York: Basic Books.

Daniels, Arlene Kaplan. 1987. "Invisible Work." *Social Problems* 34:403–415.

Deutsch, Francine. 1999. *Halving It All: How Equally Shared Parenting Works*. Cambridge: Harvard University Press.

Deutsch, Francine, Jennifer Lozy, and Susan Saxon. 1993. "Taking Credit: Couples' Reports of Contributions to Child Care." *Journal of Family Issues* 14:421–437.

DeVault, Marjorie L. 1991. *Feeding the Family: The Social Organizing of Caring as Gendered Work*. Chicago: University of Chicago Press.

Ehrensaft, Diane. 1987. *Parenting Together: Men and Women Sharing the Care of Their Children*. New York: Free Press.

———. 1990. "When Men and Women Mother." In *Women, Class, and the Feminist Revolution*, edited by K. Hansen and I. Philipson. Philadelphia: Temple University Press.

England, Paula, and George Farkas. 1986. *Households, Employment, and Gender: A Social, Economic, and Demographic View*. New York: Aldine.

England, Paula, and Barbara Kilbourne. 1990. "Markets, Marriage, and Other Mates: The Problem of Power." In *Beyond the Marketplace: Rethinking Economy and Society*, edited by Roger Freidland and A. F. Robertson. New York: Aldine de Gruyter.

Erickson, Rebecca. 1993. "Reconceptualizing Family Work: The Effect of Emotion Work on Perceptions of Marital Quality." *Journal of Marriage and the Family* 55:888–900.

Fairclough, Norman. 1989. *Language and Power*. London: Longman.

Fenstermaker, Sarah, Candace West, and Donald Zimmerman. 1991. "Gender Inequality: New Conceptual Terrain." In *Gender, Family, and Economy: The Triple Overlap*, edited by R. L. Blumberg. Beverly Hills: Sage.

Ferree, Myra Marx. 1990. "Beyond Separate Spheres: Feminism, Family, and Research." *Journal of Marriage and the Family* 52:866–884.

Finch, Janet, and Dulcie Groves. 1983. *A Labour of Love: Women, Work, and Caring*. London: Routledge and Kegan Paul.

Foa, Uriel, John Converse Jr., Kjell Tornblom, and Edna Foa, eds. 1993. *Resource Theory Explorations and Applications*. San Diego: Academic Press.

Fox, Greer, and Velma Murry. 2000. "Gender and Families: Feminist Perspectives and Family Research." *Journal of Marriage and the Family* 62:1160–1172.

Geerken, Michael, and Walter R. Gove. 1983. *At Home and at Work: The Family's Allocation of Labor*. Beverly Hills: Sage.

Glaser, Barney, and Anselm Strauss. 1967. *The Discovery of Grounded Theory: Strategies for Qualitative Research*. New York: Aldine de Gruyter.

Gottman, John, and Clifford Notarius. 2000. "Decade Review: Observing Marital Interaction." *Journal of Marriage and the Family* 62:927–947.

Grant, Priscilla. 2002. "The Breadwinners." *More*, July/August, 44–49.

Greenstein, Theodore. 2000. "Economic Dependence, Gender, and the Division of Labor at Home: A Replication and Extension." *Journal of Marriage and the Family* 62:322–335.

Gupta, Sanjiv. 1999. "What Makes Men Change Their Housework Time?" Ph.D. diss., University of Michigan, Ann Arbor.

Hartmann, Heidi. 1981. "The Family as the Locus of Gender, Class, and Political Struggle: The Example of Housework." *Signs* 6:366–394.

Hartsock, Nancy. 1983. *Money, Sex and Power: Toward a Feminist Historical Materialism*. New York: Longman.

Hawkins, Alan J., Shawn L. Christiansen, Kathryn Pond Sargent, and E. Jeffrey Hill. 1993. "Rethinking Fathers' Involvement in Child Care: A Developmental Perspective." *Journal of Family Issues* 14:531–549.

Hays, Sharon. 1995. *The Cultural Contradictions of Motherhood.* New Haven: Yale University Press.

Heckert, D. Alex, Thomas Nowack, and Kay Snyder. 1998. "The Impact of Husbands' and Wives' Relative Earnings on Marital Disruption." *Journal of Marriage and the Family* 60:690–703.

Hertz, Rosanna. 1986. *More Equal Than Others: Men and Women in Dual Career Marriages.* Berkeley: University of California Press.

———. 1989. "Dual Career Corporate Couples: Shaping Marriages through Work." In *Gender in Intimate Relationships: A Microstructural Approach,* edited by B. Risman and P. Schwartz. Belmont, Calif.: Wadsworth.

Hochschild, Arlie. 1989. *The Second Shift.* New York: Viking.

Hood, Jane C. 1986. "The Provider Role: Its Meaning and Measurement." *Journal of Marriage and the Family* 48:349–359.

Horna, Jarmila, and Eugen Leipri. 1987. "Fathers' Participation in Work, Family Life, and Leisure: A Canadian Experience." In *Reassessing Fatherhood: New Observations on Fathers and the Modern Family,* edited by Charlie Lewis and Margaret O'Brien. Beverly Hills: Sage.

Huber, Joan, and Glenna D. Spitze. 1983. *Sex Stratification: Children, Housework, and Jobs.* New York: Academic Press.

Johnson, Elizabeth, and Ted Huston. 1998. "The Perils of Love, or Why Wives Adapt to Husbands during the Transition to Parenthood." *Journal of Marriage and the Family* 60:195–204.

Kimball, Gayle. 1988. *50-50 Parenting: Sharing Family Rewards and Responsibilities.* Lexington, Mass.: Lexington Books.

Knudson-Martin, C., and A. Mahoney. 1998. "Language Processes in the Construction of Equality in Marriages." *Family Relations* 47:81–91.

Komarovsky, Mirra. 1980. "The Breakdown of the Husband's Status," In *The American Man,* edited by Elizabeth Hafkin Pleck and Joseph Pleck. Englewood Cliffs, N.J.: Prentice-Hall.

Komter, Aafke. 1989. "Hidden Power in Marriage." *Gender and Society* 3:187–216.

Kranichfeld, Marion. 1987. "Rethinking Family Power." *Journal of Family Issues* 8:42–56.

Landry, Bart. 2000. *Black Working Wives: Pioneers of the American Family Revolution.* Berkeley: University of California Press.

Lasch, Christopher. 1977. *Haven in a Heartless World: The Family Besieged.* New York: Basic.

Lewis, Susan, Daffna Izraeli, and Helen Hootsman. 1992. *Dual-Earner Family: International Perspectives.* London: Sage.

Lips, Hilary M. 1981. *Women, Men, and the Psychology of Power.* Englewood Cliffs, N.J.: Prentice-Hall.

Lorber, Judith. 1994. *Paradoxes of Gender.* New Haven: Yale University Press.

Lukes, Steven. 1974. *Power: A Radical View.* London: Macmillan.

———. 1986. *Power.* Oxford: Basil Blackwell.

Lundberg, Shelly, and Robert Pollak. 1996. "Bargaining and Distribution in Marriage." *Journal of Economics Perspectives* 10:139–158.

McMahon, Martha. 1995. *Engendering Motherhood: Identity and Self-Transformation in Women's Lives*. New York: Guilford Press.

McRae, Susan 1986. *Cross-Class Families: A Study of Wives' Occupational Superiority*. Oxford: Clarendon Press.

Mederer, Helen. 1993. "Division of Labor in Two-Earner Homes: Task Accomplishment versus Household Management as Critical Variables in Perceptions about Family Work." *Journal of Marriage and the Family* 55:133–145.

Mintz, Steven, and Susan Kellogg. 1988. *Domestic Revolutions: A Social History of American Family Life*. New York: Free Press.

Nickols, Sharon Y., and Edward J. Metzen. 1982. "Impact of Wife's Employment upon Husband's Housework." *Journal of Family Issues* 3:199–216.

Nyberg, David. 1981. *Power over Power*. Ithaca, N.Y.: Cornell University Press.

Ostrander, Susan A. 1984. *Women of the Upper Class*. Philadelphia: Temple University Press.

Pahl, Jan. 1989. *Money and Marriage*. New York: St. Martin's Press.

Parsons, Talcott, and Robert Bales. 1955. *Family, Socialization, and the Interaction Process*. New York: Free Press.

Perry-Jenkins, Maureen, and Karen Folk. 1994. "Class, Couples, and Conflict: Effects of the Division of Labor on Assessments of Marriage in Dual-Earner Families." *Journal of Marriage and the Family* 56:165–180.

Peterson, Richard R., and Kathleen Gerson. 1992. "Determinants of Responsibility for Childcare among Dual-Earner Couples." *Journal of Marriage and Family* 54:527–536.

Pleck, Robert. 1985. *Working Wives, Working Husbands*. Beverly Hills: Sage.

Polatnick, Margaret. 1973. "Why Men Don't Rear Children: A Power Analysis." *Berkeley Journal of Sociology* 18:45–84.

Popenoe, David. 1989. *Disturbing the Nest: Family Change and Decline in Modern Society*. New York: Aldine de Gruyter.

Potuchek, Jean. 1997. *Who Supports the Family? Gender and Breadwinning in Dual-Earner Families*. Stanford, Calif.: Stanford University Press.

Press, Julie, and Eleanor Townsley. 1998. "Wives' and Husbands' Housework Reporting: Gender, Class, and Social Desirability." *Gender and Society* 12:188–218.

Presser, Harriet. 1994. "Employment Schedules among Dual-Earner Spouses and the Division of Household Labor by Gender." *American Sociological Review* 59:348–364.

Pyke, Karen. 1994. "Women's Employment as a Gift or Burden? Marital Power across Marriage, Divorce, and Remarriage." *Gender and Society* 8:73–91.

Radin, Norma. 1988. "Primary Caregiving Fathers of Long Duration." In *Fatherhood Today: Men's Changing Role in the Family,* edited by Phyllis Bronstein and Carolyn Pape Cowan. New York: John Wiley.

Raley, Sara, Marybeth Mattingly, Suzanne Bianchi, and Erum Ikramullah. 2003. "How Dual Are Dual-Income Couples? Documenting Change from 1970–2001." Presented at the annual meeting of the American Sociological Association, Atlanta, Georgia, August.

Rexroat, Cynthia, and Constance Shehan. 1987. "The Family Life Cycle and Spouses' Time in Housework." *Journal of Marriage and the Family* 49:737–750.

Risman, Barbara. 1998. *Gender Vertigo: American Families in Transition.* New Haven: Yale University Press.

Risman, Barbara, and Danielle Johnson-Sumerford. 1998. "Doing It Fairly: A Study of Post-Gender Marriages." *Journal of Marriage and Family* 60:23–40.

Rogers, Stacy, and Danielle DeBoer. 2001. "Changes in Wives' Income: Effects on Marital Happiness, Psychological Well-Being, and the Risk of Divorce." *Journal of Marriage and the Family* 63:458–472.

Rubin, Lillian Breslow. 1976. *Worlds of Pain.* New York: Basic Books.

———. 1994. *Families on the Faultline.* New York: Harper-Collins.

Russell, Graeme. 1987. "Problems in Role-Reversed Families." In *Reassessing Fatherhood: New Observations on Fathers and the Modern Family*, edited by Charlie Lewis and Margaret O'Brien. Beverly Hills: Sage.

Schwartz, Pepper. 1994. *Love between Equals: How Peer Marriage Really Works.* New York: Free Press.

Segura, Denise. 1994. "Working At Motherhood: Chicana and Mexican Immigrant Mothers and Employment." In *Mothering: Ideology, Experience, and Agency*, edited by Evelyn Nakano Glenn, Grace Change, and Linda Rennie. New York: Routledge.

Sexton, Christine, and Daniel Perlman. 1989. "Couples' Career Orientation, Gender Role Orientation, and Perceived Equity as Determinants of Marital Power." *Journal of Marriage and the Family* 51:933–941.

Shelton, Beth Anne. 1992. *Women, Men, and Time: Gender Differences in Paid Work, Housework, and Leisure.* New York: Greenwood Press.

Shelton, Beth Anne, and Daphne John. 1993. "Ethnicity, Race, and Difference: A Comparison of White, Black, and Hispanic Men's Household Labor Time." In *Men, Work, and Family*, edited by Jane Hood. New York: Sage.

Sokoloff, Natalie. 1980. *Between Money and Love: The Dialectics of Women's Home and Market Work.* New York: Praeger.

South, Scott, and Glenna Spitze. 1994. "Housework in Marital and Nonmarital Households." *American Sociological Review* 59:327–347.

Spragins, Ellyn. 2002a. "His Thoughts about Her Earning Their Keep." *New York Times*, February 3.

———. 2002b. "When the Big Paycheck Is Hers." *New York Times*, January 6.

Stacey, Judith. 1990. *Brave New Families: Stories of Domestic Upheaval in Late Twentieth Century America.* New York: Basic Books.

Thompson, Linda. 1991. "Family Work: Women's Sense of Fairness." *Journal of Family Issues* 12:181–196.

Treas, Judith. 1993. "Money in the Bank: Transaction Costs and the Economic Organization of Marriage." *American Sociological Review* 58:723–734.

Tyre, Peg, and Daniel McGinn. 2003. "She Works, He Doesn't." *Newsweek*, May 12, 45–52.

Vannoy-Hiller, Dana, and William Philliber. 1989. *Equal Partners: Successful Women in Marriage.* Newbury Park, Calif.: Sage.

West, Candace, and Donald Zimmerman. 1987. "Doing Gender." *Gender and Society* 1:125–151.

White, Lynn, and Stacy Rogers. 2000. "Economic Circumstances and Family Out-comes: A Review of the 1990's." *Journal of Marriage and the Family* 62:1035–1051.

"Why a Wife's Earnings Can Strain a Marriage." 1999. *Jet*, August 2, 14–16.

Whyte, Martin King. 1990. *Dating, Mating, and Marriage.* New York: Aldine de Gruyter.

Wilkie, Jane Riblett. 1993. "Changes in U.S. Men's Attitudes toward the Family Provider Role." *Gender and Society* 7:261–279.

Wilkie, Jane, Myra Ferree, and Kathryn Ratcliff. 1998. "Gender and Fairness: Mar-ital Satisfaction in Two-Earner Couples." *Journal of Marriage and the Family* 60:577–594.

Williams, Joan. 2000. *Unbending Gender: Why Family and Work Conflict and What to Do about It.* New York: Oxford University Press.

Willinger, Beth. 1993. "Resistance and Change: College Men's Attitudes toward Family and Work in the 1980's." In *Men, Work, and Family*, edited by Jane Hood. New York: Sage.

Wright, Eric Olin, Karen Shire, Shu-Ling Hwang, Maureen Dolan, and Janeen Baxter. 1992. "The Non-Effects of Class on the Gender Division of Labor in the Home: A Comparative Study of Sweden and the U.S." *Gender and Society* 6:252–281.

Zelizer, Vivianna. 1989. "The Social Meaning of Money: 'Special Monies.' " *American Journal of Sociology* 95:342–377.

Zronkovic, Anisa, Cynthia Schmiege, and Leslie Hall. 1994. "Influence Strategies When Couples Make Work-Family Decisions." *Family Relations* 43:182–188.

INDEX

African American couples, 189
Atkinson, Maxine, and Jacqueline
  Boles, 119
authority. *See* decision making

Blood, Robert, and Donald Wolfe,
  17–19
Blumstein, Philip, and Pepper
  Schwartz, 69
Brave New Families (Stacey), 187
Brines, Julie, 19
breadwinning: assumptions about, 1; as
  burden for wives, 85; consequences
  of failing at, 182; effects of unemployment on, 65; and historical
  privileges for husbands, 5, 182; and
  husbands moving up so wives can
  cut back, 145–146, 157, 159; husbands' plans to take over role, 85,
  155–157, 169; and husbands' struggle for respect, 155–157, 173; as key
  to masculine identity, 15; as masculine imperative, 1–2, 121, 127–128,
  141–142; and potential status in
  unused degrees, 140, 156; power in,
  4; responsibility for, 12–13, 15–16,
  128; substitutes for, 130; as threat to
  woman's gender identity, 126;
  wives disappointed in husbands',
  145, 157–159, 169. *See also*
  gender boundaries; gender
  identity

Carrington, Christopher, 120
class differences: between spouses,
  170–171, 175
Coltrane, Scott, 143
Connell, R.W., 116, 191
conventional gender expectations, 9,
  13; pull of, 16, 120, 127, 146,
  160–161, 168, 177
conventional marital contract, 12–14,
  149–150; benefits for husbands, 179;
  and decision-making power, 5, 96;
  difficulty rewriting, 177; marital
  satisfaction as shaped by, 154–155;
  power dynamics embedded in, 16,
  119, 176–177, 182; same deal for
  breadwinning wives in, 58, 65; value
  of spouses' contributions as shaped
  by, 155

data analysis, 203
data collection, 31–32
decision making: assessing relative
  power in, 90, 95–96; autonomy for
  men, 98, 139; autonomy for
  women, 93, 144; benefits of acqui-
  escing for wives, 110; comparison
  wives deferring to husbands', 113;
  and conflict, 100–101, 104,
  111–112, 170; control for husbands,
  5, 99–100, 166; cost of resisting husbands' control, 110; higher-earning
  wives' ability to control, 136;

About the Author

Veronica Tichenor is an assistant professor in the Department of Sociology at the State University of New York–Institute of Technology. Her work has appeared in the *Journal of Marriage and the Family* and *Sex Roles*. She lives in the Mohawk Valley region of upstate New York with her husband, Jim, and their daughter, Michael.